INSTANT INCOME

INSTANT INCOME

Strategies That Bring in the Cash for Small Businesses, Innovative Employees, and Occasional Entrepreneurs

JANET SWITZER

McGraw-Hill

New York   Chicago   San Francisco
Lisbon   London   Madrid   Mexico City   Milan
New Delhi   San Juan   Seoul   Singapore
Sydney   Toronto

To my amazing parents, Les and Beverly.
Thank you for bringing an attitude of achievement
and sense of empowerment to my life.

To my long-time friend and mentor, Mac Ross.
You saw the vision, then gifted it to me.
Your brilliance and friendship will be missed.

Contents

PART TWO

Instant Income Overnight Audit

PART THREE

Going into Business with the Boss

PART FOUR

Becoming an Occasional Entrepreneur

Preface

It is estimated that someone, somewhere in this country, becomes a millionaire every four minutes. Your goal should be to become one of them.

BRIAN TRACY
Best-selling author of more than
40 books, including *The Way to Wealth*

MAKING MONEY IS EASY, and whether you own a small business, work for someone else's small business, or just want to earn thousands on the side pursuing what I call being an Occasional Entrepreneur, you have all the expertise and resources at your fingertips to boost your personal income immediately. How can I be so sure? Because, over the past 20 years, I've been creating quick cash for individuals and small businesses—almost on a daily basis. To say that income can be made instantly is not an overstatement. In fact, there's an entire system of strategies that tends to bring in the cash very quickly—and prepares you to make even more money in the future.

This book is about that system.

It's about the unique combination of finely tuned marketing techniques, advertising campaigns, joint-venture strategies, deal-making methods, sales pitches, and other strategies that have a 20-year track record of bringing in the cash—seemingly overnight.

It's about the words to say, the phone calls to make, the letters to write, and the offers to pitch. It's about the scripts to use, the e-mails to blast, the

Web copy to craft, and the dozens of other step-by-step tasks and techniques that ultimately compel others to give you money.

It's not about mindset, positive thinking, attraction theory, or any of the other helpful wealth-creation concepts that have been written about by countless other authors who have a system of their own.

My job is to give you the steps that lead directly to depositing cash in your bank account.

In fact, creating cash has been my job almost as long as I can remember.

For the world's best-known celebrity entrepreneurs, I've quietly produced the ads, letters, scripts, response devices, and other marketing vehicles that have transformed good ideas into great income. Day after day, I've been in the trenches creating the cash that keeps these legendary businesses going.

Along the way, I've helped everyday people, too—people who had regular jobs but who needed to make quick cash on the side. I've helped the stay-at-home mom, the weekend jewelry designer, the corporate manager, and even a sheep farmer who needed extra cash. Not only will you get to meet some of these Occasional Entrepreneurs, but you'll learn—as they did—dozens of ways to make money and pursue your passion while still maintaining the security and paycheck of a regular job.

But perhaps the most interesting people I've met were those who had discovered (or created) an opportunity to Go Into Business With the Boss. Through smart marketing and savvy business strategies, they created robust new profit centers within their employer's business—then shared handsomely in the extra cash flow while still getting paid for their "regular" job. We call these folks *intrapreneurs*, and because this is a path that I took at one time, I dedicate a significant portion of *Instant Income* to helping you pursue this path to substantially boosting your personal income while creating more job security for yourself at the same time.

Under all these scenarios—whether you own a small business, work for someone else's small business, or pursue being an Occasional Entrepreneur—you'll find that with the right strategies, making money quickly is much easier than you think.

And you don't have to be a career professional to do so. You just have to know where to look.

Part One of *Instant Income* introduces you to the seven major areas where substantial additional revenue can be found in a small business—existing customers, joint-venture relationships, advertising campaigns, prospecting and lead generating, sales efforts, Internet activity, and overlooked assets. I not only detail what to look for in these seven major areas but give you the working knowledge you need to begin creating quick cash from these pools of potential revenue.

What do I mean by *working knowledge*?

Well, many businesses and individuals that are in desperate financial straits, for example, want someone else to generate Instant Income for them. If this describes you, then Chapter 2, which discusses joint-venture relationships, identifies the three different types of joint-venture "partners" who could be sending you customers and cash flow tomorrow.

Of course, you'll need to tell these potential partners *why* they should help you, so I go one step further and give you an actual script to use to gain their cooperation. Once you have their agreement, you can use the complete tutorial I provide to calculate and negotiate how you and your joint-venture partner will split the resulting profits.

With just one or two of these joint-venture deals in place, it's easy to start making money—immediately. In fact, all it takes is a handful of proven strategies for marketing your goods and services to the other person's customers.

And where will you find these proven strategies?

Following the tutorial, of course, in step-by-step detail.

By the time you've studied all seven chapters in Part One of *Instant Income*, you'll know more about creating cash flow than the majority of business owners out there. You'll know how to write an ad today, run it in the newspaper tomorrow, and have the phone ringing off the hook with orders by the time you get to the office.

You'll know how to reactivate customers who haven't done business with you in years—for an immediate windfall of thousands of dollars.

You'll know how to find overlooked assets in your business—inventory overstocks, credit accounts, excess service capacity, and other such things—that can be turned into cash using the strategies I describe.

You'll not only have a complete working knowledge of how to generate cash in each of the seven major areas but also have at your fingertips 35 easy-to-execute strategies for creating all the Instant Income you'll ever want or need.

If you need a detailed road map of what to do before starting, Part Two walks you through the Instant Income Overnight Audit and helps you produce a list of strategies to execute, in order of priority. Simply answer the questions, use the Audit form to calculate your revenue, then rank your answers, starting with those strategies that will generate the most Instant Income for you. (If you'd like our online Audit tool to help you calculate revenue and create a start-to-finish written plan for you, including a checklist of individual tasks to be completed, log on to www.InstantIncome.com/audit.html.)

And if you're employed by someone else?

Well, get ready to boost your personal income—*instantly*. The truth is, running a small business is tough for your employer. It's time-consuming. It's intimidating. Some days, it's just plain demoralizing. But imagine your boss's reaction when you make his or her life easier by offering to generate additional income for the business using a customized, written Instant Income plan that you generated that morning—based on activities and assets that exist in the business right now. If you were hired for a specific job, imagine discussing a new and expanded role—a higher-paying one—bringing in extra money with the proven Instant Income strategies.

Part Three of this book tells you how to do this.

Part Four is for Occasional Entrepreneurs—those employees who like the security of a regular paycheck but who also want to earn thousands of extra dollars on the side several times a year.

Wherever you're at today, the Instant Income System has solutions for you.

And, as I said before, you don't have to be a career professional to do this.

Over the years, I've worked with business owners who were just starting out and with business owners who had years of expensive marketing training behind them. The strategies don't care. Whoever you are, they'll have you executing with confidence in no time.

No formal training is required. In fact, as I reflect on my own career as the "expert behind the incomes," it still seems incomprehensible to me that I fell into a line of work for which I had no formal training whatsoever.

Like many people, I went to college, worked part-time, and—after graduation—landed a job *outside* my field of study.

Way outside.

The truth is, I had studied international relations, economics, and international law. I had worked summers for a member of Congress, interned as a news reporter at the state capitol, and dreamed of going into the Foreign Service.

But while my command of the English language was good, I didn't *parlez-vous français* well enough to pass the Foreign Service exam. Suddenly, my future as America's next woman ambassador looked bleak.

What was a 21-year-old to do?

To kill time until a job offer from NATO showed up, I applied for a position as an entry-level check sorter at a small regional bank. Imagine my surprise when I was ushered into the bank president's office and offered the job of marketing manager instead!

I was speechless.

I didn't have any marketing background.

But it soon dawned on me that I had something even better: I knew what people wanted to hear. Through my work as a political campaigner, a reporter, and a public relations clerk, I had learned what people responded to . . . what they *instantly* responded to.

It occurred to me that if I simply combined this knowledge with some information on how to execute strategies and how to design various marketing devices, I'd make money for my employer.

It worked.

My first lead-generating letter returned a 26 percent response—along with the admiration of loan officers who no longer had to prospect for clients on their own. Of course, the printer ribbon often went askew and most of the letters went in the mail looking crooked, but the letter itself conveyed all the benefits that recipients would enjoy when they started doing business with our bank.

I learned that *what* you say is always more important than *how* you deliver it. It's a lesson that I've never forgotten, and it's one that I'll discuss further in the pages of *Instant Income.*

From there, I moved on to the software industry as the product marketing manager in charge of a little product called MacInTax—America's best-selling tax-preparation software on the Macintosh platform. Again the formula worked; I sent upgrade notices to our 80,000 registered users and watched the money come pouring in.

Soon after, I was hired by a small publishing and seminar company to execute marketing campaigns and help create published works. Over three years, I helped grow the company's seven original titles into more than 320 different special reports, home-study courses, audio programs, and video trainings.

In my fourth year there, I received an offer to market these published works full-time, making—on commission—a percentage of everything I brought in. I quickly wrote a 28-page catalog, worked with an outside fulfillment center, developed a national sales force of telesalespeople—and nearly doubled my income, even making a cool $20,000 from one promotion alone. I was 29 at the time.

xvi ➤ PREFACE

When it became evident that making money by making money for *other* people was a very lucrative proposition, I branched out on my own, began taking on clients, and became a hard-working consultant.

Chicken Soup for the Soul and its two coauthors, Jack Canfield and Mark Victor Hansen, were my very first clients—and they're still clients as I write these words 12 years later.

In just six hours, the first strategy I executed for Jack Canfield brought in $31,000. The second brought in $105,000 in just six weeks.

I've since replicated these same two strategies for countless other people, by the way.

In other words, you don't have to be Jack Canfield or *Chicken Soup for the Soul* to make money instantly. You simply have to know the strategies and execute them to the letter.

As I wrote in the beginning, you already have all the expertise and resources at your fingertips to immediately boost your personal income. And with a few simple changes in the way you conduct your business, perform your job duties, or pursue moneymaking projects on the side, you'll see substantial changes in your cash flow—and a substantial change in your outlook.

But be advised: Instant Income doesn't mean that money will magically flow into your mailbox without any effort. It takes action—and real-world strategies—to bring in the cash you need.

I'm delighted to be guiding you on this journey.

—JANET SWITZER

INSTANT INCOME

How to Read This Book

WHETHER YOU OWN a small business or simply work for one, whether you have a home-based business or have been merely thinking about starting one, you're living in the most exciting, most entrepreneurial time in history. New ways of making money are being tested and proven every day. Resources, technology, and services abound to help the existing millions of you succeed. And millions more will be joining you over the next few years.

Around the world, entrepreneurship is booming in places like India and China, Latin America, Asia, and Australia. The pace of women starting small businesses is accelerating faster than ever—especially in the United States, where women start businesses twice as often as men.* This includes home-based businesses, which account for 53 percent of all U.S. small businesses.† With all that's waiting for you and available to you as an entrepreneur, there's literally never been a better time than *right now* to run a business, work for a small business, or contemplate starting your own small business, either part-time or full-time.

Cash Is King for Owners, Employees, and Part-Timers

Run properly, your small business can deliver the exciting lifestyle and professional satisfaction of your dreams. That said, however, one harsh reality still remains.

---

* According to a poll by the National Association for the Self-Employed.

† According to the U.S. Small Business Administration's *Small Business Economy* report.

It takes a lot of cash to run a small business.

The truth is, cash flow is the *lifeblood* of any business. If there's cash left in the checking account, you know the business is still alive.

But paying bills, meeting payroll, and carving out a salary for yourself are only a small part of what cash does for a small business. Its bigger and much more important role is to help fund new marketing campaigns, enable new product development, pay for outside services to handle repetitive tasks, and just make business more enjoyable.

Some business owners wonder on a daily basis, *Where's the cash going to come from?* For many (especially microbusinesses and solo entrepreneurs), finding sources of outside financing is difficult. Often a credit card is the only line of credit available to start or grow a business.

But what if you had another solution . . . *an easier one*, with no strings attached?

What if you could start your business or formulate your expansion plans knowing that you had in place strategies and systems that are designed to create cash almost from the very first day—possibly even *before* you open for business or launch that new product line?

Those strategies exist in the pages of *Instant Income*. Not only are the Instant Income strategies great for leveraging the business activity you already have in place, but they're also superb for generating cash to start your business in the first place.

And if you work for someone else's small business? Don't become disillusioned whenever I detail a strategy or seem to be speaking directly to business "owners." In other words, don't bypass a strategy because you believe that it doesn't apply to you. Throughout the pages of *Instant Income*, I'm speaking to employees and Occasional Entrepreneurs, too.

What You'll Find in the Pages of Instant Income

If you've been in business for a while, *Instant Income* will help you find the cash that is hidden in those unique assets that all businesses tend to build up over time. These are "off-the-balance-sheet" assets like your customer list, your industry relationships, your current advertising campaigns, your sales scripts, and your Web site.

If you own your own business, Part One, "Strategies That Bring in the Cash," will help you leverage the business activity you're already pursuing while it helps you develop profit streams in exciting new areas. With its 35 different strategies, Part One will help you methodically improve the cash flow in your business by giving you the actual steps to take that will help to put cash in your bank account. Part Two, "Instant Income Overnight Audit," will help you to determine *which* of the 35 strategies to execute first by helping you to calculate exactly how much you'll make from each strategy.

If you're a small business owner, Parts One and Two are for you.

Employees Can Bring in More Cash, Too

If you're an employee of a small business, cash should be even more important to you because not only does your paycheck rely on your employer's ability to bring in the cash but there are also dozens of things you can do to help your employer increase the company's cash flow—while you *benefit personally* from creating these additional income streams.

In Part Three, "Going into Business with the Boss," I give you the actual steps for identifying the hidden cash in your *employer's* business, followed by a complete plan for approaching your employer and negotiating extra pay for bringing in that money. You'll be using the Instant Income Overnight Audit to help identify where your employer's business could be earning more, and you'll learn how to meet with your boss, explain your ideas, negotiate more pay, then take charge of implementing your very first strategy.

Occasional Entrepreneurs Have Countless Opportunities to Profit

If you're one of the millions of people who love their job but just want to make a few thousand dollars on the side five or six times a year, Part Four, "Becoming an Occasional Entrepreneur," has the details you need to apply the Instant Income strategies to your moneymaking project with minimum hassle, short-term commitment, and maximum results.

Part Four even gives you criteria for determining *which* moneymaking projects are the most favorable for making Instant Income using the 35 strategies featured in this book. Once you determine the income project that's right for you, read through the strategies and use the Overnight Audit to determine which strategy you'll want to execute first.

. . .

Whichever situation you find yourself in—business owner, employee, or Occasional Entrepreneur—you'll get the most benefit out of this book by reading it thoroughly, then implementing the strategies one by one, based upon the plan you create in Part Two.

Once you've mastered the strategies to create Instant Income, get ready to turn Instant Income into lifetime wealth by integrating the strategies into an ongoing business—whether it's yours or your employer's. Part Five teaches you how to maximize your Instant Income activities for the long term.

There's So Much More Waiting for You at the Back of This Book

While the first seven chapters' worth of Instant Income strategies may seem daunting to you, be sure to keep reading. There is so much more to learn beyond the 35 strategies—in Parts Three, Four, and Five—that the time you spend digesting the last third of *Instant Income* will be well rewarded, I assure you.

What can you expect to learn in Parts Three, Four, and Five?

You'll learn how to get paid more at your current job. You'll learn how to make more in your own side business. You'll learn how to implement any marketing campaign with ease. You'll learn how to develop an implementation calendar. You'll learn how to negotiate compensation deals, how to enroll others to help you make money, and how to reduce the "hassle factor" in any business you operate. You'll even learn how to integrate each and every strategy into ongoing income-generating systems that keep on working every day in your small business.

Your future as an Instant Income entrepreneur is about to begin. Let's get going.

PART ONE

Strategies That Bring in the Cash

CHAPTER 1

Getting Customers to Give You More Money

YOUR SMALL BUSINESS is a valuable asset. It gives you the ability to collect money for goods and services. It lets you create continual cash flow from loyal customers. It lets you conduct promotions, run advertisements, and broadcast e-mails that drive eager buyers to your door.

And if your bank account is in trouble, it's also your single best opportunity for generating cash virtually overnight.

The truth is, almost all businesses have tens of thousands (if not millions) of dollars in Instant Income that can easily be generated from day-to-day activities with just a few changes in tactics.

In fact, every day, thousands of small businesses like yours are losing out on money they could be making from their existing business, simply because they don't fully exploit the multitude of business assets, marketing assets, and relationship assets that the business has in place right now.

You've spent a lot of time, effort, and money to get where you are today. You probably put your own money into starting your business. You hired employees or established outsourcing relationships. You spent time and money developing a product or service, and every day of the year you spend even more time and money advertising it, selling it, and delivering it.

Along the way—without even knowing it—you created something else, too: marketable assets. These assets don't necessarily show up on your inventory printout or balance sheet. Assets include your customer list, your relationships with suppliers, your advertising calendar, your Internet presence, the knowledge of your key employees, the sales pitch your salespeople use, and so on.

Together—over this and the next six chapters—you and I are going to turn those uncommon assets into desperately needed income—instantly.

I'll teach you the basics you need to know about each of the seven areas where cash can be created in your business—joint ventures, advertising, prospecting, and sales, among others—and I'll follow each basic tutorial with individual, easy-to-execute strategies that are designed to bring in the cash. In other words, you'll not only gain the mindset and expertise you need but also "learn by doing" as you tackle the actual tasks that will turn your unique business assets into Instant Income. We'll start with the most undervalued asset of all.

Your Most Immediate Source of Instant Income

In consulting with countless businesses over the years, nothing has surprised me more than the number of business owners who fail to exploit their most valuable and reliable asset: their customer list. In fact, what's even more surprising is the number of businesses that never attempt to sell their customers anything after the first sale.

This fact is especially shocking because the typical business owner will spend tens—possibly hundreds—of thousands of dollars over the life of the business.

The truth is, the customers sitting right in your own database are the most profound source of Instant Income in your business today. When you make an offer to existing and past customers, not only is it easier to sell *them* something than to sell it to new prospects off the street, but your sales actually become more profitable because you don't have to cover the cost of acquiring those customers in the first place.

Customers Have a Lifetime Value

It's expensive to generate a new customer today. There are marketing costs, advertising costs, new account setup costs—even the time required to educate yourself about a new consulting client's business. These things all cost you—either in real dollars or in lost time that you can't otherwise spend on generating revenue.

But the good news is that you can actually forecast what you can and should be spending to bring a new customer in the door.

How?

By calculating the lifetime value of each customer.

The lifetime value of a customer is the total amount that that customer will spend over a lifetime of patronage with your business. When you know the lifetime value of a customer, you can calculate how much you can spend to bring that customer in the door—and still make money over time.

Take a look at your own customer list, for example, and calculate—on average—what each new customer will spend over a lifetime of purchases with you. Do customers purchase only once? Do they come back every week? Do they renew their annual maintenance contract once a year? Do they buy only for their children, and then only while those children are in grammar school? However they buy from you, add up the average customer's lifetime purchases in gross dollars.

Next, calculate your profits on those sales.

Then decide just how much of that profit you would be willing to spend to acquire that customer in the first place.

If you own a lawn-care company, for example, you could probably calculate the average number of years each one of your customers has been with you and the average monthly amount each customer pays you. Let's say the lifetime value of a customer is an average of three years at $40 per month, or $1,440, on which you make a profit of $1,080. Can you see how—with more than $1,000 in profits—you could easily afford to spend $100 (or maybe even more) to bring that customer in the door?

When you do the math for your own business (or your employer's), you'll discover that customers are such a valuable asset that it's worth calculating down to the penny what you can afford to spend to bring new ones in the door. Here's the formula:

Average customer's lifetime purchases in gross dollars	−	Cost of goods sold or services provided	=	Gross profit from all customer purchases

Of course, determining the lifetime value of a customer not only will tell you how quickly you can grow your customer list (based upon what you're willing to spend) but will also motivate you to do everything you can to increase the lifetime value of these folks.

Steady and frequent communication with customers is the key to greater lifetime value, by the way.

The lifetime value of a customer grows when you keep customers engaged with you and your business, when you give them a reason and the desire to do business with you, and when you stay connected with their lives. Too many business owners fall short by not staying in communication. They let past customers get out of touch with what the business is currently doing and what it can offer.

Do You Know Who Your Customers Are?

What do you need to do to start creating Instant Income from your own customers? Check your customer database to be sure you have the name and contact information for each of your present and past customers, along with a record of their purchasing history. (If you don't have a database, buy one of the many database software programs available and start inputting names from credit card slips, check photocopies, shipping manifests, and so on.) For instance, do you have the following information?

- ➤ All present customers
- ➤ All past customers
- ➤ Names and addresses
- ➤ Phone numbers
- ➤ E-mail addresses
- ➤ Purchasing history
- ➤ Reason each customer first contacted you
- ➤ Ads/promotions that each customer has responded to

If you haven't started collecting the names of customers, start doing so now, using strategies that require little or no cash outlay.

One of the fastest ways to accumulate names and use them to generate quick, no-cost sales is to ask for customers' e-mail addresses—either at the time of purchase or when they call in—and then send them prewritten special offers via e-mail that same day.

You might offer a special batch of items at a preferred price or give customers a special report containing both unique information that helps their business and an offer to do business with you. If your customers are consumers, invite them to purchase a year's worth of your services on an ongoing basis at a preferred price.

You might also commission a special e-book about the items they purchased from you or about how they can better use what they purchased from you. This "instant" delivery of quality information and offers not only is appreciated and makes you look professional but also keeps the customer engaged with you, your company and the benefits you have to offer.

Of course, there are many other ways to "bribe" customers into giving you their contact information so that you can start building a database.

Offer Something Free That Costs You Nothing to Deliver

I once developed a database-building program for the owner of an educational Web site that had millions of visitors each year but relatively few e-mail addresses for them. I advised the company to create a product "beta-test" program whereby families of school-age children could register to become test families and receive free educational products before the products were introduced to the general marketplace. The product providers were happy to get advance feedback about their products, the Web site owner was able to negotiate the distribution of these products free of charge, and the families were delighted to get free products simply for registering their e-mail address along with some information about their educational needs.

In another situation, I worked with a business owner who sold specialty hand tools to hobby shops, which then sold the tools to consumers. He sent the hobby shops a monthly audiotape of marketing advice from various business experts to help them sell more tools at retail. While each cassette cost him about 75 cents at the time, today that same audio material could be sent to the customer's e-mail address at virtually *zero cost* as an MP3 or WAV file. (You can replicate this audio strategy by downloading free Instant Income audio files to send to your business customers. Visit www.instantincome.com/freeB-to-B.html for a complete giveaway program that is already recorded and produced for you.)

What could *you* provide free that has a high perceived value but is *not* a discount, is *not* expensive to deliver, and is *not* too demanding on your time? Answer the following questions to find out:

➤ What is your typical customer's biggest problem or opportunity?

➤ What could you provide to help your customers solve that problem or take advantage of that opportunity?

➤ Where can you find that information, service, or other giveaway for free or at very little cost?

➤ How could you easily let customers know that you will give them that item when they give you their contact information?

Turn Data Capture into an Instant Profit Center

Contests and rewards programs are other easy strategies for collecting your customers' contact information. These are particularly suited for retail locations, which typically don't have a reason to ask for a customer's name, address, phone number, and e-mail address.

While only a few people will win your contest or giveaway this week, you can still turn your contest into an instant profit center by sending an offer to everyone who did *not* win the contest. Use customers' personal "wish lists" and e-mail them offers based on the products, sizes, or wishes that they wrote down. Tell customers that you're sorry they didn't win, but that you have a consolation gift of a certain percentage off on a special bundle of products that fit individual needs if they purchase these products in the next seven days.

Tell Customers It's Required

One of the easiest ways to capture e-mail addresses (which are the least expensive way to market to anyone) is to simply tell customers that they're required to provide it. If you're a retail or service company that takes credit cards as payment, instruct your store clerks to have customers put their e-mail address on the charge slip when they sign it.

Even professional practitioners can use this technique. I was recently at my doctor's office, and I was given an updated patient information form with space for my e-mail address. "Why would the doctor want to e-mail me?" I asked. The reply? "It's required."

While this sounds invasive, you would be surprised how many customers will never question why you're asking for it—they simply assume it's necessary or required. Of course, I never recommend spamming anyone's e-mail address, and you should always delete from your database any customers who ask to unsubscribe or opt out. But, by and large, if you have a legitimate business relationship with your customers, you can e-mail them information in the normal course of doing business. Check current spam laws to be certain.*

Knowing your business, what could you do to capture the name and contact information of each and every customer who walks through your door? What reason could you give for doing so?

If you're an Internet business with an international presence, or if you own a virtual company or a consulting firm without a public "storefront" location, what can you do to simply capture the customers and prospects who are contacting you now? Offer a free newsletter? A free report? A free audio file or other giveaway?

Start Turning Your Customers into Instant Income

Once you know who your customers are, it's time to start turning them into Instant Income. Of course, if you already have their names in a database, or if your retail store or order desk is currently open for business, you can literally start earning Instant Income within the next few minutes.

How?

By executing Customer Strategy 1, "Keep Track of Customer Buying Patterns, Then Call to Take Reorders." This is followed by four other powerful strategies that can help turn customer interactions into cash. And like all the strategies in *Instant Income,* they're fully explained, with enough step-by-step detail to help you begin implementing them immediately.

But don't just stop with this chapter about customers. Read through all seven chapters in Part One and take the time to digest all 35 of the proven strategies. Not only will you see immediate applications in your own business or workplace as you read, but you'll begin to develop a short list of strategies to execute.

---

* Visit www.ftc.gov/bcp/conline/pubs/buspubs/canspam.htm.

Keep Track of Customer Buying Patterns, Then Call to Take Reorders

By keeping index cards of what customers had purchased, I was able to call at just the right time and instantly sell hundreds of dollars worth of additional product right over the phone. My customers even thanked me for the reminder call.

JENNIFER SCHWABAUER
Owner of Harvest Lamb Company

One of the most interesting entrepreneurs I've ever worked with was a sheep farmer who raised fancy spring lambs for the freezers and meat lockers of private local buyers and gourmet cooks and caterers. The sheep farmer, a stay-at-home mom, provided unparalleled customer service, including coordinating all aspects of the processing, cutting, and wrapping with a specialty butcher shop hand-selected by her. She even delivered the packages of carefully wrapped chops and roasts to the buyer's doorstep.

At holiday time, she gave her buyers beautifully prepared gourmet baskets, complete with her own recipe book, jars of fancy seasonings and sauces, braids of garlic, and a special brochure reminding customers why her gourmet lamb was better than anything they would find in the grocery store, the meat market, or even the fanciest restaurant.

She continually educated her customers on how to cook each cut of meat more easily for use in everyday meals, rather than thinking of lamb solely as a special-occasion meat.

In addition to providing all this service, this sheep farmer kept careful records of how each customer wanted the lamb cut and wrapped, how thick the chops should be, how many chops to wrap in each package, whether the customer wanted leg roasts or leg steaks, how large a lamb the customer typically bought, how often the customer bought lamb, and similar comments that helped her provide optimum service to her buyers.

Her small-farm operation was a wonderful, textbook example of a well-run, customer-oriented business!

Not surprisingly, she was able to charge nearly triple the going rate for her fancy freezer lamb—and she was getting many times the average market price that commercial fat lamb producers received when they sent their huge spring lamb crops to market.

Her only problem was that each spring and fall, she waited for buyers to call her to place their orders. Often, when buyers called, she would be sold out of the size that they wanted, or else she would have too many lambs left unsold at the wrong time of year (like right after the holidays, when no one is thinking about fancy dinner parties).

To help her minimize this problem and instantly sell her lambs for cash, I suggested that she contact previous buyers either by telephone or by postcard, alerting them that she had lambs available in the size that they typically bought, then offering to handle everything, filling their freezer with flavorful, carefully packaged lamb within days of their responding.

Because she kept careful records of how often buyers bought lambs from her, she merely reviewed her records and sent notices (or telephoned buyers) *when she knew they were probably out of the choicest cuts of meat.* Her simple postcard eventually evolved into an educational flyer that she could send to buyers who had not purchased for more than a year—enabling her to reactivate customers she had thought were lost forever.

What was the outcome of this simple strategy? She began taking advance orders for lambs months ahead of when they would be ready, eventually building a waiting list for her fancy freezer lambs.

In other words, people waited months for the privilege of buying from her. Now, isn't that a problem we'd all like to have?

Applying This Proven Concept to Your Situation

The key to the success of this strategy is to maintain contact information via software that easily retrieves the information for you, reminds you to make the calls, and helps you keep notes on the results.

If you sell any kind of consumable, you owe it to yourself and your business to set up a contact management program with a "tickler" feature to prompt you to make these calls at just the point when customers will be deciding to replenish their supply. In fact, keeping records is imperative, since many customers will want to know what they ordered last time and will ask you to simply send the same amount.

Be proactive and call your customers to take reorders. You cannot afford to wait until your customers contact you! In fact, by servicing your customers this way, you will stand head and shoulders above your competitors.

If you're a consultant or a professional practitioner, not someone who sells a consumable product or service, the same strategy applies.

For instance, advertising agencies and graphic design firms can call clients months before the time their annual reports would normally be produced. Technology consulting firms can call well ahead of major software upgrades coming into use. Skin-care specialists can call two weeks ahead of when clients would routinely come in for their European facials—just by observing those clients' purchasing patterns and making a few calls in the evening.

Virtually every kind of business or Occasional Entrepreneur can immediately boost profits using this "reminder call" strategy. In fact, many companies are naturals for providing reminder calls. For example,

➤ Specialty clothing stores that know the sizes and color preferences of each customer can call when the new season's fashions come in.

➤ Interior decorators who've been able to provide only a small part of a home's total decor can call with new pieces that they know will go with the client's current color scheme.

➤ Art dealers, antiques brokers, and personal shoppers have built entire businesses on this strategy.

➤ Even trade schools and training centers can call with new courses of study that the student should be taking to advance her knowledge in a particular area.

What to Say in Reminder Calls and Notices

In any telephone call like this, you want to be sure (1) that you can easily deliver the script in a friendly way, (2) that you are providing a service and are not perceived as invasive or pushy by your customers, and (3) that you get some sort of commitment from customers to come in and look at new products, to place an order for more products or services, to agree to a meeting to review their needs, or to agree to receive samples, photos, or other printed information in the mail.

Take a look at the script and postcard that I suggested to the fancy freezer lamb grower:

HARVEST LAMB COMPANY

Recently, we noticed that, even though you've enjoyed our fresh, flavorful grain-fed lamb in the past, you haven't replenished your supply.

We now have Spring lambs in just the size you previously ordered, and can handle all aspects of the cut and wrap—delivering tender, succulent locally raised gourmet lamb right to your doorstep within a few days.

Please allow us to keep your freezer well stocked by processing an order according to your previous specifications. We'll call you within a few days to confirm your order. To reach us before we place this courtesy call, please telephone (000) 000-0000.

Sincerely,

Jennifer Schwabauer

Fancy Freezer Lamb Telephone Script

Hi, this is Jennifer Schwabauer. May I speak to [customer name], please? Hi, [customer name]. This is Jennifer Schwabauer. I'm just calling because it's the season to be replacing your freezer lamb supply. I have some really nice lambs right now and I looked up your card to see what you purchased in the past.

I have several lambs in that weight category. Can I put your name down for another lamb that size or would you like one larger or smaller?

If "Yes, Put Me Down for One":

OK, great! We'll get going on your order immediately, then call to let you know when it will be delivered. Your total will be $_____, by the way. Shall I stop by tomorrow and pick up a check? Great!

In the past, you indicated the following cutting instructions. Do you want to make any changes to these instructions or to the packaging you received last time?

If "No, I Still Have Lamb in the Freezer":

Well, I have lambs that are a little smaller now that will be available in about four months. May I reserve one for you and call you back in four months to coordinate the delivery?

Do you see how keeping track of what your current customers order and following up with them can help you generate income almost instantly? Not only that, it can help you manage your cash flow better and predict both your production needs and your workload. It just makes sense.

CUSTOMER STRATEGY 2

Upsell Customers at the Point of Purchase

I've found that the best time to ask a customer for more money is right after he or she has given you money. It seems illogical. But it works because the customer's buying emotion is still at its peak.

DAVID DEUTSCH
Top direct-response copywriter,
marketing consultant, and author of
Think Inside the Box

Whenever I present the Instant Income One-Day Seminar, the hundreds of small business owners in attendance can usually generate quick cash at the very first break simply by calling their store or office, downloading a two-sentence script to their staff, and having those employees implement the most immediate and effective technique for increasing their cash flow.

We call this powerful two-sentence technique *upselling*.

Simply put, upselling is the strategy of selling additional goods and services to customers just before they complete their purchase. Upselling means selling more products, additional services, upgraded packages, better models, and different options.

When you offer a better version or extra add-ons or any supplemental services that customers need in order to benefit more fully from the item or service that they're purchasing, you not only create more cash for yourself, but also create happier customers who ultimately enjoy their purchase more.

Think about it.

Have you ever purchased an item or service, only to find out that the one extra component you *didn't* purchase is now making it difficult for you to use what you *did* buy? Have you ever wished that a salesperson or store clerk had told you about the upgraded memory for your new laptop or the dealer-installed running boards for your new SUV?

When I went into our local consumer electronics store recently to buy a digital camera, the store clerk made certain that I knew about all the extra equipment that was available to me—including, most importantly, those items that were required if I was to have the best possible experience with the camera. He told me about the $149 memory card, the $89 photo printer, the $27 paper kit, the $18 leather camera bag, and, of course, the $38 extended warranty. As a result, $480 later, I owned a beautiful new $159 camera. My point is that this salesperson was trained to suggest add-ons, upgrades, and complementary items that would make my digital camera experience more enjoyable. But what if he hadn't done that? I would own a camera, but I would have no way to print out pictures, take extra pictures, protect my camera during travel, or get the camera repaired if anything went wrong.

That salesperson did his job of upselling. He added $321 to my original purchase—and I'm a more satisfied customer because of it.

Of course, upselling doesn't just apply to retail goods. It applies to all kinds of other sales situations, too.

➤ Newsletter publishers typically try to sell a two-year or three-year subscription at the same time they're offering a one-year subscription. They'll even provide additional bonus reports, e-mail updates, and other services to get you to choose the upgraded subscription.

➤ Specialty software companies upsell other modules, along with additional services such as training, technical support, and database transfer.

➤ High-end dress shops and evening wear stores upsell jewelry, shoes, and handbags that would "go perfectly" with that evening gown you're buying. In fact, the shop I frequent for my evening wear sells gowns, interview suits, jewelry, shoes, and even specialty lingerie to hundreds of beauty pageant contestants throughout the western United States. The saleswomen simply pull out all these extra items as customers are trying on gowns—just to make sure contestants leave the store with a look that's complete. The store's owner even travels to larger pageants for last-minute fittings and assistance with her gowns.

Upsells That Create Instant Income

Complementary Items and Extra Add-Ons

Add-ons are easy to sell, particularly when the extra component or service helps the customer get better use out of his primary purchase. Simply describe the extra items, why they're beneficial, why they're popular, and so on. Mention the price almost as an afterthought. Often the customer won't even ask about the cost until he's on his way to the cash register.

If you don't have anything else to upsell your customer, by the way, consider negotiating with another company to let you sell its add-on product or service and make a commission on each sale. See Joint-Venture Strategy 3, "Offer Other People's Products and Services to Your Customers," for more details.

An Upgraded Item or a Package

In the two decades that I've spent marketing seminars, coaching, and other information products, I've discovered an amazing phenomenon: given the choice and a few words of encouragement, people will frequently buy the most expensive package you have to offer.

Does this surprise you? It shouldn't.

The fact is, we live in a consumer-driven society. People spend money on a regular basis to both solve their problems and enjoy the possessions and lifestyle they want. They usually aren't satisfied with a lesser solution or a downgraded possession. They want the best. And *if they can justify the purchase price in their mind,* they will very often pay extra to get the upgraded package.

This is one reason why expensive cars, expensive watches, expensive homes, and other upgraded versions of life's amenities sell for such high prices, even though other perfectly functional—but less expensive—versions are widely available.

The lesson here for you is to create an upgraded option, price it high, then describe it in a way that helps customers justify the additional expenditure in their mind. We'll be talking more about techniques for writing advertising copy in Chapter 3, but suffice it to say that how you present the upsell offer is important.

Other examples of upgraded items and packages include

➤ Equipment with sturdier hardware, upgraded materials, high-fashion colors, or a high-tech look.

➤ Services provided by upper-level management rather than junior employees.

➤ Goods and services that are personalized, customized, engraved, or otherwise unique to the customer.

➤ A collection or bundle of items that go together.

➤ A two-pack or three-pack of any consumable item. (In fact, if you sell only one product, be sure to offer a two-pack or three-pack at a small discount. You'll be surprised at how many customers will buy multiple units of the same thing.)

In creating these upgraded versions or packages, the key is to build a higher perceived value into the product, then use your upselling script to communicate that higher value.

Specials of the Day

Years ago, whenever I called my Apple Macintosh reseller, the salesperson would help me with my catalog order, then upsell me by offering several specials of the day before completing the sale. The reseller always featured some nifty little software application or font collection or desk accessory priced at $49 or less. I loved those deals. To a Macintosh aficionado, they were like penny candy. In fact, this catalog company did such a good job of making these specials enticing that it got to the point where I was trained to ask for them while I was finalizing my equipment purchases.

When my niece and I were shopping recently, her favorite store offered her three different daily specials for $5 each—with colorful displays of the items right there at the checkout counter. Of course she found something she liked. And the store probably profited by another three or four dollars just by making the offer.

"How Are You Fixed for Bread and Milk?"

It amazes me that convenience stores and mini-marts don't regularly ask customers whether they need basic staples like bread and milk—especially during the late afternoon, when customers are stopping by after work. If you have a retail store, take-out restaurant, or other location frequented by folks who stop in on their way home, why not ask them if they need basic items that you stock but that they might forget to purchase otherwise?

Maintenance and Support Contracts

Perhaps the easiest upsell of all is maintenance contracts, technical support, warranties, and other long-term contracts that help customers maintain the value of their purchase and protect themselves from loss—including the loss of time, as in the case of technical support.

Large companies offer these contracts all they time—why shouldn't you?

If your company is too small to maintain a staff to provide ongoing support or repair services, you can take advantage of the many outsourcing companies that specialize in fulfilling these agreements. For instance, many Internet companies outsource their technical support and customer service to professional "help desks" in countries where costs are lower.

The Two-Sentence Upselling Script

By formulating a short two-sentence script for these various upselling situations, you can often increase a customer's sale by 20 percent or more. And while development of a successful script may sound complicated, the formula is actually quite easy—just a statement followed by a question.

Let's look at some examples:

> "Well, ma'am, that camera has pretty limited memory, so most people get a memory card so that they can take extra pictures. Can I show you the one that goes with your camera?"

> "Most companies find that their people need training on the new software, so we always offer it along with the package. Would you like to schedule your training dates along with your purchase?"

> "It's not something that everyone can afford, and, in fact, the prices are escalating every year, but we do have a limited-edition giclée of that painting signed by the artist. Can I reserve one for you?"

> "Typically, we schedule a standard audit with one of our junior accountants, but I think you'll want the extra attention of working directly with Milt Cohen, our senior partner. Can I check his calendar and schedule an initial meeting for you?"

Notice the format of these upselling scripts. The sales clerk presents a potentially frustrating situation that might occur if you're caught later without the additional item. Then the script solves the dilemma by offering you the item that will prevent that future predicament.

Also, note the tone of these scripts, which assumes that you'll naturally want to purchase the extra item. To do anything else would be foolish.

In all cases, when writing your upselling pitch, be sure to get agreement from the customer by crafting phrases like, "Shall I set it aside for you?" "Do you want to schedule that right now?" "Can I add that to your order?" You will generate Instant Income from upselling only if you get the customer's buy-in as a result of your pitch.

CUSTOMER STRATEGY 3

Convert One-Time Customers to Continuity Customers

As a chiropractor with an extensive marketing background, I created a monthly practice-building marketing service to help other doctors grow their practice. At $1,500 per month for the service, the continuity program began generating $60,000 a month within just 60 days.

DR. LEN SCHWARTZ
Founder of Marketing Domination
Specialists LLC

If you have a group of customers who buy regularly from you, or if you sell a consumable item that customers buy repeatedly, you can easily generate substantial Instant Income by upselling those buyers into a *continuity* program.

Continuity programs deliver ongoing monthly services, regular shipments of product, individual educational modules, or a special monthly selection, with customers signing up today for a series of shipments or deliveries in the future.

Not only are continuity programs easier to deliver, but they're also a lot more profitable than a one-time sale. Why? Because you don't have to constantly resell the customer on your service or spend money generating new customers.

You sell customers once and bill their card until they tell you to stop or until their contract runs out.

If you keep customers happy with your product or service, they'll keep paying you month in and month out. In fact, many businesses with continuity programs or long-term contracts include these customer revenues on their balance sheet every month as an asset or predictable revenue.

What are some examples of continuity products and services?

Nutritional supplements, pool services, janitorial services, printing, air conditioning maintenance, newsletter and magazine subscriptions, and subscription consulting, among others.

Even if you don't sell products and services that customers replace or re-order frequently, you can always negotiate a joint venture with another company to provide those goods or services. (You'll learn all about joint ventures in Chapter 2, "Getting Other People to Help Bring in the Cash.")

Common Types of Continuity Programs

There are two basic types of continuity programs that you can offer: *open-ended programs,* which continue until the customer cancels or fails to pay, and *closed-ended programs,* which require the customer to agree to a fixed number of deliveries.

Typically, business owners charge the customer's credit card automatically whenever a delivery is made. Occasionally, a business owner will ask that the entire cost of the program be paid up front.*

Regardless of the program you offer, be aware that *breakage* will occur. That is, a percentage of customers will drop out of the program or fail to use their regular deliveries. How much breakage *you* experience will depend on your product, service, program, cost, and ongoing customer-care efforts. The better the product or service you provide, and the more you do to ensure that your continuity customers use their regular deliveries, the less breakage you will have.

The easiest continuity programs to offer are those where your customers routinely purchase the same products on a regular basis, you perform the same level of service on a regular basis for the same clients, or you provide repair and maintenance services on a regular basis. Here are some other common types of programs:

---

* Check with your own attorney and accountant to be certain, but with prepaid long-term contracts, it is usually advisable to escrow any contract payments made and release them to your bank account only when shipments are made or services are delivered. Do not accept full payment if it's possible that you may not be able to make future deliveries.

➤ **Monthly shipment**. Track customer buying habits* to see how often they purchase and how much they buy each time. Then contact them as a courtesy to suggest a regular schedule so they never run out of supplies. Similarly, you can offer an item-of-the-month program that delivers a unique monthly selection.

➤ **Recurring services**. Countless services, from gym memberships to pest control to regular beauty treatments, are sold on a continuity basis. Typically, these services are sold as ongoing programs from the beginning, with no option to buy a single visit or individual house call available.

➤ **Large collection of related items delivered monthly**. If you have a group of customers who simply don't have the funds to purchase an expensive package of goods or services from you, why not split the package into individual components shipped monthly? This is routinely done in the educational field to sell correspondence courses and other large home-study editions.

➤ **Long-term contracts.** Consultants who sell their services by the hour are losing out on huge amounts of income compared to those who sell long-term consulting contracts and development programs. Simply estimate how many sessions, hours, or other work will be required for the client to get a specific result, then sell the multisession program based on the anticipated result.

Selling Continuity Offers

The most successful sales of continuity programs are made at the point when a customer is making his or her very first purchase. But you can always approach existing customers later with a "brand-new program designed to better meet their needs." Here are other offers that work:

➤ **Advertise the results derived from your long-term program.** Customer testimonials used in advertising, if they are well written, are often so compelling that consumers will call or stop in and say, "I want to buy

---

* You can read more about tracking customer purchasing habits in Customer Strategy 1, "Keep Track of Customer Buying Patterns, Then Call to Take Reorders."

what she got." In fact, they will rarely ask whether a single session or an individual delivery is available—instead, they will believe that the result advertised somehow requires multiple services or deliveries.*

➤ **Bundle goods and services that they can't buy separately.** This type of offer is ideal because it encourages customers to purchase the long-term product bundle or service contract in order to get the preferred items. Of course, you can always create new items or services expressly in order to sell your continuity program. What do you have to offer (or can you purchase from someone else) that your customers want?

➤ **Offer a price reduction, but only if necessary.** I always prefer to add extra benefits rather than drop the price of anything. But if you can truly save on delivery costs by selling customers long-term contracts, you could pass on a portion of these savings. Be sure to explain in your advertising, however, that you're discounting the total program because bundling saves you money—savings that you're happy to pass on to the customer.

➤ **Let a friend or spouse join free.** Rather than giving a discount on a continuity program, why not allow a friend or spouse to participate for free? Given the fact that some businesses experience breakage of 50 percent or more, you might easily be able to accommodate another person in your schedule so long as your fixed costs do not increase with additional customers.

CUSTOMER STRATEGY 4

Resell Customers Prior to Their Contract Renewal Date

By starting to solicit renewals well before subscribers receive their last issue, we easily get 10 times the results we would get if we just renewed upon expiration.

GARRETT WOOD
Soundview Publications, publishers of
Second Opinion, Women's Health Letter,
and *Prescriptions for Healthy Living*

---

* See Advertising Strategy 1, "Ask Your Customers to Tell Their Story," for more information on how to write results-oriented testimonial ads. Be sure to practice truth in advertising by featuring only those customers who have purchased the actual program being advertised.

Have you ever subscribed to a magazine and received a renewal notice two months later? Magazine publishers have mastered the art of reselling you prior to your contract expiration date.

When I was still working as the marketing director for the regional bank, I instructed the new account representatives to print out a list by customer of all the 30-day, 6-month, 1-year, and 2-year certificates of deposit they had sold during any given month. Then I had them carefully file these records in a simple, month-by-month accordion file so that they could pull out the list and call customers *a month ahead* of the maturity date for their CD. This way, customers perceived the call from the new accounts representative as a valuable reminder service, and the reps were able to easily roll over those funds into new CDs or other investments with the bank—before the customers started investigating other options.

Back then, we used the simple paper method. But you can just as easily use modern-day contact management software.

Include a Reorder Device with Your Product or Service

As obvious as this sounds, you'd be surprised how many business owners fail to get the next sale simply because they don't make reordering easy. If you sell a consumable product or service that is purchased again and again—by consumers or retailers or business owners—you owe it to your bottom line to include a simple and inexpensive reordering device along with each shipment or service delivery. This is especially true if your company sells to a lot of mom-and-pop retail locations that can't use sophisticated online ordering, automated inventory monitoring, weekly restocking visits by product reps, or other such sales-enhancement strategies (or if you don't offer these services).

Reorder Devices That Can Increase Sales

➤ Perhaps you sell hanger-displayed, packaged items, and the retailer stocks only one or two of each kind. To speed reorders, provide a hang-tag with your company's telephone number, the stock or part number, and the previous quantity ordered. When the business owner or stock clerk notices that a hanger or bin is empty, your tag will remain there, telling the business owner exactly how to reorder.

➤ Including a reorder form in each shipping carton is also a good way to prompt reorders. In fact, you'd be surprised how many reorders you'll get immediately following the shipment—often before the store owner's initial stock is depleted. Be sure to provide space where store owners can designate their desired future shipping date.

➤ If you sell lots of stock to a limited number of buyers that reorder constantly, take time to introduce yourself by telephone to each buyer's purchasing manager. Ask what would help him remember to reorder and what devices would make it easiest for him to contact you. A weekly or monthly reminder fax? A reminder e-mail with current pricing? A preprinted card for his Rolodex? A tablet of preprinted order forms? Determine which method would simplify the process for each buyer, then follow through on that method.

➤ If you sell routine automotive services such as oil changes, detailing, tire service, or tune-ups, provide a door sticker that alerts drivers to bring back their vehicle when they reach a certain mileage. If you service office machines, provide a sticker that alerts personnel when to call you for regular checkups.

➤ If you sell printed forms, insert a reorder form two-thirds of the way through the stack to remind administrative personnel to reorder. If you provide other kinds of printed materials, clearly mark each box with your company name, telephone number, the quantity in that box, the job or brochure number, the customer number or account name, the advance time required to reprint that form, and other pertinent information.

➤ If you sell products regularly to larger stores or chains, inquire when you make your first sale how you can be entered into that customer's automated reordering system.

➤ Depending on the customer, you may even use automatically scheduled shipments themselves as the reorder device, either shipping additional product outright or calling ahead to confirm quantities before shipping.

➤ If you provide raw materials to manufacturers, try to work with manufacturing managers, inventory managers, and purchasing staff to be designated as the regular vendor for the parts or materials you provide—even to the point of being recorded in the inventory management system. That way, you'll be contacted first with a reorder before your competitors have a chance to bid on those parts.

➤ If you provide high-end consulting, software programming, bookkeeping or accounting, telephone wiring or programming, data processing, Web site development, or other types of critical and highly custom work, provide in writing all details that might be required to produce future work and provide permanent contact information such as your phone number, Web address, and mailing address. Of course, many vendors build this kind of reporting into their contract costs, providing backup files on stable storage devices, reams of printed source code, and other details. That way, no matter where *you* end up—if you're hired by another firm, for example, or if you move your company—customers can find you even years later when they want to make changes, patches, or upgrades or to buy other kinds of services.

By offering your customers any or all of these reorder devices, you'll not only help speed the reorder process but also get reorders that you normally would have to call or send letters to get (or might even lose to your competitor). Whenever you sell a commodity item, get to the customer *first,* before she thinks about ordering additional stock or services from someone else.

CUSTOMER STRATEGY 5

Instantly Reactivate Past Customers and Patients

By automating our reactivation sequence, offering strategically timed gifts, and consistently following up using a variety of marketing methods, we saw an immediate 30 percent boost in client activity and retention. This strategy alone will represent at least $100,000 in additional revenue that had been quietly slipping away from us.

CLATE W. MASK
President of Infusion Software & Consulting

If you have yet to make an effort to reactivate past customers, or if you haven't yet looked at your customer list to see how many inactive customers or clients you have, you may be sitting on a gold mine of Instant Income.

Past customers often have no idea why they stopped purchasing from you or stopped using your services. All they need is a reminder of why they enjoyed buying from you—and a special incentive to begin doing so again.

What could *you* do to reactivate past customers?

If you're a retail location, why not contact customers with a special item that you don't normally carry but that they might be interested in? If you're a service business, you could contact past customers by phone and suggest that they come back to finish their services (if they didn't already) or that they may need your service again after going for so long without it. This is the ideal time, by the way, to sign up customers for an ongoing service of quarterly visits or monthly deliveries.

If you're a doctor, why not offer a mini-physical or some other type of test that your patients should be doing every year but aren't? Explain to them in simple language the benefits of staying on top of their health and the downside of not doing so. Offer a special package price to former patients during August and December, when things are slow in your practice. You can even contract with an outside service to bring in specialized equipment to perform tests over a two-week period, then invite past patients to come in for evaluation.

Other Ways to Reactivate Past Customers

➤ **A phone call from the owner works best.** I remember the story of an ad agency that hired a new CEO, expecting him to bring in new business. Instead, he personally called all the past clients who had stopped doing business with the agency and asked them to come back on board with the firm again.

➤ **Send an "I'm sorry" letter.** If customers and clients had a reason to stop doing business with you, apologize and ask what you could do to make it worthwhile doing business with you again. This heartfelt approach is rarely seen in business, and an honest "I'm sorry" works surprisingly well.

➤ **Treat them as you would a preferred customer.** Send to or call past customers with a special price or purchase offer on items that they previously purchased.

➤ **Be specific in your offers.** If you have built your customer database as I recommended and captured your customers' purchase history or "wish list," you know what they previously bought on a regular basis. Offer them that item again at a special price or as part of a special package. They'll thank you for knowing about their needs and for offering ways to save them money.

➤ **Invite past customers to a special event at your store.** If you own a consulting firm or professional practice, why not schedule an evening workshop with a speaker on a special topic of interest, then invite past customers to attend? Be sure to present a special offer just before you close for the evening, so that you turn the event into a true Instant Income opportunity.

Planning a Campaign to Reactivate Customers

When customers change their normal buying pattern by more than 25 percent, you should be on the alert, particularly if you are selling a consumable product or service that customers use up, then repurchase frequently.

What could you do to reactivate past customers? Answer the following questions to plan your reactivation campaign:

➤ When you look at your database, which groups of customers have stopped doing business with you?

➤ What were these customers' business or personal needs when they were doing business with you? What did they buy? What problems did they have? Do they still have those problems?

➤ What could you offer to meet their needs immediately? What kind of offer would they respond to?

➤ How can you easily and inexpensively contact them—by telephone? e-mail? postcard? letter?

Bribe Past Customers to Do Business with You Again

Whether you offer a special bonus, a free consultation, a one-time reduction in fees, or some other incentive, let your past customers know that you are eager to serve their needs again and that you have developed a special package just for them. This is important. People like to feel acknowledged. They enjoy receiving preferential treatment. By putting together a special package or offer, you can shamelessly bribe them into doing business with you again.

What kind of e-mail or letter should you send? Take a look at the example on the next page.

Don't Give Up—Customers and Prospects Have Changing Needs

Even if you don't reactivate past customers with your first letter, don't give up on them. The fact is that people's needs are constantly changing. What they weren't interested in a month ago, they desperately need today. What they didn't see value in last winter, they'd pay any price to get their hands on now. What they didn't feel comfortable with last year, they're willing to try next week.

The truth is that persistence pays off. And as long as you can generate a profit from mailing or contacting your past customers, my recommendation is: keep doing it.

For proof, consider your own buying habits. How many times have you received a catalog or letter in the mail over and over again, only to finally respond after the fourth or fifth mailing? It's common knowledge in the direct-marketing industry that the average catalog buyer receives seven catalogs before she ever buys anything. In many campaigns I've worked on, we mailed people things or called them on the phone 10 to 14 times before they ever signaled that they were interested.

If you have customers who haven't purchased from you in a long time, don't give up on them. As long as you're reactivating some of them with each campaign (add up your responses to be sure), it's probably worth mailing them repeatedly for months and even years to come.

Mr. and Mrs. John Doe   September 15, 2006
1234 Main Street
Anytown, US 00000

Dear Mr. and Mrs. Smith,

With the holidays right around the corner, 2006 will quickly be coming to a close. And after a brief check of our records, we noticed that, while we prepared your tax return in past years, 2006 was an exception. We want to be your tax preparer again—and we're willing to shamelessly bribe you to do so.

When you call our office to schedule your 2007 appointment, we'll also schedule a complimentary tax planning consultation between now and the end of the year. With the tax code getting more and more complicated, it's important to know all the options available to you. And with all too many deductions, decisions must be made before December 31.

We can help you with those decisions—and with your tax preparation needs in 2007. The year-end planning session is a $249 value, but it's yours free as our way of encouraging you to become a client again.

We'll even extend a privileged client discount of 20 percent when you pay for your 2007 tax preparation services in full at the time of your year-end planning consultation.

Our appointments desk is staffed from 7:00 a.m. to 9:00 p.m. Monday through Saturday. Year-end planning sessions are available weekdays and weekends to accommodate your schedule. The number is (000) 000-0000. Call now while you're thinking about it.

Sincerely

James Lenhert, CPA

P.S. One past client who recently took advantage of our preferred year-end tax planning session discovered over $40,000 in tax savings that she was able to act upon before the end of the year. We're willing to work just as hard to help you benefit, but you must call soon. Call (000) 000-0000 to schedule both your tax planning session and your 2007 tax return preparation session at the same time. The $249 year-end planning session is yours free as our gift.

CHAPTER 2

Getting Other People to Help Bring in the Cash

IF YOU'VE EVER launched a new business, started a new division, or introduced a new product line, you know that finding customers is your most immediate priority. But what if you don't have a large marketing budget—or the time and knowledge to spend it wisely?

Is it possible to find thousands of eager buyers and generate substantial amounts of revenue using very little of your own time, money, or effort?

You bet.

In fact, through a commonly used relationship called a *joint venture*, you can actually have other business owners eagerly selling your products and services to their loyal customers—with you paying a percentage or a fixed amount only when sales are made. And whether you're a retailer, a service business, a manufacturer, a professional practitioner, or an online marketer, a joint venture lets you benefit from the time, effort, and money that *other* business owners have spent building their database and maintaining their customers' loyalty—with payoffs that are both immediate and substantial.

Getting Started

Joint ventures can help you get started in business with little or no money. They can also give you a virtually unlimited number of ways to grow your business without putting up your own capital, without launching new product lines or service areas that you may be unsure of, and without assembling sophisticated resources of your own. In this step-by-step plan for locating, creating, and negotiating joint ventures, you'll discover dozens of strategies and opportunities for generating new customers and for selling your products and services.

You'll learn how to locate companies whose current customers would be perfect prospects to buy your product or service. Once you do, you can easily secure each company's participation simply by offering it attractive compensation to endorse your product or service to its customers—and to handle any sales as well.

What a Joint Venture Is . . . and Isn't

A joint venture is an informal business relationship in which two parties come together for a single purpose—to execute a single promotion or to participate in one small piece of each other's business, with both companies profiting from the result.

These single-purpose joint ventures may take many forms:

➤ A simple referral relationship, with you paying your joint-venture partner a finder's fee for sending you new customers and clients.

➤ A codevelopment project, where you both participate in developing and promoting some new and useful product or service.

➤ An endorsement arrangement, where your joint-venture partner promotes your product or service to its customers.

➤ A shared effort in building a side business or profit center. Both of you would bring important skills to the project, such as you developing the product or service and writing the marketing materials and your joint-venture partner bringing technical expertise, such as setting up an e-commerce Web site or launching and running a new Internet affiliate program.

A joint venture does *not* mean that you are buying part of someone else's business, creating a general partnership, taking on liability for each other, or entering into more elaborate business agreements or contracts. You are simply leveraging the customers, assets, products, services, and affinity of someone else who will benefit from an association with you. So give yourself permission to look at as many companies and potential joint-venture partners as possible.

Potential partners include any company that offers a synergistic product or service, direct competitors, and companies that are entirely unrelated to your industry but that have a similar type of customer.

Approaching Synergistic Companies

Synergistic companies are those companies that already sell a product or service that is complementary to yours.

Let's say that you're a certified public accountant with a unique marketing system for building an accounting practice that you teach to other CPAs. An ideal joint-venture partner might be an educational company that provides continuing education units to CPAs.

Why would an educational company be such a good prospect for a single-purpose joint venture? Because such companies not only acquire and teach students on a regular basis, but they also maintain an affinity with those students and graduates. Their students know them, trust them, see them as a source of expertise, and generally take their recommendations for ways to improve their professional skills. In simple terms, those students trust the company that is training them, and they are far more likely to purchase a product offering from someone they trust than from an unknown company, regardless of how good the product or service actually is.

So the first step in finding joint-venture opportunities is to locate companies that provide a complementary service or product and whose customers, members, subscribers, and students trust them to provide ongoing information and expertise. Surprisingly, these companies are very easy to find. In fact, a search on the Internet will often generate a huge list of prospective partners. Depending on your type of business, you may even find these companies locally.

Approaching Your Competitors

Competitive companies are another type of potential joint-venture partner. While it may seem crazy to approach your competitors with a joint-venture proposal, here's the reason I recommend it: At the same time your competitor is generating leads—or *prospects*—and turning them into new customers, some of these leads will never buy anything. For some reason, your competitor's product or service just isn't appealing to them. Perhaps it's too expensive, too cheap, too elaborate, or too simple. But the bottom line is, those prospects aren't buying. However, they may buy from *you* if your product or service offering is more to their liking or if your marketing materials are more convincing than those that your competitor used.

Do you begin to see the possibilities?

Similarly, customers who have bought from your competitor in the past may have simply discontinued buying. Perhaps they had a service contract with your competitor and did not renew it, or perhaps they had simply bought every product or service your competitor had to offer. Both situations are very common.

If you can convince your competitor to let you sell to its unconverted prospects and past customers, that's a phenomenal joint-venture opportunity.

Why?

Because at one time those unsold prospects were looking for a solution to their problem. They were looking for something to buy—it's just that the competitor's product, for whatever reason, did not fit their needs.

Your competitor has already spent money to create those prospects and customers, from whom it will make no future money whatsoever. Your job is to approach your competitor with a joint-venture deal that will instantly monetize those prospects and former customers, turning them into money for both of you.

Approaching Completely Unrelated Companies

Finally, look for joint-venture partners whose companies are *completely unrelated* to yours but whose customers have the psychographic profile you are seeking.

You've probably heard about demographic data—that is, age, occupation, household income, and so on—but *psychographic* data tell you what kind of buyer a prospective customer will be. They tell you where customers shop, whether they're computer-savvy, what magazines they read, whose opinions they listen to, what their hobbies are, and so on.

When you take the time to investigate the psychographics of your buyers, you can begin to compile a list of unrelated companies whose buyers are the same types of buyers you are looking for.

If you sell landscaping services, for example, you can often find new customers from the local pool company, interior decorator, air-conditioning vendor, roofing contractor, or other contractors that are providing unrelated home-improvement services to area homeowners. These customers are already purchasing services to fix up their homes, and they may decide to add a new yard to their plans. If you created a package deal for a new yard—including lawn, flower beds, trees, patio, and one year of maintenance—you could easily have these joint-venture partners promote your landscaping package along with a new roof, a new air-conditioner, interior decorating, and other services.

Another way to enter into a joint venture with completely unrelated companies is to offer your product or service as a premium or bonus when your partner's customers make a purchase. Or you can try to become the recommended add-on to someone else's product or service offerings.

Finding Joint-Venture Opportunities

Take a look at the following grid. It will help you locate those companies to which you would like to pitch a joint-venture arrangement. On the left-hand side of the grid are types of companies and organizations, and across the top are the three categories we just discussed—*Synergistic*, *Competitive*, and *Completely Unrelated*.

To find these three types of companies, use Internet search engines, ask the executive directors of national trade associations for recommended possible partners, attend industry conferences and conventions, look in your local

Type of Company	Synergistic	Competitive	Completely Unrelated
Manufacturers	_____	_____	_____
Service providers	_____	_____	_____
Retailers	_____	_____	_____
Professional schools	_____	_____	_____
Magazines and e-zines	_____	_____	_____
Corporations	_____	_____	_____
Trade associations	_____	_____	_____
Local civic organizations	_____	_____	_____
Web site owners	_____	_____	_____
Venture capital firms	_____	_____	_____

Yellow Pages, or ask at your local chamber of commerce. Of course, while the grid will help you start looking for promising companies, you'll probably find numerous joint-venture partners just by brainstorming among your employees and vendors—or by looking in your own Rolodex. When you locate potential partners, jot them down by name in the blanks provided on the grid.

Developing Potential Joint-Venture Partners

While contacting a potential joint-venture partner may seem daunting at first, remember that you'll be offering your potential partner a benefit, too—either additional revenue that it never would have had without you or the ability to offer its customers a popular product or service without the cost of buying inventory or training its staff.

To prepare for your initial phone call—and I do recommend that you make all initial contacts by telephone—make a brief script for yourself, complete with talking points and questions that you may forget under pressure.

When you call, be sure that you successfully reach the ultimate decision maker—typically the business owner or the marketing manager.

One quick way to start developing relationships with potential partners is to form a simple referral arrangement like the one in the following sample script, with you paying a finder's fee whenever sales are made. You can adapt this sample script or write one that is specific to your own offer.

> Hi, Ms. Jameson. My name is Julie Beekman. I'm calling because I notice that your company services and repairs boats and marine equipment. My company reupholsters and designs new interiors for boats, and we've noticed that many of our customers originally had trouble finding these services, especially for older boats, which you probably service frequently. I wonder if ABC Boat Repair would be interested in receiving a referral fee for any interior job we write for one of your customers. We have a complete marketing plan for notifying your customers of our value-priced services, and we've paid out thousands of dollars in referral fees over the years. The entire joint promotion requires just a simple letter, which we will take care of mailing at our expense. Can I send you a copy of the letter and put you on our calendar for a mailing soon?

It goes without saying that once the call is over, you should follow up with any information requested.

Negotiating the Joint-Venture Deal

Regardless of the kind of company you identify as a potential joint-venture partner, the fundamental idea behind a joint-venture partnership is to create a win-win scenario.

Remember, the customers you hope to sell to are not just names or contacts to your joint-venture partner. They are valued purchasers who have been acquired through years of effort and expense. Be sure to respect that in your negotiations.

One way to acknowledge both the value of your partner's leads and the opportunity you bring to the table is to split the profits 50/50 after all marketing and product costs are paid.

But be careful. Profits are often a complex calculation. Instead of selling a simple packaged product, you might be selling a long-term service contract with varying staff costs, related delivery costs, sales commissions, and so on. Be fair to yourself and make sure you cover all your costs *before* calculating how you'll split the money.

What if your partner wants to simply split the gross sales amount? Try to avoid paying your hard costs out of your percentage of the gross. Instead, try to calculate your percentage of the gross so that it covers your costs, even if your split is more than 50 percent.

For example, let's say you are offering a $495 product (that's the retail price), and your hard cost to produce the product, package it, inventory it, and prepare it for shipping is $45. Add to that any other costs of delivery, such as discounts, special offers, preannouncement special pricing, and any bonuses you want to give, and also add your marketing costs, like the costs of direct mail, Web site development, and outbound telemarketing—especially if you have thousands of names to call. When you factor in all these costs, your actual cost of delivery might be $95, instead of just the $45 hard cost for the product.

If you subtract that $95 from $495, then $400 would be left to split 50/50 with your joint-venture partner. Calculate your partner's $200 split amount as a percentage of the $495 (which in this case is 40 percent of gross revenue).

If you negotiate a deal that gives your joint-venture partner 40 percent of the gross, it will always be a 40 percent deal, not a deal where actual profits must be calculated every month.

Consider a "Cash with Names" Arrangement

Another method for paying joint-venture partners—and the best arrangement when the other party must take the orders and collect the money—is what's called a "cash with names" arrangement.

In this type of deal, you write the promotional letter, e-mail, or other device that sells your product or service. The promotional piece directs customers to your partner's Web site, store, or toll-free telephone number to buy, and your partner captures the orders and collects the customers' money.

Once your partner has received orders and payments from customers, he simply sends you a check for a fixed amount per unit, along with the list of customers you need to ship a product or deliver a service to. This is a simple and effective arrangement for two reasons: (1) it protects your partner from having to give you a copy of his list of customers to market to, and (2) together, you calculate in advance the hard cost of delivery, then agree on the amount your partner will pay you to fulfill each order.

It also protects you because you don't actually fulfill orders until you're paid to do so. And if there are ever any problems regarding fulfillment of orders or deciding who gets paid what, your partner—as the one who actually collected the customers' money in the first place—has a much greater incentive to resolve the misunderstanding quickly.

Creating Instant Income with Joint Ventures

Given all the benefits that can be derived from using joint ventures to market products and services, it's surprising that most business owners don't use them on a regular basis—especially when an individual entrepreneur has potentially thousands of fellow business owners who could be eagerly selling products and services on her behalf.

What's more, a single joint-venture promotion can create almost overnight income for both parties—particularly when you use some of the promotional strategies detailed over the next several pages.

Create Endorsed Offers

As traditional marketing and advertising becomes more difficult and more costly, joint ventures are an opportunity to generate millions in partnership with outside people endorsing our products.

CARSON CONANT
Editor-in-chief of Nightingale-Conant's
AdvantEdge magazine

The most important aspect of a joint venture is how your products and services will be marketed to the other company's customers. And while there are a number of marketing devices that work for delivering an offer to someone else's names, the key principle to remember in producing any joint-venture marketing campaign is the value of your joint-venture partner's endorsement of your products or services.

Stated plainly, the value of an endorsement is incalculable. It often means that you'll generate many times the sales you would otherwise realize from a nonendorsed marketing campaign.

In fact, an endorsement is often the primary reason to do a joint venture in the first place.

Why are endorsements so valuable?

The other company has built up affinity with its buyers and earned their trust to the point where those customers will often buy whatever your joint-venture partner recommends.

Creating Endorsed Offers

Whether you send an e-mail, mail a letter, make a phone call, or use some other delivery method, remember that the delivery method doesn't matter; it's the message itself that's most important. What should your joint-venture partner say to its customers to compel them to purchase from you?

Plenty.

In fact, the copywriting formula that you'll learn in Chapter 3 walks you through 16 different components of a well-written direct-response sales pitch. And when you add an endorser's recommendation to these components, the possibilities of generating substantial revenue virtually overnight become more and more attainable.

To begin with, the endorser's first "pitch" should be contained within the headline of an advertisement, brochure, or flyer, or in the first paragraph of a letter. Take a look at the following sample:

Mr. James Hartley
Hartley Belden Management Consulting
1234 Main Street
Anytown, US 00000

Dear Jim,

I've never written a letter like this before. I doubt I ever will again. But recently I discovered the solution to my CPA firm's client recruitment headaches, and I knew I had to write so that you could benefit, too.

The endorser should then go on to recount a problem he had and how he found the answer in your product or service:

For years, we relied on professional networking and referrals to find new clientele. But frankly, referrals can be sporadic, and networking was beginning to become time-consuming. We knew we had to do something to grow our practice.

We found the answer in a service I'd like to introduce you to.

Millennium Marketing of Kansas City implemented a professional and comprehensive promotional campaign that—over just 90 days—got us in the newspaper, on the radio, into targeted mailboxes, and even on the local luncheon circuit with a message that made us stand out from other CPA firms.

Tell the reader in specific terms what the result was, using actual dollar figures, quantities, and time frames. Don't mention the cost of the service yet. Instead, compare it to something the reader will recognize—or may have already purchased for a reasonable price:

> The entire effort generated 26 new clients worth over $100,000 in annual billings—yet we easily paid Millennium's invoice with the revenue from just our first new client!

Then make the offer:

> Now I want *you* to find out if Millennium can help drive new customers to your business. They've agreed to provide a one-hour consultation ($235 value) to all our clients as a personal favor to me.
>
> They're even giving you a special phone number to call that gets you right into the office of Jerry Baldwin—the president of Millennium Marketing. It's (000) 000-0000. I guarantee that Jerry will give you a complete promotional road map for your business in just one hour. Once he does, take my advice and get started with Millennium immediately—as I did.

Restate the benefit that your joint-venture partner experienced as a result of working with you—in essence, the real reason your joint-venture partner is writing this letter. Remind the reader how to respond. Then sign your joint-venture partner's name:

> My annual revenue grew by over $100,000 by making a phone call to Millennium Marketing. Call now to start building your business. Tell them I sent you.
>
> Sincerely,
> *Jim Dunn, CPA*

The postscript is an important device, as you'll read in Chapter 3. It's often the first thing people read when they receive a letter, so you should use it to restate the benefits, the offer, and the call to action in just a few sentences:

P.S. It's rare that I write a letter like this. But Jerry Baldwin at Millennium Marketing brought my CPA firm 26 new clients worth $100,000 a year—for less money and less hassle than we were spending trying to do it ourselves. As a courtesy to me, Jerry will give you a complete marketing plan for free over the phone, then implement it for you at a very modest price. Call (000) 000-0000 today.

As you're reading this letter, note the friendly, conversational style that says, "I'm a trusted friend speaking directly to you about something that affects your well-being."

Note, too, the use of a special phone number and "Tell them Jim Dunn sent you"—a great way to track the number of sales made to your customers.

But here's the most important point about producing a joint-venture letter campaign like this one: Always write the letter for your joint-venture partner, for two reasons: (1) you'll want to control the wording to make sure it is compelling and salesworthy, and (2) you'll want to be sure that the letter gets written, despite your joint-venture partner's busy schedule. Never leave the writing to someone else. But do give your partner a chance to review it and correct it. After all, your partner's signature is going on the bottom of the letter. She has to be satisfied with its content.

While your very first attempt at writing may take some time, once you've written an endorsement letter or brochure that brings in the cash, you can repurpose it for one of the other delivery methods described later in this chapter.

Direct-Mail Packages

Combine your one-page cover letter—like the one given in the previous section—with a lengthier announcement brochure that discusses the many benefits of your product or service.

Include in the brochure the testimonials of others who've purchased your product or service (see Advertising Strategy 1, "Ask Your Customers to Tell Their Story"), the reason why your joint-venture partner is endorsing you, the special offer that you've developed especially for your joint-venture partner's customers, plus a message from the endorser saying how he or she has personally benefited from your wisdom and had a positive experience with you.

This special message can be contained within the brochure itself, or it can be put in a lift note, which is a small folded note that has an extra, urgent message about the product or service that you're offering.

Send E-mail

By far the fastest and cheapest method of marketing to other people's customers is e-mail—a delivery method that has generated literally millions of dollars in Instant Income.

To create an effective e-mail campaign, you can simply repurpose your proven sales letter (like the example given earlier) into a simple e-mail announcement that encourages the customer to call for more information. Or you can use the e-mail to direct customers to a Web site that gives lengthy sales copy about the product or service being offered (see Internet Strategy 4, "Broadcast Internet-Only Offers via E-mail").

This e-mail to Web site strategy is particularly ideal for international customer lists, because customers don't need to call during business hours. They can open the e-mail at any time of day, click over to your Web site, read about your product or service, then register or purchase it through a secure shopping cart (credit card payment page) that you feature at your site.

Produce a Flyer or Insert for Shipping Cartons

One of the easiest ways to get the marketing message out to your joint-venture partner's customers is to have your partner insert a one-page flyer into each customer's shipping carton. It might be a flyer that advertises your product or your service with a special phone number or a specially priced package to ask for. It might be your one-page endorsed sales letter. Or it might be a letter from the joint-venture partner thanking its customer for the order and saying: "Here's something else you might want to know about."

Do Outbound Telemarketing

While most consumers hate getting phone calls from telemarketers, *outbound telemarketing,* or calling a joint-venture partner's customers directly, is a proven method for booking Instant Income over the phone, especially when it's done in good taste and when it's structured as just another part of your joint-venture partner's overall customer service program.*

Ideally, your joint-venture partner should make the calls to its customers; alternatively, your staff can. Either way, keep your script simple:

> "We're calling from Acme Home Repair Services offering all our customers a free consultation for redecorating their home. Acme has teamed up with Home Décor Unlimited to bring your home a fresh, new look in just six to eight weeks from now. We have appointments available this week. Can I schedule one for you?"

Of course, the most immediate income typically results from calling customers who are buying an ongoing service, with your product or service being offered as just an additional resource that the joint-venture partner recommends.

Write a Special Report

Here's another strategy that produces immediate results: send a cover letter signed by your joint-venture partner urging the customer to read the enclosed special report about a topic of immediate urgency. The special report presents a controversy, problem, or crisis, then features your company, product, or service as the solution.

Rather than the conversational style of the cover letter given earlier, these special reports are written in journalistic style—much the same way a feature article would be written for a major news magazine.

Your joint-venture partner can also distribute the special report in its store or office. Or, you can distill it into a PDF† file and distribute it over the Internet via a viral marketing campaign (see Internet Strategy 1, "Launch a

---

* Before contacting any customer or prospect by telephone, be sure to check current telemarketing regulations. At the time this was written, sales organizations were authorized to contact prospects for up to 90 days following their initial inquiry, and purchasers up to 18 months after their purchase. Additionally, the National Do-Not-Call Registry lists millions of phone numbers that, by law, cannot be called. Please respect customers and your joint-venture partners by adhering to all laws and regulations.

† Short for *Portable Document Format*. A PDF freezes your words, pictures, and other content in place so that your document appears just like the original on any computer system. Adobe Software (www.adobe. com) allows free downloading of its Adobe Reader software, so anyone can read PDF files.

Viral Report and Squeeze Page"). Have your joint-venture partner send an e-mail announcing the free special report you've developed for its customers. Then point readers to a Web page to view and download the report.

Be aware that special reports circulated over the Internet tend to live a long time in cyberspace, so this strategy should be used only when you have a product, service, and offer that you and your joint-venture partner will be selling for a long time.

What if You Can't Find an Endorser?

The value of an endorsement is so high that some marketers—in the absence of a genuine endorsement—use an implied endorsement in their marketing campaigns.

What kinds of promotional devices provide an implied endorsement?

A flattering article about you or about your product or service in a magazine always carries an implied endorsement, because whatever else the article might say about you, it communicates to the reader that the magazine thinks highly enough of you as a business owner to feature you in an article. This is the main reason why articles are usually so much more valuable and influential than display advertising—even display ads in the same magazine or newspaper.

Another strategy for using an implied endorsement is to simply write your direct-mail letters, e-mails, and other written marketing messages as if they were coming from another person who is speaking highly of you, then have that person sign the communiqués—even if it's just a staff member to whom you give an important-sounding title.

JOINT-VENTURE STRATEGY 2

Create a Referral Circle or Professional Consortium

These days, it seems as if everybody specializes. Doctors practice internal medicine or pediatrics. Lawyers do estate planning or litigation. Even professional organizers specialize in document management or cleaning garages. No one person can do it all. But the good news is that this trend can benefit you.

If you're a professional practitioner of any kind—bookkeeper, accountant, business consultant, insurance broker, financial planner, even personal trainer—you can generate Instant Income starting this week by linking up with others whose clients would be perfect prospects for you. Similarly, if you own a service business that provides services within a specific category, such as employee leasing or records maintenance, you should be developing your own network of noncompetitive service providers who can refer business to you—and to whom you can refer business in turn.

The Referral Circle vs. the Professional Consortium

One of the best types of joint venture is a loosely associated group of professionals who are each in a different line of work or who each specialize in a different niche area of a single industry. None of these professionals can possibly meet all the complicated needs of his numerous clients, *but someone else can meet those needs that he cannot*—which makes for an ideal referral situation.

When five or six of these busy professionals agree to proactively and enthusiastically refer clients to one another, we call this a *referral circle*.

Let me give you an example.

In the motivational speaking industry, corporations often hire three or four speakers a year for their large national sales meetings, corporate retreats, and other events. When speakers who are in a referral circle complete their presentations, they'll often ask the event organizer if a speaker has already been booked for the next event. If one hasn't, the speaker enthusiastically recommends other members of the circle.

While a referral circle is an informal group whose members typically pay no compensation to one another, a *professional consortium* is a defined group of people who act almost as business partners—visiting clients together, writing proposals that include each other's services, delivering joint services under one contract, and even distributing a brochure that details all their expertise. When an individual member lands a big contract, that member will typically pay other consortium members on a subcontractor basis for services provided.

Finding Aggressive Marketers Whose Clients Are Your Perfect Prospects

The best possible group members for you are professionals whose clients are perfect prospects for your service and whose frequent marketing activity is reaching *a constant stream of qualified clients*.

For example, if your consulting services are typically purchased by the human resources manager of companies with more than 100 employees, you're better off approaching a high-profile labor attorney whose clients have 200 or more employees rather than a local corporate lawyer who caters to small businesses.

Think for a moment about the businesses that call on *you* on a regular basis. Ask yourself, "Might they also be calling on and mailing to my prospective clients?" Is there a retail location or regular service provider from whom your prospects buy whose shopping bag or monthly invoices would be an ideal place to include your special offer?

How about some more examples:

➤ A landscaper might create a special deal for people selling their homes that, for $2,000, gives the front yard "$50,000 worth of curb appeal." By offering to finance the $2,000 interest-free until escrow closes, the landscaper can approach real estate agents with an appealing offer that helps them sell their listings faster.

➤ A CPA could generate business for a professional organizer by recommending home-office cleanup to disorganized tax clients.

➤ A math tutor could create a referral circle with other tutors whose students need help in other subjects.

➤ A car detailer could easily recommend an upholstery repair shop to work on the seats of the vintage cars it details.

➤ A graphic designer could write a proposal for a small business logo and identity package, including Web site development, ad copywriting, a trade show booth, and other services provided by other members of the designer's professional consortium.

Articulating What's in It for Them

When you first approach a potential member, remember that the relationship has to be a winning scenario for both sides. To ensure that it is, think through how you can help others yet at the same time generate lots of new referrals for yourself without feeling like you're begging or selling.

Create a plan for approaching these other businesses, then articulate an appealing offer that carries a big promise of what's in it for them.

Let's look at some examples.

If you're a graphic designer and you determine that a local print shop, public relations firm, marketing consultant, and special event planner would make an ideal referral circle, you can send each a letter with a compelling headline at the top that reads:

**If You've Always Wanted to Earn Thousands of Dollars
a Week Extra in Graphic Design Services but Can't Afford
to Hire a Full-Time Graphic Artist, I Can Help You Boost
Every Client's Order by $25 to $250 at No Cost to You**

Or . . .

**The Last Printer I Worked with Added $7,600
a Month in Pure Profit to His Business,
with No-Out-of-Pocket Expense Whatsoever.**

This Letter Will Tell You How We Did It.

Or . . .

**Our "Add-On" Typesetting and Graphic Design Services Can
Add $75 to $750 to Every Client's Order. Plus, We Pick Up Free
and Deliver Most Jobs within 12 Hours.**

The key to making a compelling offer is to put yourself in the place of your potential referral-circle member. What does each member *really* want to accomplish in its business? Here's what I've found most small business owners want:

➤ To provide their customers with additional products and services at no hassle or extra cost to themselves

➤ A job done right, on time, and with a minimum of oversight from them

➤ A better value—either a better product for the same amount they are paying now or the same quality product they're buying now for a much lower price

➤ A way to add more income to their business with little effort

➤ A more enjoyable buying experience for their customers, with something unique that doesn't require a lot of effort on their part

➤ A product or service that allows them to save money or make money or that prevents them from losing money—one that makes them more competitive, gives them more time off with less stress, and helps them grow their business with no additional work or cash outlay

Whatever you determine will be most appealing to a prospective referral-circle member, be sure to put it in bold type above the first paragraph of your letter or e-mail. Or, if you're calling on the phone, state the proposition in your first few sentences, as you tell the person who you are.

"People of Influence" Are the Only Source of Clients You'll Ever Need

When considering whom to approach, remember that a "person of influence" is an advisor that customers and clients turn to for information and confirmation prior to making a critical or expensive purchase. It may also be an individual or business that influences consumer purchases through advice or via the product or service it offers.

These people can be so influential that they keep you busy for years with their referrals. To find the names of these influencers, ask your customers whom *they* turn to when they are making a buying decision in your niche, then do some creative thinking about how to get these influencers on your side.

Marketing Your Referral Circle or Professional Consortium

There are a number of ways to successfully market your team's services.

Share the High Cost of Advertising

In some cities, the cost of newspaper advertising, Yellow Pages advertisements, and local television spots is so high that a single retailer is usually unable to advertise in these media outlets. Not only that, but the geographic area covered by the advertising is often so broad that 75 percent or more of the readers who see these ads won't be prospects simply because they live in the wrong part of town.

If this describes your situation, why not form a professional consortium and advertise jointly, listing all four or five member businesses in each ad? One group of chiropractors I know of actually formed a legal entity and advertised as multiple offices* of the same chiropractic "practice"—allowing them to share advertising costs. If this were your group, you would benefit by

➤ Being able to run larger newspaper ads more often for less money. You would probably also benefit from the substantial rate reductions that newspapers offer based on the number of insertions or total column inches purchased during the year.

➤ Being able to invest in a full-page advertisement in the main Yellow Pages directory. Instead of paying individually for a quarter-page or smaller, you could get the benefit of a full page for less than you paid for your previous small-sized ads.

➤ Moving your television ads from cable to wider-area broadcast stations without sacrificing frequency. You might even be able to afford advertising during prime time or during the local news, for a much better return on your advertising investment.

➤ Realizing more referrals from customers and patients to all referral-circle members, as customers begin referring friends and family members who previously lived too far from a location to shop or visit there.

Form a Retailer's Group

Classic examples of this are antique stores that band together to become Jackson County Antiquarians, wineries that form the Coastal Valley Vintners Society, and bed-and-breakfasts that form their own group to help increase foot traffic and bookings at all locations—particularly if some may be remotely located or otherwise difficult to market.

If you start looking at your competitors as referral sources rather than as competition, you may be able to create both a more enjoyable shopping experience for consumers *and* more business for yourself. Along with a printed map of all locations and area points of interest, you could even produce annual events, bus tours, a gift registry, buying services, and other promotional opportunities. Offer the map at each store and at popular tourist destinations and restaurants.

---

* Check with your legal advisor to see if this approach is recommended for your situation.

Provide Assistance and Ask for a Referral at the Same Time

A CPA friend of mine was a salesperson for a temp agency that specialized in accounting and finance personnel. His buyers were CFOs, controllers, CEOs, and accounting managers who continually sent him business. In fact, over 90 percent of my friend's bookings came from referrals because he used a two-part approach that you can easily replicate:

➤ Whenever the agency recruited a new temp with highly specialized skills, my friend would call his clients to let them know, just in case they had that special need. Clients who didn't have that need at the time usually knew someone who did.

➤ Whenever the agency received a hiring request for an accountant with a specialty that it didn't have in its database, my salesperson friend called his other clients to ask if they knew of anyone with that skill set who was looking for work. While most of the leads he got were not the right person for the job, at least 40 to 50 percent of them would eventually do some temp work through the agency—and virtually all of these temp professionals would eventually find a permanent job, on which the agency got paid a fee.

By simply following up on the leads referred by clients, the temp agency also developed helpful, informal relationships with all sorts of companies and professionals with whom it later developed lucrative agency relationships.

Start Asking "Whom Can I Help?"

When you send referrals to other businesses and bring them value on a regular basis, you'll become a valuable referral source that they'll want to acknowledge in turn—by sending business your way.

Offer Other People's Products and Services to Your Customers

Just as you can form joint ventures to sell your own products and services to *other people's customers*, you can also create joint ventures to sell *outside goods and services* to your customers.

Why would you want to sell someone else's goods and services to your customers? For a number of reasons.

First and foremost, doing so allows you to substantially expand your product line without spending money on extra inventory. It lets you offer unique services without investing in specialty tools, equipment, and staff. And it lets you generate substantial newfound revenue with virtually no effort on your part.

It just makes sense.

Selling Outside Goods and Services

To generate Instant Income selling outside goods and services, there are a number of powerful marketing strategies you could use:

➤ **Conduct a test with preferred customers.** Alert customers and prospects that you've located an outstanding product or service that you'd like to offer, but—as a test—you're contacting your best and most important customers first to see if they're interested. If enough of them are, you'll begin carrying the product or providing the service. Be sure to give specific directions on how to respond.

➤ **Offer special discounts.** If your joint-venture partner has offered you a special discount, you can mail a postcard, send a letter, broadcast an e-mail, or pick up the telephone to pass along the discount to your customers and prospects. An alternative is to turn the special discount into a limited-time offer and give volume discounts for any purchases of that item made during a specific week.

➤ **Look for unusual or unique items.** If you find an item that you wouldn't normally sell but that you think your customers would want (and that you can profit from), consider purchasing an option to buy the product, then use your quickest form of communication to inform your customers of the new find.

➤ **Feature the all-important story and rationale.** Tell your existing customers that you are giving them "advance notice" of a spectacular purchase, outstanding service, or rare find. Talk about it in a way that compels people to want it, then price it appropriately. Of course, the one thing you should never do is advertise that people are using or benefiting from a product that has yet to be produced.

➤ **Add it on as a bonus.** If you've been wondering whether a bonus might increase sales and win over prospects who are not yet buying, adding on an outside product or service is a great way to test your theory. Select a small test group of prospects, then quickly call or e-mail them with the bonus offer.

JOINT-VENTURE STRATEGY 4

Conduct a Teleseminar with Your Joint-Venture Partner

We've routinely used teleseminars to fill our industry conferences to capacity. Just one 60-minute teleseminar will typically generate dozens of registrations worth tens of thousands of dollars that come in that evening and the next morning.

MARK VICTOR HANSEN
Coauthor of the *Chicken Soup for the Soul* book
series and founder of the MEGA series of events for
authors, speakers, and entrepreneurs

For more than a decade, the technology has existed to hold a conference call with as many as 500 or more people on the line, all interacting with the main "speaker" or all muted . . . monitored by the telephone service provider or not . . . with full reporting of the names, addresses, and phone numbers of the people on the line . . . with the ability to require reservations for the call, and more—all at a surprisingly low cost.

Large corporations, small companies, and home-based businesses all over the world now use these calls to announce new products and programs, to provide information about a product or service to many prospective customers at one time, to trim expenses on sales calls, to hold group meetings and updates for large, geographically spread-out sales forces and dealers, and to provide "samples" of a service.

And while these calls used to cost thousands of dollars per hour, today you can hold such a call for just a few hundred dollars—or even free for small groups of 30 or less.

But first, a few details about how the technology works and how you can best use it to your advantage.

How the Technology Works

Telephone service providers all over the country rent, lease, or own what are called conference "bridges." These are huge switches that are capable of receiving hundreds (even thousands) of phone calls at the same phone number, then connecting them together into a teleconference call. As the conference host, you are assigned a telephone number that participants can call into from anywhere using their own long-distance service and paying for it on their own phone bill. Depending on the service, you may also be assigned a passcode number that lets you limit call-in capabilities to participants that you authorize.

Service providers typically charge you—the host—for the number of lines used, for the number of minutes used, and for other services such as operator monitoring, audio recording the call, and separate preconference strategy sessions.

Using Teleconference Calls as a Marketing Tool

While these calls can be used for a number of purposes, the best use of these large-group teleconference calls (and typically the highest return for your expenditure) is to convert prospective customers into paying customers—particularly for high-end products and services that need a lot of explaining in order to make the sale.

Let me give you an example.

When Jack Canfield—coauthor of the well-known book series *Chicken Soup for the Soul* and America's foremost authority on self-esteem in the workplace and classroom—first asked me to strategize on the marketing of his company, he was six weeks away from holding his annual Self-Esteem Facilitating Skills Seminar. The seminar trains people to earn an enviable income being "junior Jack Canfields"—that is, providing self-esteem workshops and consulting to all the local companies and social service programs that Jack can't possibly reach, given his speaking schedule.

When I met him, Jack had already mailed a package to his 1,200 prospects. The mailing had netted him 15 registrations. But with program tuition of $1,350, Jack needed something like 60 registrations to break even. He was seriously considering canceling the seminar.

After 30 minutes in his office, observing the incoming calls and talking to staff, I discovered that if prospects could just get past the gatekeepers and talk to Jack on the telephone, he could convince them to sign up for the seminar. Obviously, Jack couldn't spend all day on the phone closing sales, so a large-group teleconference call was really the only strategy that would get enough people on the phone with Jack to close the number of registrations he needed in the time we had left.

The Step-by-Step Strategy

Here's the exact formula I used for Jack (and it's the formula I've consistently used with every other program like this that I've done). First, I asked three of Jack's previous graduates, who were already enjoying impressive careers in the self-esteem field, to participate in the call with Jack—to be "guest speakers," to tell their stories, to present their knowledge of the opportunities available to participants once they were trained by Jack, and to help answer questions from prospects.

Then I sent out a simple postcard invitation to the 1,200 prospects that said:

> You are cordially invited to participate in an unusual and first-of-its-kind conference call with me and my team of coast-to-coast self-esteem specialists to discuss expanding opportunities and exciting new possibilities for you in the self-esteem, development, and training arenas. Join us June 21st at 5:00 p.m. (CST) for an hour or more of inspiration and information. Please RSVP by June 16th to 1-800-000-0000.
>
> Until then . . .
>
> *Jack Canfield*

You can also advertise these calls using e-mail, small ads, endorsed letters and inserts in other people's literature packages, and other low-cost or no-cost methods. If you're sending out letters and running advertisements, you'll want to capture the names and addresses of the participants on the call, either when they call in or by directing them to a Web site to opt into your database. Capture the name, address, telephone number, e-mail address, and fax number of every participant who calls in to RSVP or who opts in online. That way, you can e-mail these people follow-up messages. If you work during the day or prefer not to answer your own reservation calls, you can also hire a local "live operator" answering service to provide this service.

The Customer Service Script

I prepared answers to the most common questions for Jack's customer service staff, so that they could intelligently answer questions about the call, how to dial in, what would happen on the call, and why it was being held—particularly since I knew that many callers had probably never participated in any conference call (let alone one with 60 or more people).

The actual customer service script appears was as follows:

Answers to Questions about Conference-Call Program

I got this postcard in the mail. What is this all about?

Well, so many of Jack's previous trainees and seminar participants wanted to speak to Jack personally about how they could develop more or how they could help others, he decided to treat everyone to a telephone call with him. But, since he is out of town so much during the month, this conference call was his only alternative. Um, who is this I'm speaking to? Oh, hello, _____, would you like to reserve a spot on the call?

What's going to take place on the call?

Jack's going to talk in a general way about how you can use your self-esteem training either for your own personal growth or to help others with self-esteem issues. Plus, Jack's invited a team of people who are already out in the field teaching self-esteem in different ways. They'll be talking about their experiences—how you can replicate what they're

(continues)

doing or create your own self-esteem vehicles. Jack and his team may walk you through different scenarios and teach you some wonderful new exercises they've got, or they may field all your questions, depending on how much time they have. One thing's for certain: as long as Jack's on the phone, you know it will be a surprise. And—it won't be boring!

Is there a fee?

Participation with Jack and his team of trainers is free. You only pay your telephone charges to the conference bridge in Chicago. It's about 20¢ a minute from the West Coast, and about 35 percent cheaper from the East Coast.

How do I get on the call?

The date is June 21—that's a Tuesday. The time is 5:00 p.m. Central Standard Time. You're from (____city____), so that's _____ o'clock for you.

At two minutes before the hour, call the following number—do you have a pencil?—(000) 000-0000. You'll hear an operator ask for your passcode followed by the pound (#) sign. Punch it in to be connected to the call. And this is very important: stay on the line until Jack's staff member Janet Switzer comes on the line! Don't hang up because you don't hear Jack or Miss Switzer speaking. You will actually be on the line with a large group of people. Depending on how many people are on the call, you may be placed in a temporary listen-only mode. Don't be alarmed if you call out and no one responds to you. Stay on the line. It may be a minute or two while everyone else joins the call.

I can't make it. Is Jack recording the call?

Yes, he is. He'll send a tape to anyone who requests one—he merely asks that you send him $2.47 to defray the cost of duplicating the tape and sending it out to you. He hopes you understand about the small charge. He's expecting to have potentially hundreds of requests, and that would be a small fortune if he didn't ask you for the two and a half dollars it actually costs. Write "June 21 Conference Call" on a piece of paper and mail it with your name and your check for $2.47 to

_____.

Why was I invited?

You were selected from among Jack's thousands of customers as part of a group of about 1,200 people because you expressed an interest in helping other people with self-esteem issues. This call is not for everyone, only for special people that Jack selected. Another reason Jack selected you is that he wants to do these kinds of calls several times a year for his other customers, and he just felt he would be more comfortable trying out this format with people like you, who are more friends than customers.

How many other people will be on the call?

We're not sure yet, but it will be the same as if you were sitting in a seminar room with Jack and other attendees—it's just being done by phone. It may be 20 people, it may be 100—we don't know yet.

The Role of Your Moderator

Before starting the call, have a staff member, a friend, or your joint-venture partner welcome callers and introduce you. It sets the stage for the call and makes you appear professional. Be sure to have the moderator activate the service's "listen only" mode immediately before beginning the call.

Make No Mistake . . . These Calls Are Highly Scripted Sales Pitches

Remember, by the way, that these calls are not free-for-all question-and-answer sessions. They are highly orchestrated sales pitches that are designed to present all the information that prospects need to make a purchase decision, and then to ask prospects to make that decision immediately.

The actual script I produced for Jack appears later, but my first recommendation when preparing for your call is that you and your joint-venture partner educate and coach your guest speakers on the purpose of the call, what their role will be, how they can help you, and so on. You should also hold a short teleconference call ahead of the real one to brief the guest speakers.

Once the call begins, be sure to prompt the guest speakers to provide specific success stories, new opportunities, and experiences within their local market or industry that participants may not have thought of.

The following sample outline of Jack's actual teleseminar will provide a framework for you to produce and embellish a script of your own:

Outline of the Call for Prospective Seminar Attendees

Guest Speakers: Jane Expert, Bob Trainer, Cindy Speaker, and Jim Consultant

1. Welcome and Pointers for Participating on Large-Format Conference Calls—Janet
2. Introduction and Welcome from Jack, Background on Why He's Doing the Call
3. What's Happening in the Self-Esteem Field—Jack Canfield
4. How to Address Critics of Self-Esteem
5. Opportunities for Those Listening—Jack Canfield
6. Jack will introduce Jane Expert, followed by testimonial from Jane
7. Jack will introduce Bob Trainer, followed by testimonial from Bob
8. Jack will introduce Cindy Speaker, followed by testimonial from Cindy
9. Jack will introduce Jim Consultant, followed by testimonial from Jim
10. Jack will open the floor for questions
11. Jack will discuss Facilitating Skills Training, dates, payment plans, special offer

Spend time on your question-and-answer period. Don't limit it. This is where your participants will do the sales work for you. If you've presented an exciting enough opportunity, they'll ask intelligent questions. You'll also get immediate feedback on whether your pitch has enabled prospects to understand the opportunity presented to them. You'll know right away if they "get it."

Once there are no more questions, be sure to ask for the sale! Tell participants that your staff is in the office late tonight to take their registration, their order, or their reservation. Make any special pricing offers if they sign up within the next 24 hours. Offer to answer any additional questions, then end the call in a friendly, nonsales way. This is a soft-sell strategy. Have confidence that participants will make a buying decision.

Why These Calls Work and What You Can Expect

In every conference-call conversion program I've ever worked on, a significant percentage of the people on the call convert into paying customers—usually within 72 hours of the call. In the case of Jack Canfield's Facilitating Skills Seminar, within six weeks a total of 130 people had signed up for the program, putting $105,000 cash in the bank.

Why do these calls work so well? For a number of reasons:

1. The invitation presents the call not as a sales pitch, but as a valuable informational hour and learning experience that callers feel compelled to participate in. The format intrigues them, and they want to hear the exact strategies that others have used to be successful where they themselves perhaps have not been. They are not expecting to be pitched; they are expecting to get free information that will help them in their business or personal life.

2. Your guest speakers and participants actually help close the sale for you. The guest speakers provide success stories. They talk from experience about how easy it is to implement your program or use your product. They have no hidden agenda when answering questions (whereas your answers might be highly suspect), and they totally remove from the prospect's mind the fear that no one else has ever purchased or used this product or service before.

3. The group dynamics that are created on these calls also help support the sales process. An individual caller hears other callers who sound reasonably intelligent and who ask intelligent questions. Callers realize that they are not making this purchase decision alone.

4. Some people prefer just to listen anonymously, without having a one-on-one (potentially obligation-producing) dialogue with a salesperson. This teleconferencing format lets them do just that, then make a purchase decision if they want to. With dozens of other people on the line, they know they won't have to participate if they don't want to. Surprisingly, a large number of these "quiet ones" call in later to purchase—even though you don't expect them to.

5. You can record the call and use it later as a marketing piece. This is by far the most important reason to hold a call—even if you never do another one. You can offer the recording in mailing pieces and ads as an "audio preview," either on CD or at your Web site. Three years later, we were still using the same audio recording to help register over 200 people in Jack's seminar every year.

Resources You Should Know About

Teleconferencing services that will host your teleseminar abound. These services allow participants to call in from their own phone and use a passcode to be connected to the call in progress. Because you are given a unique passcode for your call, there's very little risk that an uninvited caller will accidentally be connected to your teleseminar.

You can purchase a single conference time—say 60 or 90 minutes on Tuesday evening—or you can pay a monthly fee for 24-hour availability all month long. Pricing depends solely on your needs and is usually negotiable. A number of these services are featured on the Instant Income Resources Page (www.instantincome.com/resources.html).

JOINT-VENTURE STRATEGY 5

Become an Add-On to Someone Else's Product or Service

We've built our company around partnering with others. CRG's personal and professional development tools enhance our partners' credibility and value in the marketplace, and become an integral part of other businesses' service offerings because we allow companies to apply their own name or brand. This business model has led to virtually all our product lines being offered on a private-label basis.

KEN KEIS, MBA
President and CEO, Consulting Resource
Group International Inc.

A seamstress provides alterations for a high-end dress shop. A graphic designer provides brochure layout and logo design for a small-town printer. A bakery provides specialty cakes and pies for a local restaurant.

These are just some examples of entrepreneurs who became an integral part of *someone else's business*. But while it's easy to become a necessary service provider or add-on for other people's products and services, surprisingly few entrepreneurs even attempt to develop these kinds of joint-venture relationships.

Becoming a Necessary Add-On or Service

Many retailers and service providers prefer not to provide every possible "extra" that a customer might need, either because there isn't a big enough return on the training and equipment necessary or because they could never develop the expertise required to perform the service properly. That's where you can be of great help to such a retailer or service provider, on either a referral, recommended, or subcontracted basis.

The truth is, many of the companies you work with won't require any revenue split for sending customers your way. In fact, it's just possible that they'll be more than happy to recommend you for free because they've been looking for a company just like yours to refer their desperate customers to.

An easy way to start finding joint-venture partners you can add on to is to make a list of every company, local or national, whose customers would be perfect prospects to buy your product or service. Then make a list of all the products or services each of those companies sells and which of your products or services would be a perfect add-on for that company.

Add contact information to your list and update or add to it regularly as other prospective "partners" open for business. Then start contacting these companies, one by one. Use the telephone, and develop a script ahead of time to help you keep on track. Assure yourself each time you call that you are speaking with the actual decision maker. Don't stop until you speak to that person.

In the beginning, offer to send samples, literature, a free service call, or a sample plan that the decision maker can read to see how your product or service enhances the company's product lines or service offerings (and its revenues).

What are some actual examples of partnerships that work? Let's look at some specific situations.

Many tiny software companies and source code programmers develop printer drivers, font utilities, report-writing utilities, or other "little" programs that address specific "bugs" or deficiencies of major software applications. If this sounds like you, start making calls now to any other software publisher whose software would work better, faster, or more intuitively with your product.

If you produce a widget, adapter, cable, or other add-on that enhances the performance of certain consumer electronics devices, ask to be introduced to the retailers stocking the electronic device for which your widget is perfect. By going through this exercise, you might even be able to negotiate a bundling deal in which your part is bundled with the other company's device or in which you actually produce the part with the other company's logo on it on an OEM (original equipment manufacturer) basis.

If you produce beautiful works of art, photography, or sculpture that can be dramatically displayed in public spaces or corporate offices, start contacting commercial space designers and interior decorators to be listed specifically in their bids and proposals. One woman I read about landed a contract with a firm that designs interiors for major cruise ship lines. Over several months, she produced more than 100 paintings that were destined for one cruise ship alone.

If you provide consulting services, offer to take over the most difficult or time-consuming part of someone else's consulting contract, such as employee interviews, audits, inventory analysis, or customer surveys.

If you've considered developing a new service or product, go through this exercise before making your final decision to move forward with production. While there may be a huge consumer market for your product, "add-on" partners will buy more quantity from you than individual consumers probably would.

Making Referring Business to You Simple for the Other Company

There are many low-cost and no-cost ways that you can help other companies refer people to your products and services. Always remember that by making it as easy as possible for these endorsers to refer people to you, you'll do more business.

> Install a display at the other company's premises—filled with brochures or with the product itself.

> Supply the referring company with a pad of order forms and teach the employees there how to write up an order. Develop a system for picking up written orders. Drop-ship product to the customer, if necessary.

➤ Offer free pickup of the customer's item from the referring party's store or business, with guaranteed return delivery within a specified time.

➤ Work out a system with the referring party where it can actually schedule appointments for your service personnel. Perhaps you'll provide services to that company's customers every Thursday from 9:00 a.m. to 2:00 p.m. Or perhaps you'll dedicate one of your service personnel to handle all of Company ABC's service orders, letting Company ABC keep its own calendar and providing your service to its customers transparently.

➤ If you're a personal trainer, give prescription pads to doctors so that they can write up "prescriptions" for a consultation with you and direct their patient to call you for an appointment.

➤ If you provide a service, visit the customer *along with the referring party's service personnel*. You can even share travel costs and other expenses required to fulfill the joint order.

➤ Provide the referring party with brochures, business cards, tear-off coupon pads, and other devices.

➤ Train the other company's salespeople, receptionists, and order clerks in the benefits of your product. Hold a companywide meeting, if necessary.

➤ Convince the referring company to provide new customer contact information, including phone numbers, so that you can call to facilitate delivery of the add-on.

➤ Develop personal relationships with professional advisors and other independent contractors who can recommend you—or even subcontract to you—to provide bookkeeping, design, copywriting, paralegal, counseling, construction, escrow, catering, landscaping, schooling, or other services. Very few customers will ever question the referral or outsource; they will generally believe that this is merely the way their professional advisor or service provider conducts business.

CHAPTER 3

Writing Ads That Make the Phone Ring

IF YOU HAVE A LOCAL BUSINESS, one of the easiest ways to generate Instant Income—and create new customers at the same time—is to write a compelling newspaper ad today, run it in the newspaper tomorrow, and watch sales and phone calls flood into your business over the next 24 hours. Similarly, if you have a business with a regional or international presence, you can use the same compelling advertising techniques to produce a sales letter, an e-mail broadcast, a Web page, a postcard, or some other device that instantly compels recipients to contact you.

To craft these compelling messages, top marketing copywriters use a technique called *direct-response advertising.* Direct-response advertising is a method that causes readers to take immediate action. It solicits a response *now.*

It's based on the premise that if you give readers all the information they need in order to make a buying decision, then add a number of scientifically tested words and phrases that trigger an emotional reaction, they will respond to your ad or letter almost immediately—and will respond in much higher numbers than they otherwise would.

Whether you're sending a sales letter, running a newspaper ad, broadcasting an e-mail, or printing a brochure, the copywriting techniques are the same. In fact, if you've ever seen a newspaper advertisement that looks like an article—with a big headline and column after column of tantalizing information—that is a direct-response advertisement. If you've ever seen an e-mail that caused you to click through for more information—to take the next step in the sales process and identify yourself as a prospective buyer—that was a "two-step" e-mail campaign, a classic direct-response strategy.

But while some business owners do their best to write direct-response copy, many fall short of the mark, with disastrous results. Fortunately, writing good copy is simple. In fact, there's an actual formula for it.

The Proven Formula for Writing Copy That Sells

In any well-crafted direct-response sales device, there are 16 different elements that will help close the sale. Each is designed to support the sales process and cause one more positive reaction on the part of the reader. Some components are designed to entice the prospect to keep reading, while others are designed to overcome those natural objections that we all have when we are faced with the possibility of opening our wallets.

I've included samples of actual advertisements, press releases, and other devices that utilize these critical direct-response components in the Instant Income strategies that follow this tutorial.

1. The Kicker

The short phrase or sentence positioned above the main headline is what we call a *kicker*—a device that comes to us from the news-reporting industry. In any major newspaper, an editor will position a two- or three-word phrase above the main headline to draw attention to that article. You've probably seen kickers such as "Conviction Overturned" or "Governor Pleads Guilty."

But for direct-response purposes, a kicker is simply a provocative statement that previews what the reader will discover in the ad or sales letter. It's a statement that compels people to read past the main headline. I've used statements like the following:

> Marketing maverick offers to share for the first time the secrets she's used to earn millions for her celebrity clients . . .

> Seasoned player shaves seven strokes off his game and reveals . . .

> In 1545, Spanish explorers discovered a rich and vibrant silver mine in the rolling foothills of Bolivia . . .

Keep your statement provocative but short—about two full lines at most. Embed within the kicker known marketing hot buttons and emotional trigger words like *free, discover, reveal, little-known,* and *secret.*

2. The Headline and Headline Stack

Perhaps the most important component of any direct-response piece, the headline is the first thing readers will use to decide if it's worth their time to read the rest of the promotion. In some cases, the main headline is followed by a series of subheadlines—a grouping that copywriters call the *headline stack.*

But whether you decide to write a single headline or a headline stack, remember that the headline is the ad for the ad. It gets readers' attention, speaks to something they are interested in, and communicates, "Reading this entire letter or ad will benefit you!"

Craft headlines that talk specifically about readers' current circumstances—about their pain or their ambitions. The reality is that all prospective buyers have problems that they would like to be rid of. They all have goals that they would like to reach, including a better lifestyle, more wealth, greater beauty, more leisure time, better career advancement, and so on. Researching your market will help you identify what their goals and ambitions are—or, alternatively, what their pain is. Are they experiencing money troubles? Do they have problems in their relationships or with their teenagers? Were they passed over for their last promotion because their skills weren't up-to-date? Is their home environment chaotic, disorganized, or in disrepair? Are they working too many hours, with no time for their family? While these are some of the more common areas of pain for consumers, researching what your buyers are dealing with in their lives and careers will help you craft the perfect headline—a headline that says, "You're in pain. Our product or service is the solution."

If your readers are other business owners, perhaps their pain is low productivity or high rates of absenteeism or dangerously high operating costs. If your product or service can solve one of these problems, put the problem and the benefits you can deliver right in the main headline.

Sometimes it's very effective to use a testimonial from a well-known person or an existing customer as the headline. Put the brief comment inside quotation marks and make the person's name large enough to be prominent. If this person is better known for the company he leads or some other designation, be sure to put that information along with his name just underneath the headline quote.

3. The Salutation

If you are sending a sales letter, you should always try to personalize it by using the recipient's full name and address (if you have it) and using the recipient's name in the salutation: "Dear James," "Dear Mr. and Mrs. Claybourne," and so on. While it's usually more expensive to print and mail individually personalized letters, it boosts the response considerably.

If you don't have the recipient's name or contact information, or if you don't have a large enough budget to pay a mailing house to personalize and print the letters from your database of names, skip the address and use just a salutation that speaks to the recipient as a prominent member of a particular niche, such as "Dear Fellow Practitioner," "Dear Valued Homeowner," "Dear Honored Educator," or "Dear Industry Professional."

Some longtime copywriters add the date, time, and city from which they are writing above the address block. They believe that this gives the letter more of a friendly, "just-typed" look.

4. Opening or Lead Paragraph

When it comes to writing the opening or lead paragraph, the first few sentences often prove to be the most difficult for most copywriters. Why is that? Well, for one thing, the copy needs to hook readers so that they continue reading. You also don't want them to have been intrigued by the headline, only to stop reading at the end of the very first sentence of the very first paragraph.

This is difficult stuff.

In fact, it's so difficult for most copywriters that I recommend you actually start by writing another part of the promotion—either the offer or the section on how readers will benefit or the discussion of what they'll receive. Come back to the lead paragraph later, when the copy is starting to take shape and become really compelling.

Of course, once you're at the point of writing that lead, there are a number of strategies you can use.

One of the easiest ways to start a direct-response message is to tell your readers why you're writing to them. Make it clear that you know something about them—something they would like to solve or achieve—and that you have the answer. If you are similar to the reader in some way (either in your line of work or in your life experience), you can actually start with your own story. Did you improve your health? Did you save thousands of dollars when purchasing a large item? Did you recently learn something that changed your life or your career? Write about that in the opening paragraph.

If you're marketing yourself and your own professional services, a powerful way to write the opening paragraph is to actually have someone else sign the letter so that this person can talk about you in the third person. This technique creates the impression of an endorsement—even if the "endorser" is just a staff person or a friend whom you ask to sign the letter:

Perhaps you've heard of Sheldon Woodruff. He's the man who quietly built the world's largest network of "green" construction companies, now hired by 90 percent of the world's most forward-thinking municipalities. He's orchestrated many of the largest developments in the world and negotiates at the highest echelons of government. He helped Wood-Rite Industries develop its revolutionary structural support product line. And he's consulted on countless other green construction products used throughout the world today. He's even one of a handful of experts who holds five Ph.D.s in the areas of environmental impact, public policy, and green research.

He knows more about "building green" than probably any other expert on earth—and yet, there's never been a reason for you to know about him.

Until now.

You see, over the next six months, Dr. Woodruff and his inner circle will be changing the way the world thinks, uses, and buys "green." In fact, he's launched a revolutionary new think tank to shape the world's green future.

But before he and his colleagues do that, you as a local general contractor have the opportunity to profit.

It's a good idea to purposely talk about all the things this expert is doing that the reader *probably wishes he or she were doing right now*.

Yet another strategy for writing the lead paragraph is to start by saying,

If you've ever wanted to accomplish [fill in the blank], you simply must read this letter as an investment in your own future.

Another strategy that I recommend is to abolish a myth or negate a commonly believed statistic:

> If you're under 50 years old and are counting on Social Security to help pay for your retirement, think again. Recent studies show that you (and 78 million other retirees) could be facing the collapse of Social Security in less than 10 short years—just as you're about to retire! Even *Fortune* magazine recently said, "You can't count on Social Security to be there. You have to pilot your own ship."
>
> That's why I'm writing to you today.
>
> My name is Marian Winters and, together with my partners at Winters Langton Consulting, I help people like you plan for an exciting and comfortable life after retirement.

Another strategy that also uses facts is this example:

> Today in America, 70 percent of school-age children read below their current grade level. I know that you're working hard to change this statistic in your school. That's why I'm writing to you today with a proven method for helping students read better.

Start with the statistic, qualify it, and then announce that you have the solution to the problem created by this statistic.

5. Body Copy

You've created a powerful headline, and you've written the salutation and the opening paragraph. Now you must fill in the rest of the paragraphs of your direct-response promotion. These remaining paragraphs are what we call *body copy.* And their content, tone, and readability are extremely important.

Equally important is the length of your promotional copy.

For decades, there has been a ongoing debate in marketing circles over whether to write long copy or short copy.

While it's possible to get some prospects to take some small action with a few short paragraphs, you're usually better off providing as much information as is necessary to make the sale. This usually means that you'll be writing what is called *long-form copy.*

It's often said that your copy should be "salesmanship in print," and long-form copy simply helps you tell the complete story better. It helps you make a more compelling case. A good way to be sure you're including all your most compelling sales points is to record the sales calls you have with customers.* As the top expert at your company, you probably sell your products and services better than anyone else does. In fact, when you talk to people over the phone, you probably find yourself saying the same things over and over. Record those calls, then transcribe them. Using a highlighter pen, go through the transcript and highlight the actual sales points you make. Then simply include all those points in whatever marketing copy you're writing.

Additionally, stick with a conversational style using fifth-grade language. It's not that people aren't capable of reading more elaborate copy; it's just that they can read at the fifth-grade level quickly, easily, and without thinking too much about what they're reading. Taking away all the difficult words and complicated sentence structure allows readers to have an emotional reaction to the copy. It allows them to read from their creative, emotional right brain, instead of their more analytical, logical, here's-all-the-reasons-why-I shouldn't-buy-this left brain.

To achieve the right tone, imagine that you're sitting down with a new friend at a local coffee shop, telling him in plain, simple words what you sell, what the advantages are, and why he should be interested. That's about as complicated as your body copy should get.

6. Internal Subheads

After the main headline, internal subheadlines are the most important aspect of your marketing piece. Studies show that a large majority of readers will skim the subheads to see if the information is worth reading. By putting your entire story and offer into your subheads, you give your readers enough information to determine whether they need the item or service featured. When writing subheads, make a provocative statement, introduce a new thought, or mention the benefits they'll read about in the paragraphs that follow.

---

* Be sure to check local laws before recording telephone calls. In many states, recording without the other party's permission is illegal.

7. Testimonials and Media Mentions

Testimonials are such a powerful element in direct-response copy that if you don't have any, you should proactively find customers who will agree to be interviewed and have a testimonial written for their approval.

The best testimonials say that a positive, specific outcome occurred as a result of working with you. What kinds of specific outcomes could occur? Specific earnings, cost savings, a specific number of new customers, actual changes someone has experienced, or lifestyle improvements. This is what a good testimonial talks about. The more detailed the results, the better. Mentioning the specific problem you solved for the customer is also powerful. Get permission to use the customer's name and a compelling professional designation that you write for him, such as:

> —Michael Huffman, Jr., founder of Athelston's Restaurant Group, Iowa's fastest-growing food-service chain and a Top 100 Employer

Equally powerful in direct-response copy are quotes from magazines and newspapers. They provide a significant perceived endorsement. But while the best media mentions typically come from major newspapers and magazines, in your particular market, prominent trade journals may actually provide more endorsement value than the *Wall Street Journal*.

8. The Offer

Only after you've made a compelling case for why people should want your product or service—and then told them in exact detail what they'll receive—should you make an offer to sell your product or service to them at a specific price. The most compelling offers are specific and simple. Unfortunately, most writers confuse readers with too many choices of pricing or components—or worse, they make no offer whatsoever, simply saying, "Come on in and do business with us."

Start writing the offer by stating specifically what items, services, or benefits a buyer will receive when she purchases your product or service. Restate what the results in her life might be if she buys it. Then—and only then—mention the price of your product or service. I like to use language such as:

> You get all this, yet your price is just $2,495!

After reading about all the benefits they're going to get and the major changes that will take place in their life as a result of buying from you, readers' natural reaction should be, "Wow, I'd pay anything for that!"

Spend a lot of time presenting your offer in a really powerful way.

After you've presented the price, immediately begin comparing it to what a product or service like this might cost elsewhere. Or compare it to the cost of not taking action at all. You might also introduce the testimonials of previous customers who have purchased the identical item and benefited as a result. Whichever methods you use, it's important to *reinforce the incredible value* that the buyer will receive.

For a more detailed explanation of the kinds of offers you might propose to the reader—a straight sale offer, a limited-time offer, and so on—see Sales Strategy 3, "Make Specific Product and Service Offers."

9. Call to Action

You'd be surprised how many copywriters give readers all the information they need to make a buying decision, then fail to tell them how to respond. The *call to action (CTA)* is that how-to language. It's you telling the reader to "Pick up the phone and call (000) 000-0000" or "Click through now to www.YourCompanyWebsite.com." You should also add a sense of urgency by telling your readers that there are limited quantities, that time is running out, that dangerous circumstances are looming, and so on.

Remember that the objective of a direct-response advertisement, letter, or e-mail is to get readers to respond *now*. And the most popular response mechanism for your instant income purposes will be the telephone. Asking readers to call you is especially good for selling higher-priced products and services because it's faster, it allows you to capture the prospective buyer's contact information, and you can dispel any last-minute objections that the buyer might have.

Be sure to have your staff or call center properly trained to take any incoming orders.

10. The Rationale

Countless advertisements attest that when you tell the reader "the reason why," you will boost sales many times. Why are you selling this item? Why are you selling this item now? Why are you selling this item under this special offer or at this price? All of these answers are positive triggers for buyers. Your rationale should always be real and truthful.

11. Answer Objections

Remember that while you are selling people on your product or service, you are also *unselling* them on every other product, service, commitment, or other use for their money. You have to overcome price objections, scheduling objections, do-I-really-need-it-now objections, I-can-do-it-cheaper-myself objections, and so on. A part of direct-response copywriting is to make a list of what the most common objections will be and answer them in a very truthful, logical way.

Of course, one of the major objections you will face is resistance to your price. If you've done your copywriting job well, however, price should never be the issue. In fact, price will be an objection only if you have failed to convince your readers of the value of what they are buying. Between the body copy, the testimonials, the offer, the rationale, the list of what they will receive (see the next section) and other components of your direct-response copy, you should create an immediate reaction on the part of your readers, with no thought of the price or whether it's good value. The right copy is as important as the right price.

But be aware: it is possible to offer your product or service at a price that's *too low*. I've read many compelling ads and sales letters, only to say to myself, "Wait a minute. What's wrong here? This price is much lower than I thought it would be. What am I not getting that I thought I would get?" Be certain you are charging the right price by speaking privately with a handful of customers, clients, or colleagues in advance of running any new promotion. Tell them what you're proposing to offer and what you're proposing to charge. Let them give you valuable feedback. Of course, the ultimate way to test the price is to simply run the advertisement itself and see what happens.

In addition to the price, an equally problematic objection is what I call the I-don't-have-time-right-now objection. People can always write a check, but they can't always find the time to take advantage of what you're offering. To overcome this objection, there are a few things you can do:

1. Create a sense of urgency by relating what will happen if readers *don't* take action now. This is particularly easy if you sell any kind of professional services where delays in filing paperwork or implementing a

system come with a penalty. You can simply state what that penalty is, then reiterate in your copy that readers should contact you as soon as possible in order to stay in compliance with laws or regulations.

2. Downplay the time commitment required to take advantage of your product or service. Present your offer in such a way that your readers know that they can be involved on a casual or part-time basis, if they prefer. Or, offer to handle the most time-consuming part of the commitment for them, if possible. You can also specifically state the amount of time that other people have spent using your product or service.

3. Compare the time required to use your product or service with the time that the reader might spend on other activities that don't benefit him as much as your product or service will. Don't ask the reader to give up other activities, but simply draw his attention to other time-wasting activities that could be exchanged for what you are offering.

A final objection that is very common in most promotions is the reader's fear that she is the first person you've ever worked with—that somehow she is a test case. Testimonials are great for overcoming this objection—especially when they contain specific details about the problem that was overcome, how easy it was to work with you, how much money was made or saved, and so on.

But what if you're just starting out in business?

Sometimes that is helpful. For example, if you're offering a brand-new service, you can call it a "pilot program." This is not only a great rationale but also a great offer. Because your program is new, you can write that you'll be working with a very small group of people who will receive more personal attention and services, prior to your offering this program to thousands of people later.

12. Bullets

Direct-response copy is often lengthy, with no graphics or other devices to break up the dense type. Bullets not only help break up this copy visually, but also let you turn features and benefits into little nuggets of sales copy that people can glance at and say, "Wow! Am I going to get a lot out of this!" In fact, if all you had room for were bullets, you would still be able to sell your product or service.

When writing each bullet point (and you should have a list of several such points that describe exactly what readers will get, how they'll benefit, and so on), always combine the item or service that readers will receive with the ultimate benefit of owning that product or experiencing that service. For instance,

- We'll conduct a complete assessment of your current accounting services, your clientele, your ancillary revenue streams, and more—finding dozens of additional ways for you to profit from the practice you have right now.

- We'll dispatch our specially trained practice-management team to train your front office staff, your junior accountants, even your senior partners in how to maximize practice revenue in every possible client situation!

- We'll provide an entire market report detailing every possible prospect for your accounting practice. You'll know exactly where to look for new clients—and how to convince them to engage your firm!

- We'll even spend the next six months coordinating your direct-mail outreach, your press relations effort, your new client intake process, and your current client retention efforts—all as part of our initial six-month Practice Turnaround Program.

Bullet points help paint a picture so that readers not only can "see" in their mind's eye what they'll receive, but will actually be able to visualize what their life will be like once they purchase your product or service. When you combine visually stimulating words and benefits with exciting copy about what the reader will receive, you have a better chance of triggering an emotional response to the copy on the part of the reader—an essential goal of direct-response copy.

13. The Upsell

An upsell is typically an extra service, an additional item or product, the customer's ability to bring a second person free, or something similar that the customer can add to his purchase of the main package being offered. It is not a product package or service combination that's *different* from your main offer—it's simply an add-on. This is a great way to add revenue to each sale you make from your direct-response campaign. (You can read more about up-selling in Customer Strategy 2, "Upsell Customers at the Point of Purchase".)

To write an upsell pitch, simply describe the extraordinary value of the extra item, then write about the additional benefits readers will enjoy when they purchase it along with the original offer.

14. The Close

Unlike the call to action, the close simply reminds readers how to respond. Repeat the phone number to call, the Web site to visit, the postcard to send back, or whatever method you are using. Remind your readers, too, that they need to act now—and why. Incorporating the fear of loss, such as restating the limited time the offer is available, the limited quantities available, or the potential penalties for waiting, is a powerful aspect of a close.

15. The Signature Block

If you are writing a personal letter to your own list of customers and prospects, you should sign it just as you would if you were writing a letter to a friend. If your direct-response device is written as if an authority is speaking directly to the reader about you, then that authority should sign the letter—even if it's just a staff person to whom you have given an authoritative title. Someone else talking about you creates a tremendous implied endorsement of you and your product or service.

16. The Postscript

Most recipients of sales letters will turn immediately to the last page of the letter to see who sent it to them. If it's from someone they don't know, they'll read the postscript to see why they're receiving the letter and what it's about. This typical reaction by readers is the reason most direct-response copywriters restate the entire offer and its benefits in the postscript. If a recipient reads nothing else, at least she'll capture what you're offering and what she'll get out of it. She may even feel compelled to read the entire promotion from the beginning.

To write a postscript, restate why you're writing—give your readers your rationale. Restate what you're offering, and briefly detail the major benefits. For instance, restate how much money people might save, how much money other people have earned, the lifelong changes that people have made, what others have gotten out of it, and so on. You can mention in the postscript an actual customer or client and the benefit he or she received from the product or service—and then say, "That's why I'm writing to you today." This technique adds the implied endorsement of someone who has already used what you're selling and was happy with it. Always remind the reader to take advantage of the upsell offer. And finally, tell the reader exactly how to respond—*and to respond now.*

While direct-response copywriting takes some effort to master, it can literally transform your marketing effort and stabilize your revenue streams. Not only could your wasted marketing dollars be a thing of the past, but you could actually begin tracking each ad or letter to determine which offers, headlines, upsells, and other components work better than others.

You'll compete more aggressively with your toughest competitors, too. And you can begin creating a marketing calendar, planning new product launches, marketing campaigns, and even cash flow around your proven advertising efforts. Rather than constantly struggling for income, you could begin concentrating on the enjoyment of growing your business. All because you learned an Instant Income technique that the world's top copywriters have known for decades.

Direct-Response Formats That Bring in Instant Income

While there are dozens of methods for distributing your marketing message, the following formats are not only the easiest for small businesses to execute but also the most reliable in bringing in instant results.

Display advertisements. Another term for the full-page, half-page, and fractional-page ads you see in newspapers and magazines is *display advertising,* one of the easiest Instant Income vehicles to write, produce, and profit from. If you've ever seen a newspaper ad that looks like an article, with a big headline and column after column of text, you've seen a direct-response ad.

E-mails and a Web page. One of the fastest ways to make Instant Income is to write a compelling e-mail, broadcast it to your list (or someone else's), and include a link that readers can click on to be taken to your *landing page—*your sales letter on a Web page. While you'll read the exact steps for writing e-mail in Internet Strategy 4, "Broadcast Internet-Only Offers via E-mail," rest assured that the same principles for writing compelling copy apply. You simply use the e-mail as the teaser to prompt a reader to click through to your Web site in order to read your long-form sales letter.

Direct-mail packages and sales letters. By far the most compelling direct-response device for high-priced products and services is a direct-mail package or printed sales letter. I usually write a brief, one-page cover letter, then include an elaborately written brochure. The brochure, of course, is the long-form sales copy printed in 8½ × 11-inch booklet form—either vertical or horizontal. I often use two colors in these printed booklets: black for body copy with blue for subheads, bullets, and bold statements.

If you're working with individual joint-venture partners who will endorse you to their clients, that's even better, since you can write a simple but compelling letter from your joint-venture partner that encourages the recipient to read the enclosed brochure.

Individual postcards. These are not the prepackaged stacks of postcards that arrive in the mail in a cellophane wrapper (known as *card decks*), but individual 6 × 8-inch postcards that contain the same big headline and compelling copy you would see in any good newspaper ad, sales letter, Web page, or other direct-response device. What makes postcards such a powerful Instant Income format is that they are immediately readable by the recipient. In other words, your prospective buyer doesn't have to open an envelope, thumb through a magazine, subscribe to a newspaper, or open your e-mail to read your offer.

Press releases. So many businesses and successful marketing campaigns have been launched with a single press release that it's almost beyond belief. And while a different writing style is required to make press releases appeal to editors, they also contain all the basic components of a long-form direct-response sales piece. For specific details, see Advertising Strategy 2, "Broadcast a Compelling Press Release."

While there are many other kinds of marketing delivery systems—from flyers to billboards to magnets and everything in between—the best vehicles for delivering your compelling message and prompting readers to buy from you are still the simplest to write and distribute—those just discussed.

Ask Your Customers to Tell Their Story

Asking one of my clients to talk about his experience in print brought us 5 new paying clients in the first three hours alone and 13 sign-ups by the end of the day—for an extra $10,387 in our bank account that day. By the end of the workweek, we had brought in a total of $29,563 from selling golf programs alone—an increase of about 800 percent.

JAMES E. SMITH, CCH
Hypnotherapist

Your satisfied customers can help you make overnight cash. In fact, even if you've just started in business and have *just one customer or client* who is willing to tell his story in print, you can write an advertisement that will bring in the money.

Remember the beginning of this chapter, where I talked about the value of a testimonial from someone who was pleased with her experience doing business with you? Well, you can turn a "nice comment" into a full-blown testimonial-style ad by following a few simple steps.

Take a look at the ad on the next page. I wrote it for a hypnosis practice that was interested in offering services to golfers who wanted to improve their game. At the time, there was a lot of talk on the professional tour about using the power of the mind to improve one's swing and to help golfers relax before important shots. I asked the hypnotherapist to find a golfer he had worked with. Then I simply interviewed the golfer and wrote the ad. The morning the ad ran in the local newspaper, the clinic was flooded with calls from other golfers, who immediately booked an evaluation session and paid that day for a series of hypnosis sessions.

Notice the style of this ad. It's written from one amateur golfer to other amateur golfers. It uses language and terminology that's unique to golfing. In fact, many of the words I'd never heard before! But it drew golfers to the practice like crazy because it spoke directly to them and voiced the challenges they were already having in their game.

Seasoned Player Shaves 7 Strokes Off His Game and Reveals...

"How I Started Playing the Best Golf of My Life...Without Changing My Swing!"

My name is Robert Hamm. I've played golf 8-10 times a month for the last 20 years. With a 12 handicap and a typical round of 84 or better, I'd call myself a serious player.

I even competed on an amateur tour in high school. But I never thought I could so easily and effortlessly take additional strokes off my game, until I discovered hypnosis.

Thanks to hypnosis, I shaved 7 strokes off my game in less than a month. I now play at a low 77.

No fudging, no mulligans.

I'm living proof that hypnosis works for golf. I continuously play the best rounds of my life!

Failed the 'Head Game'

I used to spend a fortune on lessons, drop thousands on equipment...even pay hundreds per round to play at some of the top courses in the world. But I still didn't play as well as I could have. And I sure didn't enjoy the game as much as I might.

My technique was strong, but my execution was inconsistent. I'd do great on the driving range, only to lose it by the back nine. Just when I needed a great shot, I'd muff it at the tee box. When the pressure was on, I'd land it right in the rough.

My short game was shaky. My frustration was high.

Worse yet, each failed shot set me up for failure on the next and the next. I couldn't focus. I couldn't concentrate.

Tour Pro Recommends

Then a pro friend suggested I try hypnosis. 'That hocus-pocus?' I quipped. 'Why not?' he said. 'Hypnosis is actually a proven science. In fact, it's used regularly in medical settings, for accelerated learning and test-taking, for weight loss, stop smoking — even law enforcement.' He even said the initial consultation was free.

I called and made an appointment. I was instantly impressed by their professional offices and by their evaluator's golf experience. He understood my frustration and explained exactly how hypnosis works for golf.

The program made sense and the cost was reasonable.

I signed up that day and instantly mastered the one aspect of my game I had never considered before — the mental side.

7 Under Handicap
Virtually Overnight!

Hypnosis helped me learn how to relax, concentrate, focus on the task at hand. It helped me learn how to block out distractions and diffuse the pressure, not only so I could play a better round of golf, but so I could enjoy myself more, too.

It helped me remember important shots and execute them over and over again. It helped me plan and visualize my most difficult putts.

And it helped my subconscious mind transmit all my expensive training directly into my swing.

Suddenly, I was placing ball after ball exactly where I wanted them. Slicing was a thing of the past. Mis-hits gone for good.

I found out I didn't need more power to lower my score. Hypnosis helped my subconscious mind find my authentic swing and deliver shot after beautiful shot. Within hours after my very first hypnosis session, I played seven under my handicap — easily the best round of my life!

Surprising Side Benefits

Of course, you may think using hypnosis for golf is just another training gimmick or marketing tool. Even I was skeptical— until I started playing round after round at 77 or better.

Not only that, but my life's improved off the course, too. I'm more productive at work. It's easier to relax in stressful situations. I even sleep better at night!

Hypnosis made it easy to improve my game and my life— virtually overnight. And I'm no exception.

Call Today, Play Better
Golf Tomorrow

I met dozens of other golfers using hypnosis, from high school players to one guy who'd just finished the pro tour. I even met a gal who plays local foursomes—and regularly takes home the money!

If you know you could play better golf, too, I urge you to call [name of hypnosis practice].

It's easy to find out if they can help you. In fact, the initial consultation is free. If they don't think hypnosis is right for you, they'll tell you so.

Hypnosis works and it's completely safe. Don't be left to wonder what might have been. Hypnosis helped me shave 7 strokes off my game — and enjoy golf more than I ever have.

Call now for your free hypnotic screening. Get started today!

Robert Hamm shaved 7 strokes off his game with hypnosis

Call for Your FREE Screening
(000) 000-0000

[Name of Hypnosis Clinic]
Street Address ❖ City

Mon-Thurs 10am-7pm ❖ Fri 10am-5pm ❖ Sat 10am-2pm

How to Get Your Customer to Give You a Testimonial That Sells

Interviewing customers or clients is really the best way to get the copy points you'll need in order to write a salesworthy testimonial-style ad. Of course, you should never ask your clients to write the ad; instead, ask to interview them with the intention of producing an advertisement for their approval. Then be sure to get the signed approval along with a release to use the person's story, photo, name, and city or professional designation.*

Ask your client for permission to record the conversation to help you with your note taking. To be safe, turn on the tape recorder, then ask for permission to record so that the agreement is captured on tape. Ask the client to state her full name, city of residence, and professional designation (job title, company she works for, and so on), so that, too, is captured on tape.

To write the most compelling story possible, start by asking your client what was the single biggest result or benefit from using your product, purchasing your services, or otherwise doing business with you. This will help you formulate the kicker, headline, and opening paragraph—just as the sample ad on the previous page illustrates. Notice that our golfer describes his biggest benefit in specific terms—that is, he "shaved seven strokes off his golf game without changing his swing."

Next, ask your customer to describe her background. What does she do for a living? Has she been in that industry a long time? Is she experienced in the field or hobby that you serve? Does she have a family? Asking these types of questions will help you present your client in print as a normal, intelligent person who has the kind of lifestyle or everyday challenges with which the reader can identify.

Next, ask your client or customer what her life or business was like before she discovered your product or service. Urge her to reveal what the challenges were. Try to get her to describe her woes in specific numbers, such as, "We were losing $3,260 a month in inventory shrinkage alone."

Next, ask your client how she discovered you. Is there an unusual story behind it? Was she skeptical at first? Did she hear about you from a friend or colleague who had a good experience with you? Had she known about you for years before finally deciding to call?

---

* A good attorney can provide you with a simple one-page release that will allow you to use the customer's name and story as long as you like. Don't put a time limit on the release, because you may want to use the advertisement long after you've lost contact with your customer or client.

Continuing with your interview, ask her about the first time she called you, visited your store, or interacted with you in some way. Was it pleasant? Were you surprisingly professional or in some way different from what she expected of your type of business? Did you ask questions about her situation that no one had thought to ask before?

Next, urge your client to remember the purchase itself. Was it easy? Did she save a lot of money? Did you help her select a less expensive item that was more suitable for her needs? Did you give her a complete written proposal of the services you would provide?

Next—and this is important—ask your customer what was the *immediate result of using your product or service for the first time.* Encourage her to define the result in actual terms. Here's why: prospects who have read this far into the ad and the customer's story are, by this time, interested in potentially buying from you, but they still want to know what's in it for them. If you can demonstrate an immediate payoff from using your product or service—either in actual money or in other benefits—you'll go a long way toward convincing them to pick up the phone or come into your store.

Encourage your customer to tell you about any secondary benefits she derived later from your product or service—especially benefits that might have been unexpected but were equally valuable. Ask whether she knows of other people who also benefited from working with you—and specifically what those folks said about their experience.

If you've asked questions of your customer in the order I've just indicated, you'll easily be able to write an ad with copy points that are in the same proven sequence as those in the sample golf ad.

Even if you don't use all the story points in your ad, covering all these areas in your interview with the client will help you form a more complete picture in your mind about who your client is and what her story is. After all, you're the one who needs this perspective in order to write the ad. (And if you hire someone to write the ad for you, he'll appreciate the completeness of your interview.)

I often spend 30 minutes or more interviewing a customer for these ads because I like to ask people the same question in different ways. You'd be surprised by the nuggets of information and the truly compelling phrases you'll get that can be used to substantially enhance your ad. For instance, I once had a weight-loss customer tell me, "I was so out of control, I could eat a whole bag of chips while I was heating up the frozen pizza!" Of course, I used that comment as one of my most prominent subheadlines.

ADVERTISING STRATEGY 2

Broadcast a Compelling Press Release

Today, mass-market media such as television commercials, full-page newspaper ads, radio spots, and direct mail are prohibitively expensive for most small businesses. But there's a proven, virtually free method that will blast your marketing message to the widest possible audience, building awareness of your expertise and generating revenue for your company.

Press releases—when printed by newspapers, covered by the six o'clock news, and posted on Web sites—have been known to launch entire businesses *and bring in the cash,* even when the company has virtually no money to spend on marketing.

And while you've probably seen lots of information on how to write a press release, there are a number of tricks to make your press releases more compelling and to increase their chances of getting published. Press releases—done right—are a powerful marketing weapon that you simply must have in your Instant Income arsenal.

Two of the best media experts I've worked with are Randall Blaum and David Scotland of Marketing Experts International, who unquestionably know how to generate Instant Income using the power of the press. They've created everything from elaborate movie-marketing campaigns to simple one-page press releases that have earned millions for companies like George Lucas's THX, Regal Entertainment Group, NEC Solutions America—even Madonna.

Randall and David have a three-part formula for writing a compelling press release and running an Instant Income press release campaign:

1. **Provide factual information.** Tie your press release to a recent or upcoming news event, or write about a major announcement from your company or organization that will draw attention, such as a promotion, a new product line, or a merger.

2. **Keep the message short.** Make the press release just long enough to tell the facts of the story. Remember that it's not a sales pitch or an advertisement, so it needs to communicate the point with as few words as possible.

3. **Broadcast press releases frequently.** Effective press campaigns are ongoing, with an annual schedule of regular broadcasts to media outlets.

Most publicity experts agree that one press release per month, usually broadcast around the same time each month, is the minimum.

Communicate Your Message to a Wide Audience, Even if You're in a Small Niche Market

Media outlets look for news and stories that will appeal to the widest possible audience. The more your press release speaks to a wide variety of readers, viewers, or listeners, the more likely it is to be covered by media outlets. Not only that, but once you are featured in the news, the more you'll attract new prospects to your products or services.

Of course, if you have a product or service that truly would appeal to only a very small number of people—in a specific industry or hobby area, let's say—your press release should be written to match the needs and wants of that particular niche market. If you sell gearboxes for tractors, for instance, you wouldn't send your press release to *Vanity Fair* magazine. That's too broad an audience. Instead, send it to media outlets in the farming and machinery fields, where people want to read about such topics frequently.

Make Instant Income by Driving Readers to Action and Being Prepared to Sell Them Something

No matter what your product or service, your press release should be written so that both the editor and the ultimate reader or listener want to know more about the news you've provided. Include your contact information, additional newsworthy tips, photos, and short quotes that might lead an editor to interview you—or, equally, compel a reader to respond.

Before you write one word, though, *consider what you'll do when editors and the public do respond.* How will you field inquiries from editors or Web sites? What additional information will you have ready to e-mail to them? What will you sell to people when they respond? If you offer a free item, can you deliver it in downloadable form at your Web site, thus avoiding cost and effort? These are all questions that must be answered before you launch your campaign.

The Nine Elements of Every Successful Press Release

While there are hundreds of ways to write a press release, this formula honed by Randall Blaum and David Scotland has been extraordinarily successful for small businesses in all sorts of industries. As you read the following material, take a look at the successful press release in the next section. Once you see how all of the components work together, you can begin to add your own flair to your releases. But no matter what, these nine elements must be included every time.

1. **"FOR IMMEDIATE RELEASE."** If your news can be released immediately, type the words "FOR IMMEDIATE RELEASE" in all caps somewhere in the upper left-hand corner, just under your letterhead. If your announcement is time-specific and must wait a few days, type "FOR RELEASE ON [DATE]."

2. **Headline and subhead.** Skip a line or two, then center your headline in bold type. You can also add a subhead underneath. The headline, subhead, and first paragraph, by the way, are all "mission critical" to receiving media coverage. You have only about 15 seconds of "eyeball time" with an editor before he makes the decision to cover you—or not.

3. **Dateline.** Write the city and state from which your press release is being issued, along with the day, month, and year. Editors want to know where your news is coming from and the date it was released. Also, many journalists around the world specialize in reporting news from certain geographic markets and thus home in on press releases from certain areas.

4. **Lead paragraph.** Get right to the point *in the very first paragraph* and grab the reader's attention. Answer the "five Ws"—who, what, why, when, and where.

5. **Main text or body.** Use this section to develop the message more fully. Be sure to make it interesting; tell the story, and tell readers why they should be interested. Is your product or service controversial, lifesaving, or destined to change the face of business in some way? Write about that. What are some other points of distinction or uniqueness?

6. **Recap.** Restate the main message of your release, including event information or product launch information.

7. **Company boilerplate.** List general information about you and your company, such as what the company does and the number of employees or locations it has. This is also a great place for your personal biographical statement if you are a consultant or a solo entrepreneur.

8. **Contact information.** Skip a line or two after the recap and list your contact name, contact title, contact company name, contact phone number, contact fax number, contact e-mail address, and corporate Web address. If you are broadcasting the information for release in weekend newspapers or on weekend news programs, be sure to add a contact phone number where you can be reached on the weekend. Note that some marketers prefer to put the contact information in the upper right hand corner of page one. This is also acceptable. If your release flows onto more than one page, put the contact name and a phone number on the bottom of each page, along with a page number, so that if the media misplace some of the pages, they can still contact you.

9. **End or next page information.** To end your press release, type the symbols # # # in the center of the page after your last line of text. Or to indicate that another page follows, type the word -*more*- bracketed by hyphens.

Press Release Success Story

Matt Bacak, an Atlanta small business owner known as "The Powerful Promoter," knows firsthand how effective a successful press release can be. Within 72 hours of issuing the following press release, Matt made an extra $35,000 from sales of his Lead Explosion System. Not only that, but he also saw hundreds of new prospects subscribe to his weekly newsletter—a tool he can now use to convert these prospects' interest into future sales.

This press release was sent through PRWeb.com, a low-cost, Internet-based distribution service, and was picked up by 247 national media outlets, including the *Dallas Morning News.*

Powerful Promoter Offers Tips and Breaks Myths about Opt-In E-mail

Ezine marketing guru Matt Bacak shares secrets to explode opt-in e-mail subscribers.

Atlanta, GA (PRWEB via PR Web Direct) March 28, 2005—Shedding light on why and how big name e-zine marketing gurus have tons of fans and big opt-in e-mail lists, Matt Bacak, The Powerful Promoter and recent *Entrepreneur* magazine e-Biz radio show host, reveals the secret of the "Power Squeeze" site. These special Web sites squeeze names and e-mail addresses from visitors, building a generous list of rabid subscribers.

While the average person on the Internet believes in the myth that businesses should only have one Web site, Bacak insists this is certainly not true. He says, "If you want to volcanically erupt your subscriber lists, then you must have a 'Power Squeeze' site." Bacak's Power Squeeze Site is available for view at www.unlimited-leads.com.

Bacak advises, "Keep your original site, but make another one with the sole purpose of having searchers sign up for your newsletter, e-zine or e-course. Then use the same strategies to get people to this Power Squeeze site that you are using to market your original site. The only purpose of a Power Squeeze site is for people to give you their name, e-mail address, and anything else that you want them to provide, but that's it."

About Matt Bacak

Matt Bacak, The Powerful Promoter and recent *Entrepreneur* magazine e-Biz radio show host, became a "#1 Bestselling Author" in just a few short hours. He has helped a number of clients target his specialty, opt-in e-mail direct-marketing systems. The Powerful Promoter is not only a sought-after Internet marketer but has also marketed for some of the world's top experts, whose reputations would shrivel if their followers ever found out someone else coached them on their online marketing strategies. For more information, visit Bacak's original site at www. powerfulpromoter.com.

Media Contact:
Stephanie Dial
(000) 000-0000

#

Take Steps to Reach the Right People

Now that you know the fundamentals of crafting a good press release, you'll want to broadcast your press release to the media outlets themselves and compel them to use it in their daily lineup of news stories.

The media are very protective of the stories they cover—and very careful about how they obtain information. That's because in the journalism field, a newspaper or televised news program is only as good as the newsworthiness of the information it receives from outside sources. Every editor is overworked. Editors simply don't have the time to wade through the hundreds of press releases they get every day.

So how can *you* stand out and get your story covered?

By reaching the right people with the right message. To do this, first think about how you and your business affect or interact with your local community, then write about that. Too many companies try to "go for the gold" and concentrate only on getting national coverage. But the truth is, local and regional media outlets are easier to work with. They're starving for content and are literally waiting for your e-mail or fax. Most national stories start out as local stories anyway, since journalists from other cities often scan other publications and the Internet looking for the next national headline.

Get Friendly with Local Journalists

There are two types of people who will read your material and decide if it will be used that day: reporters and editors. If you want to get covered in the news, you need to develop a strong relationship with them.

Reporters. It's surprisingly easy to connect with local and regional reporters directly. Most media outlets list their reporters right on the company's Web site along with the kind of news each reporter covers, or you can telephone the newspaper to ask who covers your type of business.

Editors and producers. For newspapers, you'll almost always want to connect with the editor of the section—business, main news, entertainment, lifestyle—where your story is most likely to be featured. With very small publications, you'll probably deal directly with the editor-in-chief or even the owner or publisher. Editors have the ultimate control over what goes into their section or paper. If you want to get on radio or TV, you'll most likely contact the assignment editor of a hard news show and the executive producer or producer of a morning show—whether on TV or on radio. One simple way to locate virtually every reporter or editor/producer in the country is to contact Bacon's (www.bacons.com). It has contact information for more than one million media contacts in almost every city and town in the country.

The Media Don't Owe You Coverage

Media outlets are not your marketing department. But you *can* encourage them to run your story by writing a press release that is so compelling, and that provides such important information for their readers, they wholeheartedly want to use it.

Choose a newsworthy story and remember to put the consumer first when writing about it. Position your business only as a helpful resource, not as the key focus of the article. Then take the time to find the best person at each media outlet to contact with your story. You'll create a successful campaign—and garner the appreciation of countless journalists who will be more disposed to use your releases in the future.

<hr>

ADVERTISING STRATEGY 3

Become an Industry Expert and Get on the Radio

My radio tour ignited my voice as a premier product coach to other inventors. With 100 percent booking, I connected with people across North America. This incredible strategy helped me gain eight new clients in a week and three joint ventures worth $23,000.

CHERYL SCALES
Entrepreneur

Every day, thousands of radio talk shows all over America interview local and national experts on topics of interest to listeners. Many of these "experts" are local business owners who have positioned themselves as authorities—strictly for the purpose of promoting their company and getting on the air.

And while I'm sure that getting on the radio is probably no secret to you as a marketing strategy, it's still one of the most effective tools I've discovered

in working with the world's most successful entrepreneurs. Just like press releases and other familiar strategies, the radio is a true Instant Income tool that
small businesses use constantly to promote their products and expertise. The
difference is the specific system of steps they use to get on the radio—and the
methods they use to be effective in generating income when they're on the air.

Entire media careers can be launched on radio. But local businesses, too,
can benefit by telling their story, creating an on-air offer, and providing authoritative information before competitors have a chance to do so.

Cheryl Scales is one business owner who mastered the use of radio to
build her business. A former product marketing strategist for companies like
Procter & Gamble and Delta Air Lines, Cheryl was shopping for a pair of designer shoes one day and wondered why no one had developed a line of pretty
fashion insoles for expensive women's shoes. The owner of an amazing collection of more than 700 pairs, Cheryl decided to combine her love of footwear
with a lifelong fondness for inventing to create a line of fashion shoe inserts
called Sassy Shoe Lingerie.

She researched the women's wear market, worked with manufacturers to
create washable designs and materials, found designs that were appealing to
women, and even had her initial customers "wear test" the insoles. Then Cheryl
began the arduous task of marketing her collection to upscale boutiques and
shoe stores, knowing from her corporate experience that mass media advertising would be expensive.

What was Cheryl's solution to the high cost of advertising? She prepared
an elaborate presentation and went to the auditions for a new television reality show called *American Inventor*. Soon, Cheryl was flown to Hollywood as
one of the top 250 inventors out of more than 10,000 across the United States.
Armed with her tremendous personal style, her natural speaking ability, and
the research she had done about what makes great TV, Cheryl even landed a
coveted spot on the promotional trailers for the show. Thus, she garnered the
mass media exposure she was looking for.

An astounding 14 million people watched the inaugural show.

And though Cheryl was ultimately dismissed from the competition, she
parlayed her participation on the show into an amazing radio "tour" that led
to an entirely new consulting business, where Cheryl now coaches emerging
inventors on their product development and marketing. On the radio, she
talked about moving from idea to market in 365 days or less. And while some
radio talk show guests wait days to get on the air, Cheryl's unique and timely
twist got her immediate bookings.

As a result of her radio appearances, Cheryl launched a speaking career, landed new retail outlets for her product line, and developed a new profit center for her business—coaching and knowledge products for other inventors. She was even invited to feature her collection of fashion insoles at one of America's most prestigious fashion shows, earning her thousands in additional revenue.

Radio delivered the Instant Income that Cheryl was looking for.

And just like Cheryl, *your* key to getting on the air will be to connect your product, your service, or simply your own industry knowledge to either a current news topic or a relevant topic that a particular talk show host is looking for. In many cases, you'll pitch your story directly to the show's host before getting invited on the air. With larger shows, you'll probably speak with the program director or producer.

Have a "Hook" That Producers Will Respond To

There are many ways to get on radio and television talk shows, but when it comes to doing things right, I turn to my own media advisor, Michelle Anton. She was executive producer for the *Dr. Laura Schlessinger Show,* reaching more than 15 million listeners. And she's produced shows for Leeza Gibbons, Montel Williams, Danny Bonaduce, and A&E Biography, among others. She's even been a freelance associate producer working on the *Oprah Winfrey Show.*

As someone who has booked interview guests for many years, Michelle recommends using one of the following "hooks" when first approaching talk show hosts and producers:

➤ **Provide on-air diagnosis.** Present yourself as an expert who will tell listeners what they need to do under certain circumstances. Tie it to a major news story for greatest impact.

➤ **Interact with your audience.** Help callers understand, process, overcome, do better, or accomplish something.

➤ **Present different ways to solve problems.** Provide tips for relating to difficult people, getting a better-paying job, improving a marriage, getting out of debt, and so on.

➤ **Use a quiz.** Write a list of questions for the show host, then have callers or audience members try to answer the questions.

➤ **Use movie tie-ins.** Tie your product, service, message, or expertise to a current movie. For example, Michael Moore's controversial documentary *Fahrenheit 9/11* provided tie-ins with political topics, patriotism, the war in Iraq, and questions about President Bush's credibility. *The Notebook* dealt with aging parents and Alzheimer's disease. *The Day After Tomorrow* highlighted disasters associated with global warming.

➤ **Relate to pop culture.** Tie your subject matter to popular culture—including what's on television, wacky news stories, baby boomer trends, and other such aspects. Ask a question that will make audiences ponder, such as, "Do reality shows like *Extreme Makeover* and *The Bachelor* reflect real life?"

➤ **Have a celebrity tie-in.** Go on the air as the expert who can talk about celebrity behaviors, beauty regimens, pets, marital issues, addiction, eating disorders, and other celebrity tie-ins.

➤ **Give an opinion.** Offer to be interviewed on the air about an unusual opinion, then defend it.

➤ **Give yourself a memorable name.** Create a moniker like "The Divorce Detective" or "The Dr. Phil of Money," then entertain listeners with stories and advice that establish you as a true expert, with products and services to match.

➤ **Ask a controversial question.** Are school lunches causing poor grades for schoolchildren? Why does the tax system penalize single people?

How to Approach Talk Show Hosts and Producers

You have just two opportunities to impress hosts and program directors enough to put you on the air: (1) when you send an advance package of literature, and (2) when you telephone them to follow up.

Your press kit—preferably sent as a PDF file via e-mail—should be professional looking, concise, and up-to-date. One strategy for ensuring that it will be of current interest (and more likely to be read) is to change the cover page frequently to highlight your tie-in to a major news event, celebrity happening, or other current topic. If your topic is date-specific, such as for a holiday or a government deadline, be sure to submit your package weeks ahead of when you want to be on the air. What should a press kit include?

> A cover page with your daytime and evening contact information

> A single page with your photo and biography

> Your Media Interview Questions page (discussed later)

When you call a producer or talk show host for the first time, have a 30-second introductory "pitch" memorized that details who you are and why you would be entertaining or helpful to listeners. Ask if it is a good time to talk. Then start with your name and deliver your 30-second speech. Take a look at the following example:

> Hi, Mr. Producer, my name is Bill Jeffries, and I'm the Divorce Detective. I give listeners strategies for discovering whether their spouse or girlfriend is cheating. I've been a private investigator for more than 23 years, and I've got stories that will captivate your audience. I love taking call-ins. In fact, in just 12 seconds or less, I can tell any caller whether they're headed for the divorce court. Did you receive the package I e-mailed you yesterday? Is this a topic that your show can use?

The key in talking with producers is to build rapport and a long-term relationship. Think long-term. If a producer isn't interested this week, don't take it personally. Find out how else you can contribute or help—by giving samples, offering your services, or even referring other experts so that the producer can build a show around more than one of you. Since a lot of shows are built around opposing viewpoints, be sure to know both sides of your topic and be willing to offer names, Web sites, and phone numbers whenever possible.

Assess the interest of the editor or producer. Listen carefully for clues and ask open-ended questions to find out what she is looking for. Work hard to turn negative responses into positive ones—or at least into future opportunities.

And finally, be fun and fabulous to work with. Life is tough enough without working with high-maintenance people who complicate things.

Be Great on the Air

Talk radio is pure entertainment. The more interesting and lively you can be on the air, the longer the show's listeners will stay tuned. And if you can keep them intrigued enough to hang on through the commercial breaks—well, you have done your job, and the talk show host may even invite you back. While becoming media-friendly is a fine art, just having a gift for chat will get you halfway there. Here are some other tips for being great on the radio when you go live:

➤ **Develop a Media Interview Questions page.** You would be surprised how many guests are on the air with hosts who know virtually nothing about them except what is contained in the guest's press kit. It's your responsibility to make the show host's job easier by providing questions that will prompt a great interview and create an interesting show segment.

➤ **Write out your sound bites and memorize them.** While you do need to intrigue and inform your listeners, you also need to steer the conversation in the direction you want it to go, in order to appear in the best light and make an impact on listeners. To do this, craft your own answers to the questions on your Media Interview Questions page, then memorize them to help you stay on track when you are on the air. Just as a sales script helps you be more "present" in the sales call, knowing your basic dialogue will help you be more present during a talk show interview.

➤ **Offer to interact with the audience via call-ins.** Talk show hosts love to get their listeners involved, with interview guests solving listeners' problems or otherwise providing interaction with listeners. If you are confident enough to answer unscripted questions, and if the talk show uses a call-in format, you can create a lively exchange on the air.

Drive Instant Income with an On-Air Offer

Although you are on the air to enlighten, inform, and entertain, talk show hosts understand that you are also there to pitch your product or service. Otherwise, why would you go to all this effort?

To make Instant Income while you're on the air, have a prewritten pitch memorized word for word, so you sound natural when you deliver it. You might offer every listener a discount if he visits your store this weekend. You might offer a reduced-price consultation if listeners call your toll-free number. You might give away free tickets to your evening workshop. Whatever you decide to offer, make it especially easy to respond.

Remember that a large percentage of listeners are hearing you while they are driving in their car. Get a toll-free number that spells something memo-rable, and register a Web site domain name that is easy to write down.

Then, be prepared to receive potentially hundreds of calls and responses within minutes of your being on the air.

Buy Remnant Space

Our advertising strategy, which included using unsold airtime, began generating a million dollars a month almost immediately from our TV spot. Eventually, our media purchases translated into about $1.8 million per week *in sales. We went from $300,000 to $63 million in sales in just five years, using a combination of unsold advertising and low-cost joint ventures with media companies.*

JEFFREY WYCOFF
Vice-president of Sirius Products, Inc.,
makers of Zap! Cleaner

Sometimes Instant Income doesn't come from outside sources. Instead, it comes from keeping more of the money that's in your bank account already. *Remnant advertising* helps you to spend substantially less on your display advertising because you're buying leftover ad space that the newspaper or media outlet is willing to sell at a smaller profit margin.

How to Speak the Language and Get Remnant Pricing

In the newspaper and magazine business, there are always two deadlines for advertisers—the *space deadline* and the *materials deadline*.

When a newspaper or magazine "closes the book" on a specific issue—say, Tuesday's paper or the April issue—that means it stops taking insertion orders for display advertising space in that issue. Once this space deadline is passed, the advertising department and editorial departments turn over all display ad orders and editorial content to the graphics department, which must put the puzzle pieces together and design the final publication layout.

But here's the inside secret: the graphics department *always* has space left over—either half-page, full-page, or fractional-page "holes" created by other advertisers and by the printing "signatures" (or page counts) required by today's massive printing presses.

Some reports say that an incredible $30 billion worth of advertising space in newspapers and magazines—and on television, on the radio, and elsewhere—goes unused every year.

Approaching Your Newspaper with a Remnant Offer

Most newspapers and other media outlets don't publicize the fact that they sell advertising space at remnant rates. But the truth is, *most do sell this space at a whopping 50 to 75 percent off their published rates.* What's more, they would rather sell the space to you at a reduced rate than be forced to run a "house ad"—an advertisement for the newspaper's own products and services—and make no money whatsoever.

If you have a copy of the media outlet's rate card showing its published rates, you should start your negotiations at least 50 percent below the *lowest published rate*—including those rates available to the most frequent advertisers.

Do the math before you call your advertising representative, so you'll know if the rate you are eventually quoted is an actual bargain. I've successfully bought on remnant for myself and for clients, including $11,000 pages in the *Los Angeles Times* for just $4,500—a savings of about 60 percent.

Be aware that newspapers typically have more remnant space available on Mondays and Tuesdays, since most other retail advertising goes into the Thursday through Sunday editions. This availability is ideal if you sell any kind of personal-improvement product or service. After a weekend of eating too much, spending too much, exercising too little, or otherwise going overboard, consumers will see your ad offering a solution on Monday morning. Advertising any products and services for men in the sports pages on Monday and Tuesday will help you to take advantage of readership of the past weekend's sports scores.

Have Your Display Ad or 30-Second Spot Ready and Waiting

Be sure to call your advertising representative just as the space deadline is looming. Tell your representative that you would like to be notified of any remnant space that might be available "after the book is closed."

Say that you can have your artwork to the media outlet immediately if it will give you the dimensions for the ad space it has available.

You can also say that you are testing this particular medium and are willing to do so only on a remnant basis. If the marketing test is profitable for you, you'll add the media outlet to your normal advertising lineup.

One thing I've discovered about buying remnant advertising from the same periodical on a regular basis is that an advertising representative will often work with the graphics department to create remnant space for you.

You must be prepared to act when your representative finds remnant space for you. Have your display ad already prepared, in different sizes if possible. Or at least have the ability to quickly reformat the artwork yourself using Adobe InDesign, QuarkXPress, or another page-layout software application. You can also ask if the newspaper's graphics department can resize your ad for the remnant space available, as long as you have a digital file of the ad, all the fonts used in the ad, and any scans or images included.

Once your remnant purchase has been approved, you'll need to submit your artwork by the *materials deadline**—the day and time by which your ad's artwork or the digital recording of your radio spot or other advertisement must be submitted in an acceptable format. Leave extra time for any legal review by the newspaper or media outlet that must take place. With some categories of products and services, this is a requirement.

Go Standby and Save Even More

Even better than remnant rates are *standby rates,* where you allow the media outlet to run your advertisement whenever it has remnant space available. You submit your artwork or commercial, along with a maximum monthly dollar amount that you'll agree to, and the media outlet keeps your ad on file for immediate use, with no notice to you. This means that you must submit advertisements for only those products, services, and offers that you honor continuously.

The beauty of running standby is that you often get more advertising than you pay for—all at rock-bottom prices.

---

* Occasionally, the space deadline and the materials deadline are the same.

Hold a Special Sale Using the "Reason Why"

Telling the story of why I needed to limit my travel generated an overnight response of young speakers for my new speaker's training program. We've since raised the price from $10,000 to $20,000, and still we're oversold for the program.

LES BROWN
Veteran motivational speaker and author
of *Live Your Dreams*

When world-renowned motivational speaker Les Brown, a friend and client of mine for many years, recently had a bout with cancer, he decided to limit his time traveling, but to make up the lost income by training emerging speakers in developing the kind of world-class speaking career that Les has enjoyed for more than 30 years.

He decided to teach his delivery techniques, his strategies for getting bookings, his formulas for creating back-of-the-room products, and other such information. "But why would someone of Les Brown's caliber agree to train other speakers when he makes millions every year from his own speaking career?" people were asking.

His desire to get off the road was his "reason why." And it proved to be a compelling one.

In the first year alone, dozens of speakers paid the hefty $10,000 program fee to be trained by Les. Today, some of them are among the most in-demand speakers in the world.

Why the "Reason Why" Helps Convince Prospective Customers

No prospect likes to think that your sole motivation as a business owner is to make tons of money from her. That idea is offensive. But if there's a compelling reason *why you're making the offer*, telling your story helps humanize you and makes your offer, your price, and your claim of urgency more credible.

In fact, the reason why is so compelling in direct-response advertising that if you don't have a good rationale for making an offer, my advice is:

Find one.

In the case of Les Brown's Speakers Training, the idea that he would offer to train others was inexplicable. Telling the reason why he would do this made the offer seem more credible and the hefty price tag more acceptable. His advertising copy even described some of the less glamorous aspects of being on the road, such as taking off his shoes for airport security and sleeping in a different city every night. It helped readers identify with Les more as a person—as someone just like them.

Decades of market testing have proven that telling the reason why leads more people to respond to your offers. It not only helps you create a stronger bond with your potential customer but also gives your offer a limited-time feel or special-circumstances slant that compels readers to take immediate action. They believe the situation won't last.

Think about your own advertising. Why are *you* offering the particular product mix or service package that you're advertising? Why are you offering it *at the price* you're asking? Why are you offering it *now*? Is it a closeout or overstock item? Do you have an unusual reason, such as

- ➤ The government recently announced new record-keeping regulations for health care providers, and your document storage company is responding with an important new service.

- ➤ Your scheduled trip to Asia got postponed, so you now have two weeks free in your schedule and are willing to do unique one-hour strategic planning consultations for half price.

- ➤ Your supplier called with a limited inventory overstock that was too small to offer the chain stores, yet the deal has now reduced the price of this item to the consumer by a whopping 78 percent.

- ➤ You recently acquired an entire estate of magnificent nineteenth-century French furniture owned by one of Hollywood's elite, and, while the prices will be high, the collection is simply too spectacular to offer it to anyone but your most loyal customers first.

Whatever your rationale is, tell the story.

Holding a Special Sale Using a Compelling Reason Why

One of the fastest ways to make Instant Income is to advertise a special sale based upon a unique circumstance that isn't expected to last. Perhaps you have a limited supply of something. Perhaps you have a unique set of goods that can't be replicated in the future. Perhaps there's a unique situation in your consulting firm that has created a once-in-a-lifetime opening or opportunity.

One consultant I worked with offered one-hour consultations at half price because a family trip had been cancelled, and suddenly there was a two-week window in his calendar. He was raising his hourly rate anyway, so he combined the trip cancellation and imminent rate increase stories into a compelling offer.

A jewelry store I consulted for held a once-a-year estate jewelry sale over two days every spring. The advertising I wrote for the store told the story of the individual pieces, how they were one-of-a-kind and sure to be sold the minute the doors opened the first morning. Rather than simply putting the preowned jewelry in the showcase and selling it over time, we made an entire event out of the fact that all the jewelry was being brought in for one weekend only.

To promote your special sale, run an advertisement in the newspaper, send a personalized letter to your best customers, e-mail your e-zine subscriber list, or use any of the other message delivery vehicles available to you. In each one, begin with the reason why, using headlines like:

> **We've Found the Only Cache Remaining of Pedro Gueraca Lithographs— All in Perfect Condition and Every One Signed by the Artist Just Before His Death in 1923**

Then write your story into the body copy, starting with the very first paragraph. Like this:

> It's rare that I write a letter this undignified to my best and most distinguished customers. But the truth is . . . I can hardly contain my excitement! Just this morning I received a call from my source in Spain who telephoned with news of an extraordinary find.

Over 200 prints from the Pedro Gueraca estate—all signed by Gueraca himself just prior to his death—have been unearthed in perfect condition during a recent inventory of the vaults at the Museum of Modern Art!

I quickly optioned all 200 prints, scheduled a full-page ad in *Modern Masters* magazine—but decided to *first* make them available to you, one of my most loyal clients, before the ad appears in the June issue. Once the general public finds out about this extraordinary discovery, I can't guarantee we'll have any of these outstanding and important prints left.

To help you get a better sense of the importance of this find, let me describe each of the selections in detail:

To begin with, there are 27 perfectly preserved lithographs of Gueraca's famed *Chica Con Su Compañero (Girl with Her Companion)*, which was painted during the artist's 1917 summer in Màlaga . . .

Be sure to make a specific offer in your promotional copy, by mentioning a unique price; listing the date by which the offer, inventory, or situation will no longer be available; and giving the reader an easy way to respond.

CHAPTER 4

Prospecting for
Instant Income

GENERATING *prospective* customers is one of the most critical activities of any small business. Yet it's also one of the least liked and most poorly performed ingredients of a solid income-generating system. One of the reasons for this oversight is that prospecting is often a natural by-product of advertising, so business owners tend to overlook it in favor of advertising that generates immediate sales, simply believing that prospects will also result from the campaign.

But intelligent prospecting is much more calculated than that.

Ideally, it's an activity that should be approached as a separate and important part of your business. It's a way to generate a database of people who know you, who appreciate what your business has to offer, and who can more easily be "closed" into buying something from you. If you aren't employing multiple strategies to create a steady stream of individuals inquiring about your product or service, your future cash flow is in danger.

Turn Haphazard Prospecting
into Strategic Prospecting

Strategic prospecting means that you choose strategies and tactics that support and enhance your other marketing and sales efforts. For example, if you have a bonus or benefit that has been highly effective in closing sales, make sure that all your marketing efforts communicate that bonus or benefit to the world. Make it the cornerstone of your marketing effort and you'll probably generate twice as many prospects and close many more sales.

Strategic prospecting also means that you perform frequent and consistent lead generation—not just when you need more business. This is especially difficult for consulting businesses, solo entrepreneurs, and other kinds of businesses that must stop advertising in order to deliver services once they land a new client or customer. This constant stopping and starting is a vicious circle, but there are ways to continuously generate prospects who will be eager to work with you when you are available.

Find a Niche and Own It

Remember that old cliché *you can't be all things to all people?* It's a well-worn comment because, regrettably enough, it's true. In today's world of specialization, it's virtually impossible to be a one-stop shop from which *everyone* will want to buy. So how do you generate the highest number of prospects who *will* want to buy from you? In other words, how can you distinguish yourself from all your competitors so that you are the one company with which a customer finally does business?

It's simple.

Find a niche market and own it.* Find the one niche in your industry that no one else has discovered or successfully exploited. Create a specialty, a uniqueness, an area of expertise that everyone needs but no one is delivering. Become the one expert that everyone turns to because you can solve a problem that everyone experiences but that no one has ever solved in quite the way you can.

You don't have to change the way you conduct your business to do this.

It's often much easier to use good marketing to change what people *believe* about you.

Let me explain.

When you sell a common item or service—dry cleaning, bookkeeping, gift baskets, hardware—you are competing with every other dry cleaner, bookkeeper, basket maker, or hardware store in town on just two things: product

---

* A niche market is defined as "an area of the market specializing in a particular type of product" (*Encarta World English Dictionary*).

and price. You have to keep track of what your competitors offer. You have to match what they charge. You have to maintain your inventory to match theirs. And, sometimes, you even have to honor the coupons they distribute.

Sadly, no matter how good you are at keeping up with your competitors, *you actually stand to lose this product-and-price war on a daily basis.* Every time a competitor runs a special that you can't afford to match or buys new equipment that you can't afford to bring on, you run the risk that your customers will go elsewhere—permanently.

With niche marketing, on the other hand, you can position yourself as better, more desirable, more capable, more professional, and more talented than every one of your competitors—regardless of your expertise, equipment, price, inventory, selection, or terms. With niche marketing, you can tell the world—in one sentence or less—how you can better solve its problems and fill its needs.

Take a look at the following four-step process for telling the world how you are superior:

1. **Put yourself in your customers' place.** Make a list of the most common needs, goals, activities, and desires that your customers have. If they could have anything they wanted at the same price as your basic product or service, what would they want? Two-hour delivery? Ongoing advice and hand-holding? Free loaner models when they bring a unit in for servicing?

2. **Make a list of the products and services you provide, especially the unique add-ons that you don't usually advertise.** Brainstorm with your staff. It's quite possible they're going the extra mile right now, throwing in little "freebies" as part of good customer service or total product quality. Perhaps they call competitors to get a widget for a customer when you are out of stock, or perhaps they have developed their own system for delivering services more quickly with the same quality. Whatever it is, make a list of these unadvertised "bonus" benefits. Could you make them a major theme of your advertising campaigns in the future? Would customers be happy to shop with you rather than the competition if they only knew about these extras?

3. **Make a list of those additional things that you don't offer now but should offer in the future to meet your customers' wants.** Most customers buy for reasons other than the tangible price, product, or services

offered. They buy convenience, dependability, delivery, training, warranty, atmosphere, finance options, retail sales support, and other such elements.

If you operate a housekeeping service, do you train, insure, and bond all your helpers; provide your own cleaning supplies; keep track of and arrange for timely cleaning of special items like carpets and drapes; then provide a free special cleaning right before the holidays? If you're a bookkeeper, do you put on extra staff at the beginning of every month so that you can deliver financial statements by the fifth? Talk about these bonus benefits in your prospecting campaigns.

Your added value, by the way, should *not* be that you provide better "quality" or "service." Those are empty promises these days.

4. **Tell your customers and prospective customers how you will meet their needs better than your competitors.** If you can successfully tell the world how you are different, you can develop a niche and own it. It will force you to start providing solutions that you can clearly describe to your customers and prospects in your advertising. Stop asking customers and prospects, "What are you looking for?" Instead, ask them, "What are you trying to accomplish?"

One More Way to Be Seen as Different by Your Marketplace

If you provide a common product or service, distinguishing yourself in the marketplace is often as easy as describing the way businesses like yours work—before your competitors have a chance to do so in their advertising.

You can tell prospects how you select your raw materials, why you use certain kinds of fasteners, the 18-point quality check that every unit goes through after manufacture—even about your packaging and shipping methods. Of course, you may not do these things any differently from your competitors, but you'll stand out from your competitors *simply because you have described the process and they haven't.*

The natural inclination of prospective customers will be to believe that you are superior and that your competitors do *not* follow these careful procedures. Why? Because *they* haven't described the process in their advertising.

Finding the Pools of Prospects

If you articulate what your business can deliver and then craft your advertised offers* using the techniques you learn in this book, you'll become a lot more successful at recruiting prospective customers.

But communicating the message persuasively is only half the equation. You must also make sure your message is read, heard, and seen by *qualified buyers* rather than by the unqualified masses.

Remember the concept of *niche marketing?* Your prospective buyers will always exist in a niche that you can identify. They have hobbies, they work at certain kinds of jobs, they have pets, they own specific kinds of businesses, they travel to certain places, and so on. When you identify their niche, and then approach each potential customer as just one person in a niche market of other like-minded prospects, your advertising and prospecting campaigns will become easier and a lot more successful.

Of course, depending on your business, your prospects might exist within a niche that is local to your store or office, or they might live nationally or even internationally. But they will always be part of the niche you identify.

Let's look at examples of how you can find these prospects:

➤ A winery could rent a list of *local* subscribers to food and wine magazines, then invite them to special events at the winery.†

➤ A nutritionist could rent a list of *local* consumers who subscribe to fitness magazines or who buy supplements through mail order.

➤ Interior designers who specialize in decorating estate homes know that their perfect buyer also owns an expensive car, subscribes to upscale magazines, and doesn't clean her own pool. The names of local car buyers and magazine subscribers can be easily rented. And there are dozens of pool maintenance companies to approach with a joint-venture deal.

➤ An advertising firm looking for new clients could read the Yellow Pages and easily determine that any business with a half-page or larger adver-

---

* See Chapter 3, "Writing Ads That Make the Phone Ring," for details on how to write advertisements. See Sales Strategy 3, "Make Specific Product and Service Offers," for more information on crafting compelling offers.

† Standard Rates and Data Service publishes details on thousands of companies, magazines, and catalog publishers that rent their customer names for your marketing campaigns. You can find SRDS at large public libraries, online at www.srds.com, or by calling (800) 232-0772.

tisement is probably a great prospect because it already spends serious money on its advertising.

To get started, make a list of what your perfect prospect is doing, reading, buying, watching, and listening to. Then identify how to rent, acquire through a joint venture, or otherwise access these people's names from other companies that are already selling to them or advertising to them.

Using Multiple Prospecting Methods to Improve Your Credentials

Using multiple methods, such as a direct-mail campaign followed by telemarketing followed by an invitation to an evening seminar, makes you look better to your potential prospects. These multiple efforts improve your credentials and make your business look more professional and more established. Multiple impressions simply give potential prospects more confidence in you.

Of course, the methods for reaching prospects (and various ways to spend your advertising dollar) are almost endless. I've discussed five of the best strategies—based on my experience—following this tutorial (those in italic type in the following list). Here are different ways to prospect:

Affiliate programs

Business cards/CDs

Direct mail

Display advertising

Distribution of free information

E-mail*

Inserts/carton stuffers

Press relations

Preview workshops

Radio commercials

Radio interviews

Referrals from customers

Statement stuffers

Telemarketing

Teleseminars

Television commercials

Trade shows

Two-step campaigns

Web site traffic

---

* Please see an important notice about e-mail prospecting and current CAN-SPAM regulations in Internet Strategy 4, "Broadcast Internet-Only Offers via E-mail."

Getting More Leverage from Your Time, Effort, and Money

The prospecting strategies I've listed come from many different industries. Yet if you looked around your industry, you'd probably find that your competitors are all prospecting the same way. Don't invest in simply getting better at prospecting the same way everyone else does when "getting better" will improve upon what others have already refined by perhaps only 5 to 10 percent. Instead, try something new and different beyond the industry "norm."

First Market to a Smaller List

Never spend a large amount of money on mailing to 100,000 names or on buying a full-page ad before testing on a smaller scale.

For example, perhaps you've discovered a list of 100,000 homeowners who are looking to refurbish their homes. You wouldn't want to rent this list and then send all 100,000 names a marketing piece about your construction services until you know which message will give you the biggest return on your marketing investment. Instead of "rolling out" to the entire list, why not rent a small group of names and start marketing to this smaller and more qualified list more effectively and more often? Your results when you do finally send those 100,000 pieces are likely to improve.

A good case in point is a friend of mine who lost everything in a bad franchise experience. While he could have looked for a job or spent months prospecting for new clients, I suggested instead that he offer to trade his services for an endorsement from a consultant to the consultant's clients—knowing that he'd probably make more money in a week doing that than he would in a month doing something else.

My friend could afford to send only 100 letters out of the 30,000 names on the endorser's list—a sample so small that it could have yielded no results at all.

But it *did* yield results.

In fact, over the next six months, my friend mailed only 600 letters total, yet more than 50 of the 600 recipients became clients of his—with the average client buying more than $1,500 in services in just the first six months!

By starting small, you get to test what works, and you get to develop a follow-up system that converts prospects to buyers. Ask yourself which is likely to be more effective: one letter to 100,000 prospects, or focusing on 20,000 prospects and sending them two different postcards offering free reports, followed by an invitation to a teleseminar, followed by an educational letter, followed by a call from your sales team.

Don't Forget to Do "More"

Prospecting intelligently is important. But even more important is the *frequency* with which you conduct your prospecting campaigns. Why? Because your business is just too big an investment, too valuable an asset, and too time-sensitive an activity to rely on a single, random strategy conducted infrequently or haphazardly. You can't just run one ad or mail one letter or produce one commercial and hope that it will continually provide robust cash flow. Even the most successful campaigns eventually decrease in effectiveness.

A much more secure way to run a business is to have 4, 5, or even 10 sources of new prospects. When your revenues are derived from consistent, smart, and targeted prospecting methods that gather prospects from lots of sources, you won't be so vulnerable to a single source that could eventually fail.

PROSPECTING STRATEGY 1

Conduct Preview Workshops and Start Speaking

Since 1990, we've provided a turnkey Seminar Marketing System to professional practices nationwide. Seminars are the most cost-effective method of marketing; they attract the highest response at the least cost per lead. On average, when we promote a seminar, we generate 92 seminar reservations at a cost per lead of just $43.

KATHRYN DUNN
K. Dunn & Associates, a performance-based marketing firm

I f your business recruits clients, patients, or customers from your hometown or local market area, offer free evening workshops and weekend "how-to" classes, which are a superb way to let prospective customers sample your product, service, or expertise before hiring you.

Not only do these workshops and classes help you draw in new customers but they help you retain existing customers who feel that you are going above and beyond the service they normally get from businesses in your industry. Home-improvement stores, skin-care salons, bookstores, garden centers, computer resellers, and other such businesses are providing free lectures, demonstrations, and classes, knowing they'll be the first place attendees will turn to for help and purchases later.

If you sell supplies for construction projects, own an art supply store, run a kitchen store, sell landscaping supplies, teach scuba diving, or do just about anything else that customers install themselves or could have an interest in trying their hand at, offering a do-it-yourself class or a learn-the-basics class can help bring you Instant Income by

➤ Getting your customers to start a project or hobby for which they'll need to purchase tools and supplies immediately following the class

➤ Giving your clients a new appreciation of your expertise in an area that they may not know about, resulting in their hiring you for that new service or referring others to your firm

➤ Reactivating past customers who may have always wanted to take that class

In addition, classes are a great way to establish a bond with your customers, find out why they patronize your business, learn why they refer or don't refer others to you, and look for potential endorsements or joint-venture opportunities with those customers who own their own business.

Done right, these preview workshops can also be powerful selling environments.

Start with Back-End Revenue in Mind

When you decide to hold evening workshops, how-to seminars, and other kinds of programs, approach your decision with the back end in mind—that is, the product or service that you'll ultimately sell the customers once they attend. Determine what you'll offer to the crowd, calculate your potential revenues, then create a plan for presenting that offer to attendees. Use the following checklist to guide you:

➤ Determine what you'll offer, what the price will be, and what you'll bundle into the package.

➤ Write your advertisement, flyer, or other workshop promotional copy to attract the type of buyer who will purchase that package.

➤ Set up a response mechanism, such as a call center, Web site, or trained front-desk staff at your office or at another point where people can purchase.

➤ Use every promotional outlet possible to attract prospects to your event, from e-mailing your current clients so they can invite their friends and family to getting on the radio* to display advertising, press releases, endorsed mailings through joint-venture partners, and any other outlet you can think of.

Make Instant Income from Workshops and Classes

Most successful workshop scripts include industry information, how-to demonstrations, and other helpful details that provide real value to attendees. But they also go one step further and present a compelling offer so that attendees can instantly purchase the products used, the services described, or the consulting work you talk about from the podium. To generate maximum instant income, you can

➤ **Sell products at the back of the room.** Be sure to bundle a kit or package that includes everything that attendees will need to replicate the process you just demonstrated in your class.

➤ **Offer consulting services at a special package rate.** Whether it's advertising services, business consulting, or another type of work, try combining all possible services you would typically provide into a package that you discount for attendees who purchase that evening. A common practice is to include bonus items that have a high perceived value but cost little to deliver, then incorporate the value of those bonuses into the overall price.

➤ **Sell an advanced program.** You can sell a refresher course, executive summary, or other specialty program that is held *immediately following* the main program. You can also sell it in advance—at a reduced rate—by mentioning it in the same marketing materials you use to sell your main program.

---

* See Advertising Strategy 3, "Become an Industry Expert and Get on the Radio," for more details on booking radio interviews.

➤ **Sell one-day workshop participants into longer programs.** These can include more intensive lessons or class schedules that run for months afterward.

➤ **Follow up with telemarketing.** Those attendees who don't purchase at the end of the workshop should receive a phone call within a few days to sell them the package offered.

Speak Locally about Your Business

You don't need to limit yourself to workshops that you can do at the local mall or inside your store. Service clubs, churches, youth organizations, and all kinds of other groups need speakers for their weekly and monthly programs. Speaking locally about your business and how it serves an immediate need is an ideal strategy for selling your professional services to local prospects.

Speak at Industry Trade Shows and Conferences

Similarly, if your business operates in a vertical market or industry that routinely holds conferences, trade shows, and other events, you should start contacting trade associations and organizers to be added as a speaker to the conference's educational forum.*

PROSPECTING STRATEGY 2

Run a Two-Step Campaign

Educating prospects is a big part of selling them something. Yet occasionally, a product or service takes so much education that you simply need more space, more time, and more conversation than can be adequately handled by a full-page display ad or even an elaborate Web site. You need the prospect to contact you directly for more extensive information.

That's when it's time to run a *two-step campaign*.

---

* If you're uncomfortable speaking before a group, have an employee prepare and deliver the presentation. Or hire a professional speaker who can conduct local workshops or represent your firm by delivering a breakout session at national conferences.

A two-step campaign starts with a teaser device—an advertisement, letter, e-mail, postcard, or voice broadcast—that convinces a prospect to *take the next step* and contact you. When people respond, you deliver a special report, teleseminar, live sales call, evening workshop, e-mail short course, or other communication that closes the sale.

Of course, in addition to being a powerful selling tool, a two-step campaign is also a powerful list-building activity that fills your prospect pipeline with informed and interested people who have said, "Yes, I'm interested in hearing more, and I may even purchase from you." Those are qualified leads.

What Does a Two-Step Campaign Look Like?

There are many ways to conduct a two-step campaign and numerous circumstances under which a two-step campaign can instantly create thousands of qualified leads for your sales conversion process. Here are some of the more common ways:

➤ **Generate leads from an endorsed joint-venture list.** Customers and prospects who are mailed, e-mailed, or telephoned by your joint-venture partner—who enthusiastically endorses you to her customers—are much "warmer" than other leads. Leads generated on an endorsed basis are often presold, particularly if you have crafted a well-written introduction letter or e-mail for your joint-venture partner to sign. In this kind of campaign, respondents call you directly to request an informative booklet, get more information, book an exploratory consultation, or see if they qualify to do business with you. (See Chapter 2, "Getting Other People to Help Bring In the Cash," for more details.)

➤ **Generate entry-level "sampler" buyers.** An ideal way to pay for your two-step program is to sell an inexpensive sampler item, then upsell those leads into more expensive products or services using other Instant Income strategies. I've advertised everything from $49 special reports to $2.47 audiocassette tapes. And the beauty of this approach is that not only do you generate hot prospects who are inclined to find your company and its more expensive products valuable but your two-step campaign is *self-liquidating,* which simply means that it pays for itself. One recommendation is to offer your sample at your exact cost, such as $3.68. Add up all your costs—the hard cost of the sample, the mailing envelope, the postage, the call center, your staff costs—then truthfully tell respondents that you're providing the sample at your actual cost. Don't round up to the nearest dollar. The odd number actually makes your offer more believable and gains you more favor with prospects because it conveys to the buyer, "I'm not here to gouge you. I'm not making any money off this. I just want to get this information into your hands."

➤ **Generate opt-ins to your autoresponder series.** You can read more about this powerful technique in Internet Strategy 1, "Launch a Viral Report and Squeeze Page," but in summary, you can create subscribers (opt-ins) for a multipart, educational e-mail series where each e-mail is automatically delivered according to your predetermined schedule via an *autoresponder*. Embedded within the e-mails, starting with e-mail 6, is sales copy that converts these online prospects to buyers of your offline product or service. A well-written press release, e-mail to an endorsed list, or e-mail broadcast to rented e-mail addresses* will drive prospects to your Web site to subscribe.

➤ **Prospect among your customers for a new product offering.** You can use the same techniques you use to prospect for new customers in the marketplace to prospect among your existing customers for any new product or service you might offer.

Crafting Your Compelling Two-Step Offer

A two-step offer that convinces someone to take the next step—to call for more information, to click through to a Web site, or to schedule an appointment with a customer-care representative—will be successful only if the "next step" item is valuable and appealing. What can you offer?

➤ A free teleseminar about a controversial new law or some other matter that affects the prospect's livelihood, lifestyle, health, or career. You can also record the teleseminar and make that recording available for download at your Web site for future prospects.

---

* E-mailing to people who do not have a previous business relationship with you and who have not requested (opted in) to receive information about a particular topic is called spamming and is illegal. Please abide by CAN-SPAM laws and rent only confirmed opt-in names from reputable sources. For more details, visit www.ftc.gov/bcp/conline/pubs/buspubs/canspam.htm.

➤ A free audio CD or DVD explaining a new process or service. You can also sell the CD as a $9.95 sampler product.

➤ A free printed special report or, less expensively, a colorful PDF file that you can e-mail to people (or have them download at your Web site) once they identify themselves to you.

➤ A free sample monthly issue of your e-zine or other periodical.

➤ A free buyer's guide that helps the prospect compare all suppliers of a particular item or service, written in such a way that your product or service ranks near the top. You can easily create this document using colorful graphics, then distill it into a PDF file for easy, free delivery via e-mail.

➤ A free 14-day business short course on a specific topic, delivered via e-mail using an autoresponder service.*

➤ A free weekend seminar or evening workshop where you present an expensive service or consulting package for sale.

➤ A free evaluation by one of your specialists (who are, in reality, trained salespeople).

➤ A free session with your assessment team to see if the prospect qualifies to become your client or customer. If you have a high-profile consulting practice, sell exclusive dealerships by territory, or otherwise limit whom you sell to, you can run a "see if you qualify" campaign to sift through prospects and choose only those with whom you really want to work. This technique also works to instantly boost sales from these prospects because it employs what's called the "take-away" close: it sets up the notion in the prospect's mind that he might not be able to have what you're offering. And how do people react when they think they can't have something? They want it even more.

---

* Visit the Instant Income Resources Page for recommended services. Go to www.instantincome.com/resources.html.

What's So "Instant" about Two-Step Income?

Income from two-step campaigns, while not as "instant" as income from some other sources, often gets generated more easily. When you do the advance work of getting people to contact you for more information or to get something free or to see if they qualify, you completely change the sales dynamic and make it much easier to sell to these leads. An especially good technique is the "see if you qualify" offer, since it often turns the tables and causes the prospect *to start convincing you* to let him buy what you're offering.

Two-step campaigns, while more time-consuming, can also help you sell to a larger percentage of readers than you might by advertising at one time your entire offer with a big price tag—which you can't possibly explain or justify in the limited space of a display ad.

These campaigns very often save on advertising dollars, too, since you can run a much smaller ad or mail a short letter with a compelling headline and a few lines of marketing copy—ending with an invitation to "call or click" (by telephoning or visiting your Web site).

PROSPECTING STRATEGY 3

Place Your Literature in Targeted Locations

We've been able to place our special offers and guest passes in over 100 different locations around town by approaching other business owners and offering to put their literature in our facility in return. This win-win approach not only persuades them, it brings us thousands of dollars in immediate revenue.

ERNIE SALAZAR
Manager, Newbury Park Athletic Club

A Laundromat puts coupons in the lobby of local motels. A golf pro leaves business cards in the pro shop at the local municipal golf course. A massage therapist places brochures in the waiting rooms of luxury car dealerships.

It seems that you can find business information nearly everywhere these days because—if it's done right—placing literature where it will be seen and taken is perhaps the least expensive way there is to get information into the hands of people who have an immediate need for your product or service.

Not only can brochures and business cards be distributed this way but so can audio CDs, application forms, catalogs, and other such items.

To be truly effective using this strategy, make a list of those places where your prospects might be thinking about your product or service as they are shopping, running errands, or pursuing their favorite hobby or sport. Don't put your literature just anyplace that has a message board or use an expensive distribution company that will drop off bundles of literature at dry cleaners and delicatessens. Be much more targeted than that by choosing locations where prospects will be in the right frame of reference to act upon what they see. Let's look at some examples.

I once took golf lessons from a woman golf pro who had placed a small display of her business cards on the counter of the pro shop I frequented. I was in the pro shop to buy a bucket of balls, I wanted to take lessons, and her business cards held an appealing message for me, so I took one and called her up.

A short time later, I was in a small hotel in Florence and, after two weeks in Italy, needed to do laundry. A local *lavanderia* had wisely put coupons for one free wash on a small table in the lobby. When I asked the concierge where I could do my laundry, she handed me a coupon and sent me on my way. I wasn't so surprised that the coupons were there, but I was more than impressed that the owner of the *lavanderia* had placed coupons written in both Italian and English—complete with prices, a map, hours of operation, an explanation of the coin-operated machines (so that I'd bring enough change), and other details I'd need. Apparently, he knew that many English-speaking travelers frequented that hotel. Very smart.

A massage therapist I know placed attractive and informative brochures for her day spa in the waiting room of the Mercedes-Benz dealer down the street. Ladies who had to wait while their cars were being serviced could bring in the brochure for a 40-minute, specially priced massage or facial treatment just a block or two up the street. The flyers cost just a few cents apiece to photocopy, they appealed to the upscale ladies who were stuck waiting for their cars, and the massage therapist typically had at least one therapy room free where walk-in clients could wait in a luxurious spa robe—with a fashion magazine and an herbal tea—until she could do their massage. It was much more appealing than waiting in the car dealership's back room, and, needless to say, the therapist did a huge business this way—with virtually every penny of those massages and facials being pure profit.

A foreign-exchange company I consulted for distributed pads of tear-off coupons to local bank managers, just in case customers mistakenly came to the bank to exchange dollars for foreign currency. The coupon offered to exchange currency for no service fee, the exchange company was locally situated, and it saved the bank managers a lot of grief in explaining to customers why the bank didn't exchange currency or how to get currency by mail (the only other alternative). Other logical places for distributing these coupons were travel agents, luggage stores, and the travel section of bookstores.

Placing Your Flyers, Cards, and Brochures

To get your literature into the hands of prospects who might purchase your product or service, find locations where they would be open to your offer while they are on-site or where they might call or visit your business immediately afterward.

Here's a formula that works:

> ➤ **Start by making a list of the kinds of activities your prospects might engage in on a regular basis.** Do they frequent a certain kind of sports location? Do they make regular purchases of certain items at specialty stores? Is your product or service hobby-related, so that prospects might frequent a bait shop, batting cage, antiques mall, ice rink, or other unique property? Do you cater to travelers, senior citizens, young mothers, job seekers, or other prospects who frequent identifiable places? What are those places?
>
> A great memory jogger to get on track with this step is to look through the Yellow Pages, newspapers, or coupon mailers to identify locations that your prospects would be likely to frequent.

> ➤ **Create a unique strategy for each location.** Think about each location from the perspective of the owner and the consumer. How can you make sure that everyone benefits and that the business owner's environment is enhanced, not harmed? You may need different approaches for different businesses, such as an acrylic brochure rack, countertop display, poster, or other device. Develop a few different ways to present your offer to suit the business owner. Also, you may have to buy, trade, or barter for the space, so decide in advance what you are prepared to do.

> ➤ **Script your conversation ahead of time to keep you on track.** You'll have to ask the owner's permission, so plan ahead how you'll present the placement of your literature as a service to that business's customers, clients, or guests. Then visit in person or start calling the owners of

those locations. Offer to keep your small display well stocked on a regular basis—and be sure to maintain a list of locations to help you keep this promise.

In a very real sense, you are capitalizing on the foot traffic being generated by the marketing expenditures of the location's owner. Respect this privilege by providing appropriate material, attractive and not overly large displays, regular maintenance, and offers that benefit the business's customers.

Use Your Knowledge to Provide a Benefit

A chiropractor I once read about took all of the articles and newsletters he had written over the years and turned them into stand-alone health reports he classified into groups based on demographics. He created entire "health library" rack displays that could be placed in logical businesses as a free service in their lobby or waiting room.

For example, he had 20 different articles on treating childhood illnesses via alternative methods, and he set up libraries in the day-care centers that were close to his office. The very first month he got 45 new patients—triple the response in any month during his previous five years in practice! He similarly placed articles about seniors at local senior centers and for athletes at sporting goods stores. The strategy was so successful he developed specialized health libraries for golfers, new moms, weight lifters, and even pet owners with allergies.

Make Compelling Offers in Your Literature

Since these displays are meant to be maintained year-round, they really aren't appropriate for limited-time offers, special closeouts, and other time-sensitive offers. What does work well are offers that build your prospect list, that can be honored at any time without relying on potentially unavailable merchandise, and that are appealing enough for prospects to take your coupon, brochure, or other response device.

What also works well is the distribution of unusual marketing pieces, including preview audio CDs, how-to booklets, and free samples (especially where the prospect must bring in a coupon to get the free item). Depending on what you're selling, one sale might be worth the hundreds of dollars you'll spend on these higher-priced marketing vehicles.

Ask Customers and Vendors for Referrals

Three days ago, I asked my past consulting clients to recommend me to their friends and customers. I even gave them a special report named Internet Business Manifesto *they could distribute as my business card. Now, just 72 hours later, over 5,000 people a day are downloading the report from my Web site and asking how they can become clients, too. The instantaneous response has been almost beyond belief.*

RICHARD SCHEFREN
StrategicProfits.com

Most companies get referrals by chance. But smart business owners proactively contact customers and guide them to enthusiastically refer family, friends, coworkers, and colleagues. Similarly, the vendors and suppliers you buy from are an ideal path to other companies and consumers who should be buying from you.

Get Customers to Refer Instant Business to You

First, it's a simple process to contact customers and ask them to recommend new customers to your business. You can

- ➤ **Include a special letter** in their next shipment thanking them for their business and asking them to pass along an enclosed flyer to their friends and family. Feature a special offer on the flyer with a deadline for responding.

- ➤ **Ask your Web site visitors or e-zine readers to forward a link** to friends who can register for your free advisory service. Then send a special welcome offer to these new opt-in names.

- ➤ **Provide referral rewards.** When a customer refers someone else, give both people a discount on your services.

- ➤ **Send personalized letters** to your customers who are professional practitioners and ask them to mention you to their client base. Offer to provide a free consultation to any of their qualified clients who respond.

➤ **Credit the customer's account** when she sends you new business. Many customers could send you enough new business to enjoy free products and services.

➤ **Promote bring-a-friend offers.** When a customer brings a friend or spouse to enjoy your services with him, both people get a discount. It's an ideal strategy for instantly generating income on slow days (or during slow months) at your personal services business.

Give Away Gifts for Customers' Friends and Family Members

If you're in an industry that is highly price-competitive or where everyone is providing the same basic product or service, you can generate a substantial number of new prospects by giving away something with a high perceived value that a customer's friends, family members, or colleagues can use in their daily lives.

For instance, if you're an estate-planning attorney, why not send a letter to your clients offering a free book on wills and trusts that they can pass on to their adult children, who probably haven't established a long-term plan yet? Be sure to include a free consultation as part of the gift so you can immediately schedule an appointment when the adult son or daughter calls to claim the free book.

To generate Instant Income from this strategy, be sure to

1. Choose gifts that cost you little, but that customers will believe are expensive or valuable.

2. Don't include the gift with the letter; instead, describe it in an appealing way. Tell the customer how you specially selected the gift for her, why it's valuable, what it can do for her, how it works, how she'll benefit from it, and what the retail value would be.

3. Tell the customer why you've singled out his family member or friend to receive the gift. Tell him why he's special!

4. Ask the customer to help her family member or friend respond in some way—either by bringing in an enclosed gift certificate to get the gift or by telephoning to request the gift item. Keep track of those customers who call in or redeem the coupon so that you can send them additional information later.

Ask for a Testimonial Letter and Three Referrals

What a simple strategy this is—yet it routinely gets Mark Victor Hansen and other high-priced speakers booked for expensive keynote addresses at major conventions and corporate events.

Within two days of delivering his speech, Mark's booking agent telephones the client to ask for a testimonial letter—and provides Mark's Federal Express number so that it can be sent overnight. At the same time, she asks for three referrals to other organizations or departments that might be interested in having Mark speak at their event. Once the agent receives the letter, she sends a copy (with her own introductory letter) to the three referrals.

Get Vendors to Refer Instant Income to You

Those vendors and suppliers who sell goods and services to you are in a unique position to know which of their customers might need your product or service.

An easy way to convince vendors to contact their customers on your behalf is to approach them with a specific offer, free gift, or other bonus, then convince the vendor that it will make more money when its customers do. Your job is to show how your product or service will help build other businesses' revenue streams.

PROSPECTING STRATEGY 5

Create Instant Income at Trade Shows

Preshow, at-show, and postshow marketing is the formula you need to stand out against your competition. And it ensures profits.

MITCH CARSON
Impact Products

Studies show that the cost to acquire a customer through *exhibit marketing*—or trade shows—is actually far less than the cost of acquiring that customer through other marketing means.*

---

* This statistic comes from the Center for Exhibition Industry Research, which says that it takes an average of 3.7 field calls to make an actual sale in most industries. By exhibiting, it takes an average of just 1.6 contacts.

Trade shows are more time-efficient. They greatly reduce the sales cycle required to motivate a prospect to buy. And if you spend a conservative $5,000 to exhibit, but you get 500 eager prospects, you've just built a list of highly qualified leads that your salespeople can follow up on for around $10 each. This is far lower than the staff and overhead costs of making a phone call, sending a salesperson, or mailing an elaborate literature package.

Two Types of Trade Shows—and Two Kinds of Exhibitors

If you sell products or services to *other businesses,* you probably have major national and regional trade shows that bring together thousands of buyers and other sellers within your industry. As a *business-to-business* trade show exhibitor, your options—and your chances of success—are virtually unlimited.

If you sell to *consumers,* on the other hand, your trade shows tend to be more local in nature, such as home-improvement shows, small business expos, craft fairs, bridal shows, art walks, baby expos, and so on. Your prospects may not be as concentrated among the attendees, but your options for making Instant Income are just as numerous as if you were exhibiting at a big North American show.

Become One of "The 35" with Preshow Marketing

Smart marketers start working about 16 weeks ahead of a major trade show in order to maximize their exhibiting time there. While this doesn't necessarily translate into "Instant" Income, being prepared does tend to substantially shorten the sales cycle with booth visitors, making it more likely you'll write large orders on the spot during the show. More important than the usual trade show "strategies" you've read about—such as getting featured as a speaker in the show's educational forum or doing preshow press campaigns and advertising—will be the *preshow marketing* you do to bring buyers into your booth.

Studies show that a staggering 80 percent of trade show exhibitors *never promote* their product, service, or special offer ahead of the show—even though additional research says a whopping 76 percent of attendees *arrive with a predetermined list of booths they plan to visit.* Since most attendees can visit only about 35 booths over a three-day show, you must conduct preshow marketing to ensure that yours is one of them.

Show management will usually provide you with a list of registered attendees well in advance of the show. If the list isn't available yet, request last year's list. Then start marketing to the people on that list—along with marketing to your own database of customers.

Mitch Carson, a 23-year veteran of trade shows and one of America's top exhibit marketing experts, has worked with countless small businesses, helping them generate millions of dollars' worth of sales at trade shows all over the world.* Mitch's preshow formula is a proven one that any small business owner can use.

Preshow Giveaways

Mitch Carson's favorite preshow marketing campaign is to select only those attendees who've indicated that they're interested in your type of product or service, then send a direct-mail package detailing a compelling show special and including "part one" of a two-part giveaway item—the second part of which must be picked up at the booth. (Show management will usually provide you with a list of registered attendees well in advance of the show. If it isn't available yet, request last year's list.)

This mailing creates in the recipient a sense of obligation and interest in at least stopping by your booth and collecting the gift. You could even add a third part to the giveaway, sending it as a follow-up after the show is over.

What are some ideas?

➤ Send a decorative coaster ahead of the show, with an invitation for prospects to collect the matching coffee mug at your booth.

➤ Send an elegant fountain pen or other fine writing instrument, with an invitation to receive the matching pencil and presentation case at the booth.

Telemarketing Follow-up to Your Giveaway Mailing

If you have a sales team, have them follow up by telephone on any direct-mail package you send to a registered attendee. Additionally, have them call to invite

---

* You can learn more about Mitch's trade show system at the Instant Income Resources Page (www.instantincome.com/resources.html).

existing customers to your booth—or even set up meetings at the booth to discuss your new products or to discuss the upcoming year's order.

Faxed Invitations

Faxed invitations to visit the booth and take advantage of your show special are very effective—particularly since they are usually read more often (and sooner) than direct mail. Be sure to fax to only your own list, registered attendees, or other names that have been qualified in some way as having a business relationship with you. Fax blasting to "cold" names has been illegal for more than a decade.*

E-mail Promotion

If you're lucky enough to get the e-mail addresses of upcoming attendees—and if you have the e-mail addresses of your own customers and prospects—you can use good direct-response copywriting techniques to craft a compelling invitation by e-mail. See Chapter 3, "Writing Ads That Make the Phone Ring," for e-mail copy strategies that generate responses.

Of course, with any preshow communication, it's critical to combine the right message with the right offer and deliver it to the right people. Furthermore, if your message and your offer are compelling enough, you're likely to generate *preshow orders* with your advance marketing.

What are some offers that are compelling?

➤ Special pricing on your most popular product bundle

➤ New products at a special price during the show

➤ Territorial exclusivity on a new product for a limited time

Prospects Will *Not* Call You after the Trade Show

Just as important as preshow marketing is your postshow follow-up plan. Don't let your salespeople (or yourself) come home to a pile of work that

* Just to be safe, include a disclaimer at the bottom of the fax, such as, "If you wish to be removed from this list, please call (800) 000-0000."

causes you to ignore the prospects you so carefully generated. It's said that an astounding 80 percent of leads are never contacted after a show. Use the following strategies to make sure your leads aren't among them:

➤ Print a full-color postcard of your booth and staff members with an area on the back for a personal message. Then, in between meeting people in the booth, have your staff write messages and address these cards during the day. Bring postage stamps and mail each day's stack of cards that evening after the show closes. When your prospects arrive home, your postcard will be waiting for them—reminding them of your booth, your company, and your special offer.

➤ Send the third part of your three-part giveaway with a personal note encouraging the prospect to place an order.

➤ Send a prerecorded audio CD with a generic message about the benefits of doing business with you and details on your special offer. It will help you stand out from every other booth the prospect visited. Handwrite a message to go along with it.

➤ Send a fax broadcast, since you've captured the prospect's contact information, had a conversation with him, and now have a business relationship with him.

➤ Have a professional call center telephone to thank the prospect for stopping by the booth and to tell her that her literature or other materials will be arriving shortly.

➤ Assign the prospect to a salesperson who can follow up. If you don't have your own salespeople, add the prospect to your regular marketing schedule so that he'll receive constant communication from you. Better yet, see Sales Strategy 1, "Conduct Follow-up Telemarketing and Voice Broadcast Campaigns," for details on how to personally follow up with thousands of leads in your own voice, using your own words.

CHAPTER 5

Helping Your Sales Force Earn Instant Income

YOUR LIVELIHOOD is based upon your ability to sell. And whether you alone provide the sales function for your small business or you recruit others who can sell on your behalf, your primary goal is to generate new customers and sell more products and services to existing ones.

This makes your business a sales and marketing entity, aside from whatever other business you might be in. In fact, virtually every other element of your business—including your own expertise—can usually be taught, delegated, outsourced, purchased, or recruited in the marketplace.

But not sales.

This means that you must find a way to master the sales process, recruit others who can duplicate your passion and knowledge about your product or service, then support those people in generating a substantial income from selling it.

Not surprisingly, some of the most substantial Instant Income can come from changes or additions to your sales process. And if your salespeople are regularly calling on enthusiastic customers and prospects generated by other Instant Income strategies, the potential for exponential increases in revenue is truly vast.

Creating a Culture for Salespeople to Earn Instant Income

Outstanding sales organizations have a culture that not only supports and inspires their salespeople to work hard and earn more; it also tends to attract *superstar salespeople*—those top 5 percent of sales professionals who typically produce about 70 to 90 percent of all sales.

What does this robust kind of sales culture look like?

For one thing, it's based upon aggressive, out-of-the-box marketing that generates prospects who are eager to buy from you. If you simply started using the direct-response advertising techniques in Chapter 3 to presell consumers on owning your product or service, for example, imagine how much easier your sales representatives' job would be. If you started making specific offers for a certain product or service bundle at a fixed price, your salespeople would effectively become order takers. And if you negotiated joint ventures where an endorser sent special, limited-time offers that compelled its customers to call you—well, nothing makes salespeople happier than an easy sale.

Unfortunately, when recruiting potential sales superstars, many companies make claims such as "We've got great leads" or "We've got a loyal customer base," but they often don't or can't deliver on that. Salespeople find out too late that making sales is difficult or takes a lot of extra steps, so they end up failing to perform at their highest level. They don't really get the opportunity to be rewarded in a big way.

Sales superstars know this, so they proactively seek out companies whose aggressive marketing strategies will make their job easier. This means that your company—even if it's a very small business—can easily attract a stellar salesperson away from her current job (and possibly away from your competitor) with a little cutting-edge marketing.

Of course, under this scenario, you would never ask salespeople to generate their own leads (unless they came to your company with their own book). Rarely can a salesperson orchestrate effective lead-generation campaigns or single-handedly generate enough leads to make a living while at the same time working to close sales. With the exception of network marketers, whose businesses naturally require a one-on-one recruitment process, salespeople should stay busy closing the leads that your aggressive marketing campaigns generate.

What else can you do to create an optimum sales culture?

Keep Your Customers Happy

Top-earning sales organizations benefit from customers who are appreciative, enthusiastic, and happy. In fact, while your main job as the business owner is to generate new prospects for your salespeople, your other responsibility is to ensure that the rest of your staff optimizes the experience for existing customers, to whom salespeople will probably have to sell more products and services in the future. Providing a top-notch customer experience will also help when you approach customers for referrals—which are some of the easiest leads to convert into sales. Plus, happy customers who know that they are being well taken care of will typically have far fewer objections to price, product selection, add-ons, and other features that salespeople have to overcome.

Pay Your Salespeople Well for Closing Sales

As a business owner, I'm happy to pay professional salespeople a lot of money to do the most important work of my company—making sales and providing good service to the customers they sell to. I like to reward them for doing a job that, frankly, I don't do as well and, given my other duties, shouldn't be doing in the first place. So I never worry that my salespeople might be making "too much" money, or more money than I thought they would, or even more money than I make in some weeks. Every time I write them a big check, I know that they have generated massive sales for me.

Unfortunately, all too many business owners seem to have a preconceived notion of how much a salesperson should make. They let their ego interfere with good judgment to the point where they invent complicated compensation arrangements that limit the salesperson's pay. For some reason, they never want their salespeople to make anything close to what the business owner makes.

I, on the other hand, like to keep things simple. My sales representatives work on straight commission, and they know—as I do—that when they sell a lot, they get paid a lot. I have no ego about how much they make, which is one more hallmark of a company culture that attracts and keeps top salespeople.

Instantly Transform Your One-Person Business

If you're currently a one-person micro-enterprise, your business will change—for the better—the minute you turn over your sales function to a trusted professional.

Suddenly, you'll have time to develop your marketing calendar. You'll be able to schedule your own workload, rather than be pulled away to talk with prospects whenever they call or stop by your store. You'll have quiet time to concentrate on more lucrative client projects or on launching a new product line or service offering. You'll be free to work *on* your business rather than *in* your business.

Building a Sales Force Designed to Generate Instant Income

Countless small business owners have asked me how they can hire a sales professional who will grow with their business. My reply is that (aside from those sales superstars who you might attract through good marketing) the best "salespeople" are very often everyday folks who are circulating in your universe right now. They've used your product or service. They're enthusiastic about you and your business. They may not be experienced salespeople, but they have a natural aptitude, friendliness, rapport with people, passion for the industry, and so on. With a little training, they could become sales superstars.

If you've done sales for your own small business or managed your sales organization for any length of time, you know the traits, skills, and sensibilities that are required to sell your product or service. Why not turn that knowledge into a process for identifying and recruiting people who can be trained to sell for you?

Simply create a checklist of the traits you're looking for and use it during the interview process. Have the candidates answer questions related to those traits.

If candidates look promising, send them home with a copy of your sales script (more about this later) to study. Schedule a time when they can call you or your sales manager to role-play—*as if they were conducting a sales call using your script.* They won't be that well rehearsed, of course. But you'll be able to tell whether they have what it takes to sell for you. See whether they have potential *before* you invest the time and resources to train them.

If you decide to hire them, offer a 30-day trial period. While many sales organizations follow this practice, most tend to focus on scrutinizing the new recruit's performance, rather than on supporting, growing, and training the new salesperson during this time. Make it clear that you have a very specific sales culture in your company and that you expect to work with the new recruits over the next 30 days to evolve them into sales superstars. You expect to deliver certain things to them—training, support tools, motivational resources, qualified leads, and so on. This announcement alone can have a huge impact. You want your new recruits to be motivated and to "take ownership" of their job and your product or service. But if they find they can't work within this supportive, exacting culture, it won't be a good fit in the long run—for either of you.

Good Salespeople Are Entrepreneurs Just Like You

If your sales professionals work on any type of commission, they are, in effect, working for themselves. Like you and your business, their income is directly related to their efforts and their ability to find new ways to sell more goods and services in less time.

If you add "thinks like an entrepreneur" to your list of criteria to look for in a candidate, it will make your job of recruiting salespeople much easier.

One way to determine if an applicant has this tendency toward self-motivation is to find out whether he or she has invested in his or her own knowledge and training, beyond what was provided by previous employers. Has she taken sales training on her own? Does he listen to motivational CDs or training tapes in his car? Does she passionately pursue sales excellence by reading books on the subject? If he's never been in sales before, has he at least searched out new ways to make money or expand nonsales projects that he's been involved in?

Just as you pursue your own business with a passion, entrepreneurial salespeople pursue sales strategies and tactics with a passion. They constantly improve their abilities in their spare time.

One Final (Sneaky) Way to Recruit Salespeople

Aside from the possible salespeople circulating in your universe and those who will find you via your good marketing, one final way to recruit sales professionals is simply to recruit them away from the jobs they have now. This is done every day. In fact, so many salespeople become disillusioned with their employer, you'd be surprised how successful you can be in convincing them to leave their job to work for you.

One woman I knew who sold personal-improvement services recruited attractive young saleswomen for her clinic from the cosmetic counters at upscale department stores. She knew that they received frequent and comprehensive sales training as sales reps for the big-name designers and cosmetic companies. All she had to do was recruit them and teach them to sell her clinic's services instead.

Another business owner I know of appraised the salespeople who came to sell *him* goods and services, then pitched the more talented ones on joining his sales force—particularly if he suspected that they were not earning the substantial income that he knew his commission structure could pay them.

Support Your Sales Force with Instant Income Tools

Even if your salespeople are real self-starters, they still need support in the form of product descriptions, sales scripts, reference sheets, faxable sales kits, sales training, and other such tools.

As the business owner, you are the best person to produce these tools, particularly during the early stages of the business. In fact, unless you have exceptionally poor people skills, you are actually the best possible salesperson in your organization.

Why?

Not only do you know your business better than anyone else, but you have the greatest amount of passion for your business. You were motivated to start the business in the first place. You have a passion for the work you do, for the organization you've built, and for your posture and reputation in the marketplace. Consequently, there's no better salesperson in your business.

So how can you transfer that passion and knowledge to sales professionals who must do the job that only you can do best? By using your own sales dialogues and tactics to train them.

One way to capture the words you say that culminate in a successful sale is simply to tape-record 10 or 12 of your sales calls.* Ask the prospects' permission, if necessary. Then combine your best opening scripts, your best handling of sales objections, your best answers to questions, your best close, and so forth into one perfect sales call. Then use that to train salespeople, role-play sales calls, practice handling objections, and so on.

---

* Many states have laws against recording phone calls and in-person conversations without the other party's permission. Please check applicable laws before you decide whether to record sales calls.

Additionally, determine if there is something special or different that you do during a sales call that is really effective in closing sales. Is there something about your product knowledge or perhaps a personal story or anecdote that works to demonstrate the value of the product or service you are selling? Identify those aspects, then use them to train your sales team.

Of course, one reason you want to teach your salespeople to mimic your sales abilities—aside from increased sales—is that you want them to "take ownership" and act just as you would in any sales situation. You want them to provide all the information about your product or service that you would. You want them to help their customers solve a problem, not just help them buy something. You want your salespeople to be enthusiastic. It's what you would do as the owner. And it's what you want your salespeople to do on your behalf.

You can also model your top sales stars in the same way—by observing and documenting and distributing their successful strategies, either in audio form, in writing, or in a group sales meeting with your sales superstar role playing for other members of the team.

Scripting for Top-Notch Sales

Owners of small companies often have a bias against sales scripting. But a sales script is really just the sales process written down—from the introductory dialogue through each objection and its appropriate response to the close. It doesn't turn your salespeople into robots. In fact, it helps them learn the dialogue well enough to eventually be more "present" during the sales call itself.

Today, the art of sales has evolved to a more consultative approach. Your salespeople are there to listen, ask questions, and solve problems. They can't do that if they're trying to remember what to say next. A script helps them stay on track with crucial details that need to be covered, language that works well in your industry, and methods of dealing with objections.

Salespeople who sound like they are reading a script are in fact just learning the script. When they learn the script to the point where answers, questions, anecdotes, offers, and other information become second nature, they'll become more effective in selling your products and services.

Written Materials That Create Instant Income

Salespeople also need "cheat sheets" detailing product pricing, possible sales objections, answers to frequently asked questions, product comparison charts, and other such tools that they can use as guides when they are on the phone. They also need additional materials that can be faxed, e-mailed, or handed to prospects during the sales process itself. And if you work with independent sales reps or own a virtual company with remote salespeople, you can even use these materials to help your salespeople represent you as if their desk was right across the hall:

➤ **One-page product sheet that salespeople can e-mail or fax.** While you may have beautiful color brochures or an elaborately written Web site, many prospects will still want "more information." A faxable sales page or a PDF file that can be e-mailed gives your salesperson a way to handle the "I need more" objection.

➤ **Product comparison chart.** If you have numerous comprehensive packages at different combinations and prices, a product comparison chart in Microsoft Excel or another spreadsheet program is indispensable. Distill it into a PDF file for easy e-mailing.

➤ **Frequently asked questions and sales objections prompter.** New salespeople especially will value having prewritten answers to questions and objections that they may be hearing for the first time.

➤ **Complete sales letter or offer in a PDF file.** If your current offer is on your Web site, be sure to produce it in sales letter or brochure format, then distill it into a PDF for easy e-mailing.

➤ **A testimonials sheet.** If you've followed my advice in Chapter 3 and collected testimonials from satisfied customers, you can easily compile these into one sheet, then distill it into a PDF file for easy e-mailing and faxing.

Conduct Follow-up Telemarketing and Voice Broadcast Campaigns

Recently, my sales team used telemarketing follow-up to upsell a $5,000 item to 78 percent of customers who purchased our $199 entry-level product. Telemarketing follow-up is an extremely effective tactic. Now, we don't even plan a new product or service offering without first considering how we'll telemarket as part of the sales equation.

GARY HANDWERKER
Chief executive officer of Handwerker Consulting

Once you have a sales force in place that is prepared with training, scripts, and other tools, it's time to add an important second function to their job duties: *follow-up telemarketing.* When you call prospects as a follow-up to their initial, unsuccessful visit or inquiry, your chances of selling to them skyrocket. In fact, because it's both personal and personalized, telemarketing follow-up to sales leads not only outperforms all other forms of follow-up, but can actually increase your close rate from 3 to 10 times.

Think about it.

How many times have you telephoned to inquire about a product or service, only to buy weeks later when you were called by a friendly salesperson from that store or business?

Your customers are no different.

When you call to rekindle their interest, answer their questions, meet their needs, and overcome their objections, your sales will increase.

The key to successful telemarketing follow-up is to have your salespeople conduct each sales call with a script that helps them focus on the customer, listen to the customer's needs, and adjust their sales strategy based on the customer's feedback.

Anatomy of a Sales Call

As I mentioned earlier, using a sales script doesn't turn your salespeople into robots. It actually helps them stay on track with important information, with answers to questions, and with closing strategies to the point where—once they learn the script—they can be "present" in a consultative, focused selling situation.

A successful sales call is based upon (1) the salesperson's ability to ask questions, and (2) his ability to listen to the answers and adapt his tactics and dialogue from there.

If your salespeople can ask the right questions and really listen to the answers, they'll have all the information they need to close the sale—or find another way to help the prospect. (This "other way" may be steering the prospect to a less expensive product than the one she called about or even steering her to another company that has what she needs. Save yourself the grief of customer complaints, returns, and refunds by *not* selling prospects something they don't need.)

The sequence of questions to ask on a follow-up call is given here. And, by the way, even if you don't have any formal selling skills or training, you'll be surprised by the positive response you get from your prospect just by virtue of asking these questions.

1. Reengage the Customer in Conversation

Greet the customer, then remind her why she called you in the first place or (if you don't know) ask her what motivated her to call you. Was she responding to an ad? If so, what was it about the ad that prompted her to call? How did she find you?

Sometimes you will be following up with virtually no information about the prospect. A good icebreaker in these circumstances is to ask, "Did you come from a referral?" That alerts the prospect that your company gets lots of referrals, making him more comfortable almost immediately.

Of course, what you really want to hear from these opening questions is the customer's motivation. What did the customer read in the marketing piece that prompted him to call, or what about his referral conversation with an existing client resonated for him?

2. Ask a Question That Identifies the Real Problem the Customer Is Trying to Solve

Be aware that most people won't have originally called to buy a specific product or service, *even if you advertised a specific product or service package in your advertisement or sales letter.* Instead, they are calling because they have a problem, need, want, or ambition—and they believe you might have the solution.

Of course, many callers *will have yet to identify for themselves* what their problem or need is. You may have to help them discover it. Regardless, your true goal at this point should be to identify whether your company's solution fits their problem.

3. Find Out Who This Person Is as a Buyer—and What's Important to This Prospect

At some point in the conversation, you'll need to build personal rapport with the prospect. It will help you to understand who she is and what's important to her. It will help you to identify the exact and specific language she uses to illuminate the goals she's hoping to achieve through purchasing your product or service. It will help you to determine how much she knows, what level of expertise she already has, and what she is already doing so that, later, you can speak with her at her level about the features, benefits, and components of your product or service. You wouldn't speak to a 30-year industry veteran as if she had started in business yesterday. Only by asking questions can you ascertain her level of expertise.

Once the customer tells you her story, begin explaining what your product or service really has to offer. Use this time to build positive expectations, too. If you have a consulting business, for instance, one way to build positive expectations is to ask your prospect if she conducts business in a certain way or has certain profit centers that you effortlessly help clients with. It's just possible that you could end up working on an additional aspect of her business that she might never have thought of before. That's a substantial sales hook in itself.

Further build the prospect's desire by using stories, anecdotes, and case studies of other customers and clients. You can even start painting a word-picture of what the prospect's life will be like once she owns your product or service.

Be helpful, open, and forthright with information so the prospect will conclude early in the conversation that she's reached the company that can help her. Providing insights, advice, and information almost always leads to prospects wanting to pay for more. In fact, if you don't give prospects any real information, they're not going to want more.

Some salespeople hold back because they're afraid of giving away too many of their "secrets." But the reality is that giving away information and expertise often leads prospects to determine that you know more than other companies they called. "If he's giving away this much for free," they'll believe, "just imagine what I'll get when I hire him."

4. Determine What It Takes for the Prospect to Make a Buying Decision and What It Takes for Her to Make a Buying Decision Today

Everything you do up to this point must prepare you—and the prospect—for a sale to be made. In fact, a good closer won't even try to close, won't even send out a trial close, until he's effectively gone through the progression—the questions, the listening, the helpful information, and the advice—and seen the buying signals from the prospect.

This is the point where the sale actually starts. And hopefully, by now, you have created the desire, heightened the sense of urgency, and deepened the need to the point where the prospect believes that your product or service is more valuable than the money she's about to spend.

Now send out a *trial close.*

A favorite of my sales team is "Wow. This sounds so perfect for you, how am I going to talk you out of it?"

With this trial close, you'll discover right away what the prospect's objections are. Once you hear her objections, start selling again. Continue reading her signals, sending out a different trial close, handling her objections, and so on—until you get to "yes."

Be aware, by the way, that an objection is really just *an expression of interest, coupled with a challenge that the prospect is asking you to overcome.* A price objection, for example, means that you simply need to show the prospect how to make more or save more than the amount she'll be spending with you—or, alternatively, how to easily recoup her investment once she gives you the purchase price.

Voice Broadcast: Telemarketing Follow-up for Solo Entrepreneurs

The beauty of telemarketing follow-up is that a salesperson can adjust the script based upon what he hears from the prospect. But what if you don't have your own sales force or are too busy with the other aspects of your business to follow up?

You *can* follow up—in your own words and using your own voice—with a readily available technology called *voice broadcasting.*

Voice broadcasting lets you record a follow-up message of up to 60 seconds or more, then broadcast it to all your customers' or prospects' phone numbers—all for about 20¢ per name or less. You don't even need expensive software, since these services are available today on the Internet. Also, the technology will play the message if the prospect picks up the phone, leave it on her voice mail if she doesn't pick up, prompt her to press "3" to be connected to your customer service department, or follow any one of many other scenarios.

What makes for a good voice broadcasting script?

Well, if you wrote a compelling offer and got responses from prospects who read the advertisement but did not purchase, you can simply record a friendly message reminding them of the most compelling aspects of the offer and the most compelling benefits of the product or service. Be sure to tell them how to respond—by calling back during certain hours, by pressing a number to be connected to your customer service department, or by going to your Web site to order.

Be aware that many of the voice-broadcast campaigns you hear today are done in very poor taste—using exaggerated language delivered in a phony-sounding, overly enthusiastic voice. Stay above the fray by keeping your recording professional-sounding, friendly, and in good taste—just as you would speak to customers and clients in your store or office.

SALES STRATEGY 2

Start Bundling Products and Services

Once I bundled my music CDs into 4-pack and 10-pack collections, I instantly began selling my music for more money in less time. Not only that, but I also became a more valuable joint-venture partner to other businesses, because I had higher-priced product bundles to sell.

MARK ROMERO
Musician and inspirational speaker,
www.markromeromusic.com

Remember the technique of upselling from Customer Strategy 2, "Upsell Customers at the Point of Purchase"?

I told you that, given a choice, prospects will often buy the most expensive package you have to offer. They're simply not satisfied with a lesser solution or a downgraded possession. They want the best. And if they can justify the purchase price in their mind, they will very often pay extra to get the up-graded package.

Bundled products and services are often the most appealing packages to buyers—providing an instant increase in revenue over selling individual items alone.

A good case in point is the first strategy I executed for *Chicken Soup for the Soul* founder Jack Canfield. As Jack was getting ready to leave for his biggest speaking engagement ever, I exclaimed, "You can't just sell that book at the back of the room!"

To help him generate more cash, I convinced him to let me create an expensive Success Library selling for $299 that bundled *Chicken Soup* with a collection of Jack's audiocassette programs and videos.

With Jack's protests ringing in my ears—"Nobody will pay that," he said—I spent five hours writing and printing a four-page catalog that described the library in glowing terms. Then I listed Jack's lower-priced products individually on the opposite page. After speaking for just one hour, Jack generated $31,000 in product sales—the most he'd ever generated from a single event up until that time.

And what was the most popular item? The $299 Success Library, of course.

This was understandable when you consider that, by the time Jack had finished speaking, audience members wanted the life benefits he had talked about on stage. They didn't want to shortchange themselves—they wanted to be sure they got the result that Jack talked about. In their minds, there was no other option than to buy the "gold package."

The Expectation of a Greater Benefit Is Essential

Since I do a lot of work in the high-end seminar field, I can tell you firsthand that no one sells just a seminar anymore. They sell expensive "training programs," with a workbook, audiotape recordings, postseminar consulting or coaching services, a hotline update, a secret Rolodex of contacts and resources, a reference library, and other goodies that boost the perceived value of the overall package. Of course, the company would ordinarily sell all these services separately, but many more people will purchase the full menu of services if they see them combined and described in such a way that *they expect a greater benefit from receiving all these services together.*

Carpet cleaners, service stations, appliance repair shops, portrait photographers, consultants, insurance agents, and other service providers use this same philosophy every day by offering a package of services at a discount. They offer to clean the carpets and the furniture on the same visit. They include a tune-up with a lube and an oil change. They sell you a portrait sitting with a portfolio of different-sized prints. They combine your home, auto, disability, and life insurance into one package for a more reasonable, single premium.

Bundled Packages Help Salespeople Make Instant Income

Bundling is a powerful sales aid because it allows salespeople to verbally "unpack" the bundle and show the prospect how expensive everything would be if they purchased it separately.

What to Bundle

If you have numerous products that a customer would logically use together, start packaging them into multipart units, either assembled inside the same box or described together in your catalog or store display. Then price the bundle at a legitimate discount to encourage sales—and watch the extra revenues pour in.

Survey customers and determine what they would respond to if you offered bundled packages. You can conduct written in-person surveys, send letters, or have your order clerks or service personnel ask customers individually. Important survey questions include the following: What do we provide that you haven't tried yet? What would motivate you to try it? What do we not currently provide that you would want us to provide? What services do you typically use all the time?

Pricing a Bundle

Once you have informally surveyed your customers and prospects, choose the most popular items to bundle. Do the math and decide what you can afford to subtract from the combined price. Research your competitors to determine if they are offering a similar bundle at a comparable price.

One of the easiest ways to compete with other businesses that are offering something similar is to assemble a bundle with individual components for which prospects can't easily determine your cost. Or, include components that you don't offer individually as a bonus that prospects can't easily compute a value for.

Also effective is to include in the bundle items that cost you virtually nothing yet have a high perceived value as part of the bundle.

Selling Product or Service Bundles

One way to make your salesperson's job easier is to describe the individual items that are included in the bundle elsewhere in your product literature as expensive stand-alone products. Then, simply list the bundle as a separate product, with perhaps a one-sentence reminder description of the individual components that you've described in detail elsewhere.

Coach your order clerks, reservation agents, food servers, and other customer service personnel on the exact components of the package so that they can easily upsell the package to customers (particularly when customers inquire about one or more of the items in the package).

Offer at least two or three packages, no matter how simple. Even if it's just a dozen of the same item; or the customer's choice of soup, two deli salads, and a drink from your menu of 17 items; or a Florida vacation with discount coupons, rental car, and silk-screened travel pack—package it and you'll increase your income.

The Bundling Concept in Reverse: Breaking Your Product Down into Smaller, Less Expensive Parts

Often customers just don't have the money to purchase everything they would like from you. So instead of bundling products into multi-item packages, try breaking down existing multi-item products or services into smaller parts and delivering each different part on a pay-as-you-go basis. Like continuity offers (see Customer Strategy 3, "Convert One-Time Customers to Continuity Customers"), these pay-as-you-go packages let customers buy more goods and services from you, yet your salespeople still close the sale once rather than having to resell the customer every time the next component is ready to ship.

This is not the same as simply selling each component individually. You still describe and sell the entire "package," but you provide the components over time, shipping each part or providing each service on a monthly, weekly, or quarterly basis, and billing the customer's credit card each time a shipment or service call is made.

What are some examples of pay-as-you-go product and service packages?

➤ Consulting contracts with deliverables provided and invoiced over several months

➤ Correspondence courses and online degrees with additional "class" modules sent when the student completes the previous module

➤ Home construction jobs that are done in phases with separate invoicing

<u>SALES STRATEGY 3</u>

Make Specific Product and Service Offers

Read any newspaper or magazine and you'll find that the majority of the ads in it are very general in nature. "Come on in and buy from us," they say. "We provide quality, service, and low prices." Unfortunately, the sales function at these businesses often takes the same position. "What can we sell you today?" their salespeople ask. "What are you looking for?"

Compare that, on the other hand, with offering a specific package at a specific price in your ads, e-mails, and letters, with salespeople specifically trained to sell that product bundle, service contract, or consulting package.

For one thing, by offering a package, you would be able to cut down on your inventory and better manage your service calls and work flow. You wouldn't have to stock thousands of items for consumers to choose from or have staff available to perform countless different tasks for clients. And your salespeople could be trained and primed to sell just the current offer—with prewritten language that works and closing techniques that bring in the money.

Imagine the excitement, too, among your salespeople when they reach a steady selling rhythm, actually competing against each other for total "packages" or "contracts" sold.

That's exciting. And—when combined with Chapter 3's direct-response advertising techniques for producing presold prospects that contact you—it's also one of the most tried-and-true formulas for generating Instant Income in a sales department.

Determine Your Bundle and Its Price Beforehand

When writing ads, sales letters, postcards, and e-mails, it's best to have the specific product bundle or service package you'll be selling in mind (see Sales Strategy 2, "Start Bundling Products and Services," for more details). What do your customers tell you is the most popular package? What are the most logical add-ons? How can you provide everything a customer needs to go along with that specific product or service and make the bundle attractive at the same time?

Then start calculating the price you'll charge for the bundle. Be aware that in your advertising, you'll have to justify that price in some way—either through testimonials, through comparisons to other packages, by talking about other customers who have saved more than the purchase price after acquiring the item or using the service, or by some other method. Be sure that the price you start with can be justified by facts, case studies, or other good copy.

Whenever you are pricing anything, by the way, it's best to use a specific number, not one that's been rounded up to the nearest hundred or some other "package" number. For example, saying that you really put a pencil to it and value-priced your most popular heating and air-conditioning installation package at just $3,682 is actually more believable in print than a nice round price of $3,500. A specific number makes it appear that you carefully did the calculations and are truly charging a fair price based on your costs, labor, and a small margin. Of course, you might be building in an outrageous profit for yourself, but because it's a specific number, it looks fair. Go figure.

Offers That Generate Instant Income

Once you determine your bundle and your price, there are a number of proven offers that bring in the money. And unlike the two-step offers discussed in Prospecting Strategy 2, "Run a Two-Step Campaign," these advertised offers actually mention the price, justify it with additional information that makes it seem like a superb value, and provide a sense of urgency—a reason why the reader must call your sales department immediately.

While the bulk of your sales function will be done in print with these types of straight-sale offers, your salespeople will also need to be trained on the offer itself, including all possible objections concerning the price, the product or service, and other aspects of the transaction.

What are some of the proven types of straight-sale offers that compel the reader to act immediately and make a purchase from you?

Limited-Time Offers

Remember the "reason why" from Advertising Strategy 5, "Hold a Special Sale Using the 'Reason Why'"? A good rationale will help you justify offering this particular product bundle or service contract only for a limited time.

Salespeople love selling limited-time offers because these offers take away the "not-right-now" objection used by so many prospects. Salespeople have an added advantage in making the sale—a price or product package that will go away soon.

Discounted-Price Offers

I personally do not like discounting the price of anything, as I think it sends the wrong message to your prospects. After all, if you don't think your product or service is worth anything, guess what? A lot of other people won't think so, either.

But if you have a *legitimate* reason to discount your product, this kind of offer works well.

Let me give you an example. If you sell home electronics but you recently made changes to your product offerings, you might say:

> We've just started offering a new line of home stereos. But we have lots of units left over from our previous top-selling brand. These units are still excellent stereo systems—new in the box. We've invested heavily in promoting the new line, and we now want to sell our previous inventory immediately. We have 127 state-of-the-art stereo systems left. As a favor to you, we're offering them—not at the original price of $495 or even the discounted price of $295, but at our cost . . . just $122.49.

Note the specific price of $122.49, which is much more believable than $129. Note the rationale for why you are dropping the price.

That is what a discounted-price offer reads like.

Limited-Availability Offers

One of my favorite types of offer, a limited-availability offer is very effective for any kind of product, service, or consulting contract that people should be eager to purchase.

It is so effective, in fact, that sometimes it actually pays to limit your availability on purpose. For example, if you're offering a type of consulting that develops a new profit center for a business, helps to turn around a failing business, or prepares a company for a merger, by default you can't work with an unlimited number of clients. In fact, if you calculated the amount of time you would spend on each client and added the time needed for all your other activities, including marketing your services, you would probably find that you couldn't work with more than 15 to 20 companies a month. Since you're forced to limit your client list anyway, why not make that limitation part of the offer?

The "Don't Let Competitors Respond First" Offer

One of the most successful offers I've ever used, this kind of offer creates a tremendous sense of urgency for your salespeople to "sell into."

Being naturally competitive, most people will jump at the chance to be the one and only person who captures the product or service you're offering. It causes them to act more quickly—to not think about it too much. Allowing just one person to have an advantage creates a powerful marketing situation that we call *scarcity*. And it works especially well if you have an ongoing service or product line that you truly want to sell to just one business owner per town.

I once wrote an ad for a consultant who offered to help expand local alternative therapy practices by $50,000 a month or more. The headline, which limited the opportunity to just one therapist per market area, created tremendous scarcity. We had people calling in and offering to send their check by overnight delivery, simply so that their competitor across town wouldn't be able to lock in the training opportunity first. The sales staff was elated.

SALES STRATEGY 4

Create a Downsell Position

I always lead with my medium- or high-priced service package so I have something less expensive to sell when those options are too expensive for my prospect. The bonus is that a business owner will always take a call from someone they've paid money to. Downselling becomes my foot in the door for doing future business.

JOEL BLOCK
President, Growth Logic Inc.

When your salespeople hear price objections from a prospect so often that it seems as if a sale will never be made, smart sales organizations move the prospect to what is called a *downsell position*—a lower-priced item or payment plan that rescues the sale and makes at least some money from the prospect.

Downsell positions are imperative in a sales situation. Not only that, they're a great Instant Income strategy. The moment you add these strategies to your live sales calls, you can expect both your close rate and your revenue to increase dramatically. I've seen close rates jump to more than 90 percent by adding downselling to programs I've been involved with. Plus, downselling motivates salespeople, too. An experienced salesperson who is given permission to downsell will often become an unstoppable cash machine.

You can also write downsell offers into your advertising so that readers who might not buy because of price can purchase a less expensive option yet still access your company's product line, service offerings, or expertise.

For many years, I developed the highly structured marketing campaigns for Mark Victor Hansen's "Mega" events for authors, speakers, and owners of small businesses, and we downsold $295 audio recordings of the seminar to prospects who could not afford the seminar tuition or the travel expenses to attend the event itself. Mark sold countless hundreds of recorded programs as a result—to authors and entrepreneurs who never attended. But even better, many people who bought the recordings the first year actually attended in person in subsequent years—proving that downselling is a great tool for familiarizing a prospect with what you have to offer, with future additional sales being a common result.

Developing Downsell Offers and Pricing

The price of your downsell item or package has to be low enough to (1) put the item in an entirely different price category and (2) completely remove any barrier to the prospect's purchasing *something* from you. Most consumers are accustomed to there being different prices for different levels of quality— economy, standard, and premium, for example. So if your salespeople are unsuccessfully trying to close a sale on a premium item, offer an economy or standard version instead. Offering just a slightly less expensive premium item typically won't work. The price difference has to be great enough to matter to the consumer.

In addition, your downsell item must be priced low enough to totally remove any concern the prospect may have about price. This means that your salespeople must be able to ask enough questions to "read" the prospect's buying ability. If it's clear that funds are an issue, it's much better to save the sale by offering the prospect a lower-priced item that still delivers tremendous value and gets her comfortable with buying from you. One of the key functions of a downsell position is that it lets prospects "sample" your company's quality, service, and value. If you deliver on these features—even at a lower price—a prospect is much more likely to buy more expensive items from you later.

Some Common Downsell Strategies

➤ If you sell consulting services and typically write large contracts of $10,000 or more, you could offer a single one-hour consultation by telephone for $1,000—but turn it into a product offering where you deliver a printed guidebook with general information, a questionnaire that new clients can complete before the consultation, a recording of the consultation, and a complete "road map" over the phone of strategies the client can follow to reach his goal. Not only is this a great downsell strategy, but it effectively makes you one of the highest-paid consultants in your industry—at $1,000 per hour.

➤ If you sell high-end equipment, furniture, or other hard goods, you can easily sell a less expensive version—even if you have to go into a joint venture with someone else to make those cheaper units available. If there truly is no "junior" version of your product, offer to finance the cost over three or four payments or more, depending on the price. Consumer finance companies abound that will handle the financing transaction for you, paying you the majority of the purchase price immediately upon completion of the sale, then managing the paperwork and payments with your customer directly.

➤ If you are a wholesaler or a manufacturer that sells directly to retailers, financing plans are common, as are different product lines with different price points.

➤ If you conduct expensive live training, seminars, or professional education of any kind, you can offer a home-study or online-study version of the proceedings for less than half the cost of the live, in-person training.

Create Instant Sales with Nontraditional Salespeople

The real growth of our business came about because we deemphasized traditional sales channels in our industry and instead hired nontraditional sales representatives to target nontraditional customers. We engaged a former corporate executive and a former marketing executive. So far this year, we have increased sales to nontraditional customers by almost 350 percent.

DAN MOZERSKY
President and publisher, Patron's Pick
Publishing Inc.

In every industry, there are salespeople calling on prospective customers to whom you would like to sell things. They may be sales reps from other companies, consultants, service providers—even visiting nurses. These unlikely "salespeople" can be your sales pros, once they are properly compensated and are informed of the value of what you have to offer their contacts.

Finding a Motivated Salesperson with Customers Who Will Buy Your Product or Service

When I was hired to strategize on the growth of an advertising agency that had just launched a Web site development division, I immediately began brainstorming with the agency's owners about the types of people who were calling on, speaking to, selling to, visiting, or advising the CEOs, CIOs, MIS managers, and vice presidents of marketing at the small to medium-sized technology firms that the ad agency wanted as clients. Not only would these people have the goodwill of their clients, but they would be in a position to know if a company was considering developing a Web site in the near future.

Who were these potential nontraditional salespeople?

➤ Magazine advertising sales reps

➤ Authorized retailers of computer hardware and software

➤ Value-added resellers (VARs) who took existing hardware and software and combined it into customized information-processing systems for individual companies

➤ Joint-venture partners that bundled their own products and services with those of a prospective client's company

➤ Internet service providers (ISPs) that had already developed e-mail services for prospective companies

➤ Editors of newsletters and advisory services who had these prospective client companies' managers as subscribers

➤ One-person-shop Web site developers who did not have the expertise or personnel to develop the more complicated Web sites that companies might desire

➤ Other ad agencies that did ad work for prospect companies, but did not have a Web site development division of their own

I crafted a letter to go out to each of these prospective types of "salespeople," advising them of our need to reach their customers, describing how recommending our Web site development service would deliver untold benefits to their customers, explaining why recommending us and the idea of developing a Web site would make the salesperson a hero with his or her customers, and offering to pay for each lead the salesperson brought in.

Prescription for Healing

In the case of another client of mine, a *Chicken Soup for the Soul* coauthor, I developed an entire program to pay visiting nurse associations when any one of their nurses sold a book to the family or friend of a patient. I called it the Prescription for Healing Program and designed gummed, tear-off prescription pads that were really coupons for ordering the book. Nurses could carry the pads in their nurse's bag, recommend the book (perhaps even carrying a copy with them), and simply tear off a "prescription" for the patient or a family member—even helping to place the order by telephone, if necessary. The book was already popular with nurses, and one organization of visiting nurses offered to be the test group for the program.

Getting Your Accounts to Become More Enthusiastic "Salespeople"

If your customers buy your products or services to resell to someone else, your revenues are driven by your customers' ability to sell these goods and services profitably and then keep repurchasing them.

The key to generating Instant Income in this case is to help your accounts sell more to their own database of names. We call this *cooperative advertising*. You put up money or supplies or promotional items and bonuses that help your dealers and distributors sell more to their end users. While these co-op programs are often complicated to set up, you can create simple ones that are easy to manage and don't cost a lot.

Start by surveying your dealers and distributors with the message that you want to help them sell more. Ask them what they need in order to sell your products and services. Do they need training, stand-up displays, or special incentives for their sales force? Do they need a smaller-sized package, different case quantities, or a different bundle of services from what you offer? Start surveying your least active customers now.

Based on that information, offer to deliver on those requests if the dealer or distributor will participate in a special offer to its customers or purchase a larger quantity from you. This is a co-op program—that means that both of you are taking action.

Be aware that co-op advertising programs—and requests from your accounts—will often take the form of rebates directly to the customer or manufacturer's discounts. Avoid these cash giveaways, regardless of what your accounts say they need. Investigate other ways to sell your products and services instead.

Another way to help your accounts sell more is to give them actual marketing campaigns that you devise. You must be careful to test these campaigns at selected dealers' locations prior to distributing them to your other accounts, but by and large, dealers and distributors appreciate these turnkey programs all thought out for them—even if they don't use them. And the truth is, they might use them.

CHAPTER 6

Making Instant Income on the Internet

MAKING MONEY ON THE INTERNET is not much different from making money anywhere else. It's just that delivering your marketing message—and sometimes even delivering your product—via the Internet is faster, cheaper, and more effortless.

From that standpoint, it's a beautiful thing.

But what frustrates so many small business owners—and keeps them from using the Internet more effectively to make money—is the sheer size and perplexity of it all. Technical idiosyncrasies too often leave business owners immobilized when it comes to implementation. And this is sad, because it prevents many of them from fully exploiting the income streams that are out there waiting for them.

Luckily, you don't have to learn everything about the Internet. By simply following a few basic principles about setting up your Web site, communicating with prospects, recruiting affiliates (the Internet's version of joint-venture partners), and enrolling the media, you, too, can begin making money on the Internet.

This tutorial is about those basic principles.

Good News! Internet Consumers Are Trained to Buy

First, let's start with the good news.

Consumers on the Internet are now trained to buy. Of course, we have the dot-com boom of the late 1990s to thank for that. In fact, back then, lots of big companies set up consumer Web sites, carefully trained consumers to use a credit card to buy things, then promptly went out of business and left these customers to small businesses like yours and mine.

But even though the Internet now boasts 694 million users (and the number is growing), the truth is that not all of them are your perfect customer. Just as in your offline market, you have to use geographic or psychographic factors to narrow down your marketing efforts so that you reach just those people who would be interested in what you have to offer.

Even on the Internet, the Whole World Is Not Your Market

Whenever I begin advising a small business owner, the very first question I ask is, "Without using the word *everyone*, who is the market for your product or service?" What I'm trying to determine is which *niche market* this business will ultimately be pursuing via newspaper ads, direct mail, press releases, and other offline methods.

Well, the Internet as a market is no different—just bigger. This means that, while you can easily sell your product or service to buyers around the world, you still need to find your niche on the Internet and proactively seek out ways to reach those unique customers.

Niche marketing just makes your work a lot easier.

Find Your Niche by Asking Prospects What They Want to Buy

Unfortunately, many business owners develop products or services that the marketplace doesn't want. They approach their entire future by saying, "This is my product. Now, how can I sell it to the marketplace?"

What they should be asking instead is, "What result does the marketplace want? And how can I use my expertise to develop the product or become the service provider who delivers it?"

Notice the difference between these approaches. The first approach sets you up for tremendous hardship—spending time, effort, and money to force your persona and your message on the market—while the second approach simply sells people what they already want to buy.

To find out about the *exact* products and services that *your* market already wants to buy, try using some of the following strategies:

1. Interview 25 to 30 randomly selected business owners or consumers in your intended market.

2. Approach the executive director of your industry's trade association to ask about the problems that most member businesses and their customers are facing.

3. Program your online news feature to deliver news articles containing industry keywords. Call anyone listed in those articles with questions you may have about prospective customers' wants.

4. Determine which customers are new to this industry or consumer category, where those customers come from, and where they're getting information, and then talk to the people who are their first point of contact with the market—whether it's schools, certifying boards, magazines, or some other entity.

5. Find out who is leaving the market and why. Perhaps you have the product or service these businesses need in order to survive and be successful in this field.

6. Talk to potential joint-venture partners about the average person on their customer list. When you see desires that are not being met—even by those potential partners—you know you've found a niche that's not being served.

Can You Take Away People's Pain or Fulfill Their Dreams?

In any market, there are really only two ways to make money: (1) take away people's problems or (2) help people fulfill their dreams. In marketing jargon, we say *speak to their pain* or *speak to their ambition*.

When you sit down to write a Web promotion that will sell your products and services, you must know for certain what your market wants and what motivates the purchasing decision: pain or ambition.

Buyers Will Spend Money to Get Tangible Results

Remember that buyers always want the *result* your product or service will provide. You are not selling tangible goods or services, you are selling an intangible result. So when you ask the market what it already wants to buy, let me give you a checklist of answers to look for. For instance, consumers want to achieve

More money, easier money
More time with family
Exciting experiences
Time to pursue hobbies
Acknowledgment
Financial independence

Less work, fewer hours
Freedom, security, safety
Comfortable retirement
Being part of the "in" crowd
Being able to help others
"Walk-off-the-job" money

Consumers are in pain and want relief from

Money problems
Health challenges
Too little time
A job that is not challenging
    enough

Relationship problems
Legal matters
A life with no purpose
A complicated job

Business owners want

Easier money and
    better cash flow
Most burdensome aspects
    handled by others
To be recognized as first
    among their peers
An autopilot business

To work fewer hours for
    more revenue
To be successful in their
    chosen field
To be able to focus on what
    they love to do

Once you know what the market already wants to buy—including the result it's ultimately looking for—you can begin to refine your product or service so that it's attractive to online buyers.

You can also begin to map your Internet campaign strategy to explain how your product or service meets the market's needs, populating your Web site, Web campaigns, e-mails, and affiliate programs with the sales language, hot buttons, free giveaways, and other elements that will be most compelling to these buyers.

You'll need a simple Web site and a few other tools before launching such a campaign. But don't get discouraged. While marketing on the Internet may seem daunting at first, in my experience the roadblock that stops so many businesses is simple lack of knowledge about what their Web site and related tools are supposed to do.

What Your Web Site Must Do

Your Web site is a delivery vehicle for your message, just like postcards, telemarketing, newspaper ads, or direct-mail packages are delivery vehicles. And like these other devices, the Internet has its own checklist of requirements you must follow to make any campaign a success.

To begin with, there are four functions of any Web site that must be fully operational before you launch any sales or marketing campaign (and in order to take full advantage of the strategies that follow this tutorial). These functions needn't take long to develop, but they must be in place.*

Function 1: Your Web Site Must Capture Prospects' Names

In the very first strategy that follows this tutorial, you'll be reading about distributing a free report that drives readers to a "name squeeze page" at your Web site. This squeeze page is designed to do one thing only: convince visitors to provide their names, e-mail addresses, zip codes, and other information in order to access a free online tutorial, audio interview, downloadable checklist, e-zine subscription, or other instant giveaway that has value.

To create your squeeze page, start by writing a compelling headline about the material visitors will be downloading for free. Then describe the actual item they'll receive, explain who you are, tell them why you're providing this item free, and mention testimonials from others who have benefited from the material. Then feature a fill-in form and give visitors *exact instructions* for completing it—along with a promise that they'll receive their information instantly.

---

* To see these functions in action, please click through the individual pages of my Web site for authors at www.howexpertsbuildempires.com.

While this seems like a lot of copy, even giving away free stuff on the Internet takes a lot of convincing these days—mainly because registrants know that they'll be e-mailed advertisements and promotions later.

Once they fill in the form, visitors should be taken to a simple confirmation page that tells registrants how to download the free item. This confirmation—or "thank you" page—should also feature information on a lower-priced, entry-level product (if you have one available), then provide a link where visitors can read more about it.

Along with giving the visitor access to the free item—or if the free item is a series of reports or tutorials—you should immediately add the registrant's e-mail address to an autoresponder that delivers prewritten generic messages every two or three days. Within these messages should be other helpful information and—starting with the fifth or sixth message—marketing copy about the first product or service that you plan to sell to these subscribers.*

Function 2: Your Web Site Must Sell Products and Services

Remember that in Chapter 3, "Writing Ads That Make the Phone Ring," I detailed how to write the elaborate direct-response copy that generates Instant Income? Well, virtually all successful Internet marketers use this same kind of direct-response copy to sell their products and services online. They think of a Web page as just another delivery vehicle for these sales letters—except that the letters can be read on a computer screen.

You'll be writing a lot of copy as you create your Web site, but if you divide your writing effort into creating these three sales elements, it will make your task easier.

Sales Element 1: A Sales Page That Compels the Visitor to Buy

In crafting this sales letter—which begins with a compelling headline and continues through all the components of a well-written direct-response piece—take as much time as you need to tell the story and offer proof of why

---

* You can subscribe to a stand-alone autoresponder on a monthly basis or use the autoresponder function that is included with your shopping cart (more about shopping carts later in this chapter). All autoresponders will manage your opt-in list and let you send out single messages, too.

the reader *must buy* your product or service. Don't worry about the length. Instead, focus on providing all the compelling copy you learned to write in Chapter 3, "Writing Ads That Make the Phone Ring."

You should also include proven credibility builders, such as testimonials from past customers, video or audio testimonials (which are even more compelling), photographs of your product or service in action, scans of letters or documents that make your case, and so on.

Somewhere in the first quarter of the sales letter, offer your free newsletter, short course, or other autoresponder giveaway, and include a fill-in form that readers can complete instantly without clicking over to a separate page. Sprinkle your sales letter with phrases such as "click here now to order" that —when clicked—take the reader to a secure shopping cart.

At the bottom of the sales page, put your company's name and address, your copyright line—for example, "© 2007 Success Resources International"—and the following links:

<u>Place Your Order By Phone</u> | <u>Policies</u> | <u>Become an Affiliate</u>
<u>For Media Professionals</u> | <u>Contact Us</u>

Sales Element 2: A Shopping Cart That Instantly Captures Orders

A shopping cart allows visitors to your Web site to click on links embedded in your sales letter and buy your product on a secure page that captures their credit card number and other order information. If an affiliate originally generated the visitor, the shopping cart will credit that affiliate with the purchase so that you can pay a commission on the order. The shopping cart I use not only processes my online orders but also manages my entire affiliate program, even reporting on how much to pay each of my affiliates each month (more about affiliates in a moment).*

Sales Element 3: A Thank-You Page That Upsells Other Products

Once visitors complete their order, you can—and should—elect to take them to a thank-you page where you congratulate them on their purchase and tell

---

* The best shopping cart I've found (and the one used by countless Internet businesses) can be found at the Instant Income Resources Page (www.instantincome.com/resources.html).

them how their order will be shipped (or how to download it online). Smart Internet marketers also add an upsell offer to their thank-you page that buyers can click on to make an additional purchase.

Function 3: Your Web Site Must Recruit Affiliates

Once you have your shopping cart operational, you can write a page that recruits others to help you sell your products and services. On the Internet, a joint-venture partner is called an *affiliate*. And throughout the Instant Income strategies following this tutorial, you'll find proven steps for broadcasting powerful promotions to your affiliates' customers, members, students, clients, and subscribers.

Ideally, your affiliate sign-up page should contain a personal letter from you introducing your affiliate program in language that convinces another Web site owner to promote your products and services. The letter should also contain a link that takes readers to your shopping cart's affiliate sign-up page to register.

Once prospective affiliates register, you can approve or reject them* and provide tools that they can use to promote you. The most common tools include banner ads and announcement e-mails that direct readers to your sales page.

Function 4: Your Web Site Must Promote Media Exposure

Because I've worked with so many celebrity entrepreneurs, I'm accustomed to writing Web pages that facilitate media exposure—in print, on the radio, via speaking engagements, on television, and, of course, all over the Internet. You, too, can benefit substantially by adding a single "For Media Professionals" page to your site that contains links to the following small documents and features:

➤ Your electronic press kit, or EPK, containing your biography, company history, previous articles, suggested radio-TV interview questions, and contact information, distilled into a PDF file.

---

* You should never approve an affiliate whose customer list, promotional tactics, or business activities would detract from your product or service.

➤ Free prewritten articles that visitors can publish in their newsletter, magazine, or newspaper. (Put multiple articles in a single Microsoft Word file for ease of downloading, but describe them separately on your media Web page.)

➤ A fill-in form that allows journalists to request an interview or guest appearance.

➤ A link that lets the media download color photos of you and your products or services (ideal for printing with your prewritten articles).

➤ A link to your affiliate sign-up page (for e-zine publishers).

It's Only About $500 for a Six- to Eight-Page Web Site . . . Honest

While these functions seem elaborate, the reality is—if you have just one or two products and services to sell—your Web site needn't be any larger than about six to eight pages. Plus, you can always add other pages as needed. The four functions discussed here are just the basics.*

And here's another bit of good news: once you develop the content, getting your pages created and uploaded to the Internet by a professional shouldn't cost more than about $500—particularly if you hire one of the many competent design firms outside the United States via Web sites like www.elance.com and www.guru.com.

The truth is, if you've thought through all the copy, drawn a map of how the pages link together, and already programmed the shopping cart yourself, then creating your Web site and uploading it to the Internet shouldn't take your Web designer more than about 12 to 15 hours. Honest.

What Your Web Site Doesn't Need to Do

Because so many people around the world still pay for dial-up connections to the Internet, your site should load fast and be easy to navigate quickly. You also want it to climb the search engine rankings quickly as you conduct

---

* Two other pages you will need to add are a policies page (stating your data collection and use policies) and a contact page (so that visitors can reach customer service and other departments). These pages are required by regulation and by certain other Web sites that may be your affiliates.

campaigns to drive traffic to your site. For these reasons, expensive flash animation, music, frames technology, and large graphics are not advised. Use simple sales letters with easy-to-read text and headlines. That's a tried-and-true moneymaking format.

Instant Income Strategies on the Internet

We've talked a lot about how to develop a Web site that delivers your marketing message effectively and gets others to help you sell. But now the real work begins—the work of actually getting people to say, "Yes, I'm interested. I want more information. I want to be led by the hand in making a buying decision." The strategies that follow this paragraph will help you do that.

INTERNET STRATEGY I

Launch a Viral Report and Squeeze Page

By combining name squeeze pages with viral reports and articles, our opt-in rates went from 8 percent to as high as 74 percent, which helped us build a list of over 20,000 targeted prospects in a few months with very little effort.

STEPHANIE FRANK
Author of *The Accidental Millionaire* and
founder of www.StephanieFrank.com

For entrepreneurs, the Internet has changed not only how we deliver products but how we sell them, too. Results can happen lightning fast. Promotional timelines are typically accelerated. And substantial income can be made in literally hours, not days.

These are just a few reasons why many of the fastest-growing companies today are Internet-based.

And, by far, one of the smartest strategies used by Internet marketers is to produce a special report that teaches readers about the benefits of your product, service, expertise, or other offerings. In Joint-Venture Strategy 1, "Create Endorsed Offers," I taught you how to write a special report that endorsers could send to their customers. Well, on the Internet, a special report—distilled into an easily downloadable PDF file—becomes an incredible tool that endorsers can use to help earn you Instant Income.

What Is Viral Marketing?

On the Internet, *viral marketing* is based on the pass-along principle. Like a virus that causes colds or flu, a viral marketing campaign also passes something along—in this case, your special report, which is largely designed to sell the reader on your products and services. Viral reports are passed along in two different ways: (1) when someone broadcasts an e-mail or publishes an article that drives people to your Web site to download the report, and (2) when someone posts your report on another Web site or otherwise gives it away because you've authorized that person to do so.

Viral marketing actually capitalizes on the very best feature of the Internet—that is, that information spreads very quickly in this freewheeling environment. In fact, as you'll see in a moment, many viral strategies actually enhance how quickly your name, reputation, and message can spread. Not only that, but once you unleash your viral marketing campaign, it literally takes on a life of its own and cannot be stopped. Like the real-life viruses of centuries ago, it will affect hundreds of thousands of people before it fades out.

The Seven-Step Process for Launching a Viral Campaign

While you'll need only a few resources to get started, they must be in place before you can launch your viral campaign.

Step 1: Set Up Three Web Pages to Run Your Viral Campaign

Whether you set up a brand-new Web site or simply add these pages to your existing site, you'll need three critical pages to do the work of giving away your special report and ultimately selling your product or service:

> ➤ A squeeze page that offers your free report as an instantly downloadable document, but that first requires visitors to give their name, e-mail address, zip code, and any other information you want before they can download it.

> ➤ A confirmation page that thanks visitors for providing their contact information, then gives instructions for downloading the free report. The confirmation page also tells visitors to click on the following link once

they have downloaded the report. That link should take the new subscriber to your product sales page.

➤ Your product sales page, which features a well-crafted sales letter— written in direct-response style—that compels visitors to buy your product or service.

You can see these three Web pages, along with a viral campaign in action, by visiting www.instantincome.com/freecourse.html.

Be sure to put your contact information at the bottom of every page. One additional page you'll want to add is a policies page, which is required by law.

Step 2: Subscribe to a Shopping Cart Service

You'll want to add to your Web site a shopping cart mechanism that processes individual sales and tracks which affiliate—or Internet joint-venture partner—sent the customer to you.

At its simplest, an *affiliate program* means that other Web site owners— hopefully with large customer lists—will proactively promote or give away your special report to their customers, many of whom will read it and click through to your Web site to buy.

When they do buy, it's customary to pay the referring affiliate a commission on each sale. The commission paid depends on the product or service you are selling and its price point. Many affiliate programs pay between 1 and 8 percent of the price of each item when what is being sold is a tangible physical product. Programs that sell e-books, software, and other instantly downloadable—or *digital*—products often pay commissions as high as 20 to 50 percent, since there is no hard cost or delivery cost of the product.

Regardless of what you decide to pay, be aware that few affiliates will pass along your report unless you pay them a commission on the resulting product sales. This is understandable—and reasonable—when you consider the time and effort that affiliates have spent on developing their customer list.

A good shopping cart service will include affiliate-tracking software that monitors all sales, tracks where they came from, and gives you a monthly report from which you can calculate commission checks.*

---

* A shopping cart service must include the tools and functionality you need to sell your products and track where your sales come from. You can read more about carts at www.instantincome.com/resources.html.

Step 3: Write a Special Report That's Salesworthy

The success of your viral marketing campaign will depend upon how frequently and how quickly other people pass your report along to their own customers, subscribers, friends, members, and clients.

This means that you must start with a report or other device that is informative, that contains information not readily available in other places, and that can be promoted as a valuable resource for consumers or business owners in your niche market.

In other words, the better your report—and the better looking it is, with colorful graphics and rich, useful content—the more eager others will be to give it away.

One secret that smart online marketers use to boost the perceived value of their report is to give away "reprint rights" to the report, allowing thousands of online marketers to give it away as a bonus along with information, products, or services of their own that they are selling.

You can also give away an MP3 file, e-book, podcast, video clip, or other such item, each with embedded links that direct people to your Web site for more information, products, and resources. Whatever you decide to give away, spend time making sure that it contains valuable information but also converts prospects into sales by encouraging them to click through to your Web page and buy when they get there. Affiliates won't continue to give away your report if few sales result from it.

Step 4: Make Your Report Fully "Brandable"

Today, the software exists to allow any affiliate to insert its own custom links into your report before passing it along. When readers click on these links, they're taken to a custom Web page where they can buy your product—and where the affiliate who passed along the report earns money on each sale. You can read more about branding software on the Instant Income Resources Page at www.instantincome.com/resources.html.

Step 5: Create an Autoresponder Series

Once a visitor lands on your squeeze page and signs up to download the free report, you've captured an e-mail address, which you can—and should—use to continue to market to that visitor. An autoresponder (included in most shopping carts) can be programmed to automatically send out a series of e-mails at a predetermined frequency. You can create a free tutorial series, a daily checklist for pursuing the goal talked about in the special report, or any other regular communication that provides value. Whatever you call it, its purpose is to follow up with prospects and encourage them to buy the products or programs that you're selling.

The key to a successful autoresponder series is to first gain the prospect's trust. Deliver valuable content, not just sales copy. By the fifth or sixth e-mail, you can start to mention the product you have for sale.

Step 6: Make It Easy to Give Your Report Away

Develop press releases, prewritten e-mails, and other simple marketing tools that affiliates can send to their customers after embedding their unique tracking link (generated by the shopping cart mechanism). Each marketing tool should convince readers to visit your Web site and download your free report.

You can also build an affiliate support page at your Web site, with cut-and-paste tools that help affiliates begin sharing your report with others immediately. Provide

➤ Endorsement letters that affiliates can send to their list

➤ A text link, pop-up window, hover window, or banner ad that affiliates can add to their site

Step 7: Start Contacting Superaffiliates

Superaffiliates are list owners with hundreds of thousands of names (or at least tens of thousands of names that respond). To entice superaffiliates to give away your report, offer them a substantial percentage of the gross revenues on sales generated by the special report. Make sure they know that you provide tools that make it easy to give away your report and make sales.

Why pay such high commissions to superaffiliates? Because they'll help you build a massive "opt-in" or subscriber list in a very short period of time. Your business will prosper more from your list in the long run as you begin to sell other products to the names you acquire.

To find these superaffiliates, visit the Instant Income Resources Page at www.instantincome.com/resources.html for details on software that can help you locate top-ranked Web sites that are more likely to have big customer lists.

Get Ready for Lightning-Fast Results

Many Internet marketers experience response times of mere hours between the time a superaffiliate promotes their free report and the moment readers begin to click through to the Web site and buy. This kind of speed is one of the biggest benefits of the Internet. When it happens, be prepared with product fulfillment capabilities, customer service capabilities, and other resources that you need.

When I launched my first viral report system on the Internet, my team was prepared with these important resources. But what we weren't prepared for were the instant orders for my *other*, more expensive products and services.

And can I tell you another secret? Looking back on the experience of setting up the viral report system itself, I think we made virtually *every mistake* it was possible to make. In fact, just getting the Web site up and running was a lot more work than I expected. Three different programmers couldn't get the pages to work with each other. Half of the e-mails in my autoresponder short course were too lengthy. And, when at last we were ready to launch, I uploaded 1,600 e-mail addresses collected from people who had given me their business cards—only to find out that the shopping cart immediately sent these folks a confusing e-mail *congratulating* them for opting in to a list they didn't even know about yet. Wow. Lots and lots and lots of lessons.

But in the end, it all came together—which is the most important lesson for *you*.

In the first full month of operation, hundreds of people visited my Web site at www.HowExpertsBuildEmpires.com. And not only was the response instantaneous—it was downright shocking. Visitors who opted in to receive my free report series *immediately* clicked over to buy a unique $97 marketing plan I was offering to help industry experts, authors, and entrepreneurs become the leading expert in their niche. Of course, generating sales for the $97 product was the reason I wrote the free reports in the first place.

But nobody was supposed to buy it right away.

They were supposed to download the free reports, marvel at their quality, pass them on to friends, and slowly—over time—convert from report subscribers to $97 buyers.

Instead, to my surprise, by the afternoon of the very first day, dozens of $97 marketing plans had been sold. And in the first full month selling the marketing plan on the Internet, a total of 1,043 visitors opted in to receive the free reports, and more than 270 of them purchased the digitally downloadable marketing plan—a conversion rate of more than 26 percent. Not only that, but my office was flooded with callers who happily bought an *additional* $26,000 worth of consulting time and more elaborate products in that first month alone. All this occurred during August, too, which is typically a "down" month for most businesses.

Today, the Web site at www.HowExpertsBuildEmpires.com looks essentially the way it did when I first set it up to run the viral campaign. Take a look and replicate the process, if you like. Just remember that, while the viral report system may seem daunting to set up, it remains one of the most reliable Instant Income Internet strategies available to you.

Recruit Affiliates for a 24-Hour Strategy

Once I learned this strategy, it became my business. I've personally helped hundreds of people use this strategy to sell tens of thousands of books and become bestsellers. One particular author, over two 24-hour campaigns, sold 6,828 copies at $27 each—earning $187,356 in revenue without spending a dime on advertising. This strategy has proven to be one of the best methods of marketing.

PEGGY MCCOLL
Online promoter and president, Dynamic
Destinies, Inc. www.destinies.com

If you've been recruiting affiliates for your other online promotions—or even if you're just starting out—there is one promotion you can conduct where everybody wins and affiliates become heroes to their customers.

It's called the "24-Hour Strategy." And the excitement it creates is almost uncontainable.

When Jack Canfield and I launched our *New York Times* bestselling book *The Success Principles: How to Get from Where You Are to Where You Want to Be,* we recruited 363 friends who owned e-mail lists ranging from 100 names to more than 500,000 names. We offered 80 free downloadable bonuses that readers could access once they purchased the book online.

And in the first 12 hours after affiliates broadcast our prewritten e-mail, we sent more than 4,400 buyers to online booksellers, skyrocketed to the number one position at BarnesAndNoble.com, and happily added thousands of new names to our own personal e-mail lists—*all at virtually no cost whatsoever.*

You, too, can create this kind of buying frenzy for your product or service.*

Here's How It Works

The strategy works because hundreds of dollars worth of free bonuses are given away as an incentive for buying a product or service during a specific 24-hour period. The bonuses are provided by your affiliates, who are happy to supply free samples in exchange for the exposure they'll get to lots of other lists. Then on a specific day, at a specific time, all affiliates send a prewritten e-mail to their lists promoting your product and the free bonuses.

If the bonuses you gather and the lists that participate are of superior quality, you can expect thousands of qualified prospects to go to your Web site, buy your product, download the free bonuses, and opt in to multiple affiliates' lists.

Because it combines the promotional power of hundreds of list owners with the undeniable value of the free bonuses and the concentrated buying power of hundreds of thousands of eager consumers, this is one promotion where everybody wins.

The Step-by-Step Formula

To set up your campaign, follow this step-by-step formula:

1. **Recruit affiliates with sizable e-mail lists.** Since the ultimate goal of the campaign is to attract prospects who will purchase your product or service, start by approaching list owners that have customers and prospects who would be ideal buyers for you. Since this is a numbers game, recruit large lists whenever possible. Try also to recruit list owners within a certain niche market so that all e-mail recipients will have at least some interest in the free bonuses and what other affiliates have to offer.

2. **Secure bonuses that can be downloaded over the Internet.** Since many people will buy your product just to get the free bonuses, you can maximize the impact of this aspect of human nature by securing the most

---

* To see a 24-Hour Strategy in action, visit www.instantincome.com/free-gifts.html.

valuable bonuses possible. *But make sure buyers can instantly download the bonuses at your Web site.* This helps drive sales. And, additionally, it encourages affiliates to participate, since there is no cost involved.

What are some bonuses that work? E-books, guides, checklists, business plans, journals, teleclasses, Webinars, and online courses. Bonuses to avoid are discount coupons that require recipients to spend money to exercise the bonus—and any other bonus that reflects poorly on you.

3. **Build a simple Web site or add two pages to your existing site.** The first page should feature a short personal note from you about the product or service being offered; it should then highlight the bonuses that will be available once visitors purchase that product or service. It should instruct readers to click on a link, buy your product, then return with their order confirmation number to download the bonuses.

Send buyers to your own shopping cart to buy or to an online re-tailer who is selling your product or service for you. Feature a brief fill-in form at the bottom of the first page asking for the buyer's name, e-mail address, zip code, and order confirmation number. Completing the form and hitting the Submit button should take the buyer to the bonus download page.

On the first page, be sure to talk about how valuable and useful the bonuses are. Ask each affiliate to provide a description of its bonus, a dollar value, and the bonus itself, either in PDF form or via a link to the affiliate's Web site.

4. **Schedule the launch date.** Choose any Tuesday or Wednesday of the year, except during late August or the last two weeks of December. Con-tact affiliates well in advance so that they can schedule your promotion.

5. **Write instructions plus an e-mail for affiliates to broadcast.** Tell the affiliates which day to broadcast the e-mail to their list and at what time of day. In the case of *The Success Principles* campaign, Jack Canfield and I wanted to concentrate buyers within a very narrow time frame in or-der to drive our book up the bestseller rankings. You may wish to spread out orders over two to three days to better manage order taking and fulfillment.

Be sure to write the e-mail for your affiliates, so that all they have to do is personalize the first paragraph (if they wish) and add their name to the bottom. Notice the e-mail below. It talks almost as much about the bonuses as it does about *The Success Principles*. It includes—among other elements—a call to action, a personal endorsement by the affiliate, and a dollar value on the bonuses that far exceeds the price of the book itself. Value is key.

SUBJECT LINE: URGENT . . . I Have Dozens of Gifts for You, But You Must Respond NOW

Dear [firstname]:

Today I'm sending you one of the most important announcements I've ever broadcast to [name of affiliate's list].

This week, my good friend Jack Canfield—co-creator of the famed *Chicken Soup for the Soul* book series—is announcing the definitive guide for those of us who want to become more successful in our lives, careers, finances and relationships.

It's called "The Success Principles: How to Get From Where You Are to Where You Want to Be"—and Jack and his coauthor Janet Switzer have $3,060 worth of bonus gifts in store for you when you purchase the book online during this initial launch period.

What will you receive FREE when you purchase Jack and Janet's newest book during this limited time offer?

- Exclusive programs you'll rarely find anywhere else . . .
- Private mentorship courses worth hundreds of dollars . . .
- An entire library of e-books, manuals and resources . . .
- Plus so much more . . . !

These are gifts from the most renowned experts of our time: Real-estate guru Carleton Sheets . . . One Minute Manager author Ken Blanchard . . . fitness expert Kathy Smith . . . Brian Tracy . . . Mark Victor Hansen . . . Michael Gerber of E-Myth fame . . . and so many other experts you've heard of.

All it takes to start enjoying these valuable gifts is a few minutes of your time RIGHT NOW . . . plus the order confirmation number you'll receive when you purchase *The Success Principles* at your favorite online book retailer.

You can read all about the FREE bonus gifts at:
www._____.com/book.

But don't wait! You must act soon to take advantage of this outstanding offer. More than $3,060 in gifts are waiting for you—yet *The Success Principles* book costs less than $20 when you buy it online.

Visit www.jackcanfieldtrainings.com/book for details.

Of course, I've read *The Success Principles* and it's something I'm delighted to recommend. Along with co-author Janet Switzer, Jack has detailed 64 principles of success used by top achievers from all walks of life. Jack and Janet have even detailed dozens of strategies you won't find in other books on success— and many that only top entrepreneurs and world-renowned athletes, scientists, philanthropists and others know.

I want to make 2007 your best year EVER—by getting this book into your hands today . . . along with the $3,060 worth of other resources that can take you from where you are now to where you want to be.

Read about the free gifts you'll receive now at:
www._____.com/book

Then purchase *The Success Principles* using the same link. Please hurry.

In friendship,

[name of list owner]

INTERNET STRATEGY 3

Drive Buyers to Your Web Site with Articles

Like many new Web publishers, I started with no real budget for online advertising, so I optimized my site with my own articles instead, then diligently submitted many of these articles to directories. In less than five months, my articles appeared on over 500 other Web pages—all indexed on the major search engines. Plus, I was able to sell my site to a seasoned Web publisher because of my Web site's original content.

KRIZIA DEVERDIER
CEO and publisher, Project Sixty-One
Media & Publishing, Toronto, Canada

There are many different ways to drive traffic to a Web site today. Unfortunately, most of them cost a lot of money. If you're new to the Internet or you don't really have the technical knowledge to navigate these expensive traffic-generating methods, you could end up spending hundreds of dollars a day.

But there *is* an alternative that's actually *more* effective. And the good news is, it's practically free.

A Proven Strategy That's Worked for Over a Decade

Jason Potash, the expert and inventor behind the Article Announcer software and training course, likens article marketing to a stately old tree with thousands of branches and leaves that gather sunshine to nourish the trunk and roots. Your articles have the ability to be these "feeder" sources, too, since a single article might be picked up by a newsletter, e-zine, directory, or discussion forum and passed on virally to potentially millions of people.

Submitting articles to Web sites, e-zines, and other online forums has generated cash for small businesses almost since the day the Internet became a thriving commercial community.

Why Article Marketing Works

When you submit a high-quality article to a Web site that serves the needs of your potential customers, your article will typically be "published," or added to that site's newsletter, blog, or other regular communications. Rarely will it be published in print using this formula. (For print publication, see Advertising Strategy 2, "Broadcast a Compelling Press Release.") Luckily, online publication is much faster than print—in fact, it's nearly instantaneous.

Of course, aside from merely informing readers of your expertise, article marketing has many other substantial benefits. Most importantly, it tends to get you higher rankings on the search engines.

Here's why:

Search engines determine the quality and relevancy of your Web site based on how many *other* Web sites link to yours. It's like a voting system. If instead of having only five votes (that is, five other Web sites that thought well enough of you to talk about you at their site), you have 300 votes (300 other Web sites that are linking to you because they posted your article on their newsletter page), your ranking in the search engines will skyrocket. Whenever someone searches for products and services in your industry or area of expertise, your Web site will appear higher up on the list than that of a competitor who doesn't do article marketing.

To begin creating massive traffic using articles, follow these steps.

Step 1: Decide What Your Objectives Are

While most small business owners want to turn their article-marketing effort into product sales immediately, others simply want to build a large opt-in list for a future sales effort. If you don't have a product to sell yet, you can still profit from article marketing by building a list and offering consulting services, a subscription series based upon your expertise, or some other knowledge product.

Suffice it to say that article marketing works beautifully regardless of the business model under which you operate—even if it's simply to help build interest or memberships in an online or offline special-interest group or hobby club.

Step 2: Build a Web Site That Sells Your Product or Service

The best use of article marketing is to drive prospective customers to your Web site for additional information in the form of a free report, a short course delivered via autoresponder, a fact sheet, a checklist, or some other giveaway item—which then does the work of converting the reader into a buyer. Remember the two-step campaign strategy from Prospecting Strategy 2, "Run a Two-Step Campaign"? Article marketing is a classic two-step method.

But you must support your article-marketing effort and your free giveaway item with a Web site that features compelling sales letters that convince readers to buy. Put links to these sales pages in your free giveaways, so that readers can click over and buy. That is how articles ultimately get turned into cash.

Step 3: Make a Short List of Topics

If you've been operating your business longer than a few months, you have the ability to become an expert in your industry. In fact, you know more than you think you do.

To begin developing your expert articles, look around at your own customers and clients. What are their challenges, opportunities, and interests? What problems keep them awake at night? What do they respond to? Make a list of these topics.

Next, list those subjects that you already know something about or need to research—even if you're only somewhat familiar with them.

Step 4: Create Subthemes of Your Topic

If you are a therapist and relationship expert, for example, you can develop articles about teen love, divorce recovery, workplace hostility, and single motherhood. While all these themes are related to relationships, articles on them would be submitted to very different Web sites. Make yourself an expert in *multiple* markets by locating subniche markets with Web sites where potential customers might congregate.

Step 5: Write the Articles or Hire Someone to Write Them

If you're not a natural-born writer or you just don't have an interest in writing these articles, consider hiring a professional. For about $200 for a series of articles, you can find freelance writers—many of whom are career journalists looking for some side work—at Web sites like www.elance.com, www.guru.com, or www.rentacoder.com. You can even review portfolios of their past work prior to hiring them.

Don't worry about optimizing your article with many of the Internet tricks that worked a few years ago. Just use the most common phrases and buzzwords that would normally be used in your industry, then craft the rest of the article in normal, everyday language and grammar. The search engines have gotten wise to keyword stuffing and other optimization tricks, anyway. Let your good content rise to the top of the search engines on its own.

Each article should be about 500 to 700 words* and contain these four parts:

➤ An introductory paragraph that gets readers excited about the rest of the article and presents what they'll learn in subsequent paragraphs.

➤ Three body paragraphs that contain the most important points about the topic and present your opinion, recommendations, or information on the subject.

➤ A concluding paragraph that summarizes the subject discussed and presents a solution or suggestion.

---

* For best results on the Internet, be sure your word count is no less than 450 words and no more than 1,000 words.

➤ A resource box that contains two to four sentences about you and your services, then offers a valuable free report, checklist, audio interview, discussion forum, or other giveaway via your squeeze page.* Don't talk about yourself; talk about the benefits of what readers will receive free when they click.

Ideally, selected topics should be turned into a multipart article so that you get follow-up publication at Web sites that publish the first segment.

Step 6: Submit Your Articles to Free Article Directories

There are hundreds of article directories that will accept your articles and post them for free downloading by registered users. These directories are a good way to get the process started.

But the best way to submit articles is to submit your subtheme articles to specific niche Web sites that speak directly to avid readers. To find such sites, do an online search using keywords that help narrow down the results to those niche sites. Then contact the Web site owner by telephone to ask that your article be used.

Many sites today also have submission forms that you can complete online with your name, Web site name, article headline, and body copy. To make this process easier, Jason Potash publishes a software program that not only automatically completes these forms for you but also helps you manage Web site contacts for future submissions and even teaches you how to craft superb articles that get published.[†]

Step 7: Repeat the Process

Articles also tend to live a long time on the Internet. They get indexed, archived, and sent virally by many thousands of people. This is one reason why, while massive traffic *can* be generated virtually overnight by broadcasting a single article, "critical mass"—according to Jason Potash—typically occurs after you have 20 or more articles circulating around the Internet.

---

* See Internet Strategy 1, "Launch a Viral Report and Squeeze Page," for more details on how to develop a squeeze page.

† You can read more about Jason Potash's Article Announcer tool at the Instant Income Resources Page (www.instantincome.com/resources.html).

Broadcast Internet-Only Offers via E-mail

Consumers are continually looking for the absolute best bargain. By sending our current deals directly to our members via e-mail, we stand out from the millions of other online shopping options available to them, and increase our sales and conversions significantly.

JOEL COMM
Founder of InfoMedia Inc.

E-mail continues to be the best friend of solo entrepreneurs and other small businesses. It's virtually free and quick to execute, and the income it can produce is typically more immediate than that produced by virtually any other delivery method you might choose for your message.

Like every strategy, e-mail has its own unique requirements. But it also starts with solid direct-response copy—a skill that you can easily master by executing many of the other strategies in this book.

Jeff Johnson, a solo entrepreneur who generated $454,000 in revenue in just 90 days on the Internet, has mastered the art of using e-mail to sell products and services. What's his secret? "Knowing what would benefit your customers and sending them offers that would appeal to them is key," says Jeff, "especially since only 30 to 40 percent of your e-mails will be opened—if you're lucky."

Jeff—a former manager in the financial brokerage business who wanted to step away from his grueling management position so that he and his wife could raise a family—began exploring alternatives that would allow him to earn the income he wanted yet require just a few hours a day of effort. "I wanted to watch my kids grow up," says Jeff.

Through his research, Jeff knew that the Internet would be the ultimate leverage tool—both for leveraging his time and for leveraging other people's resources to help him grow his business. Jeff understood early on that using the Internet was simply a matter of (1) building a Web site that would generate customers 24 hours a day, 7 days a week, then (2) e-mailing those customers special offers that would appeal to them. Jeff launched his first Web site—but with this unique twist: instead of selling his own products and services, he became a "professional affiliate" who now specializes in *creating customers and sales for other online businesses*. He lets these other businesses handle the ongoing customer relationships—the customer service, the billing issues, the phone calls and product delivery—while he spends all his time generating customers in the first place.

In Jeff's first six months online, he created enough traffic to earn between $1,500 and $2,000 per day at his first Web site—without selling a single product of his own. He set up additional Web sites that advertised products for two large companies, and those sites generated $454,000 in sales commissions to Jeff in the first 90 days.*

Jeff compares affiliate marketing to just being a salesperson for somebody else, without all the work of fulfilling on a product or service—not very different from his experience in the brokerage business.

And using e-mail, he says, has been key. Success with e-mail marketing requires generating contact names, building a relationship with each person on your list, and then finding a reason to e-mail that person again about something else—a new product offer, a free gift, a special event, and so on.

Ideal for All Types of Businesses

Pizza restaurants can use e-mail to drive people in for a discount offer on a slow night, says Jeff. Consultants can e-mail their clients about a special evening workshop or teleseminar with an expert, he continues. Or a retail business can create a special offer, then ask its e-mail customers to tell a friend.

In other words, you don't have to own an e-commerce business to use e-mail. If you own a retail store, a consulting office, a service location, or some other "brick-and-mortar" business, you, too, can use e-mail to drive customers to your door (or to your Web site to read the complete offer, download a coupon, or get product details).

And if your business is home-based? Then e-mail will often be your first and most favored marketing method.

A Reason to Collect Their E-mail

E-mail reduces your marketing costs and the delays involved with sending letters or making phone calls to customers. Telling customers that they'll be eligible to receive Internet-only specials is a good way to capture their e-mail addresses. In fact, many of these new e-mail addresses will be among your best

---

* You can read more about Jeff and his techniques by visiting the Instant Income Resources Page at www.instantincome.com/resources.html.

respondents, especially if they just enjoyed a positive shopping experience with you.

Well-crafted e-mails can generate literally thousands of dollars in income. But just like composing any other direct-response device,* writing e-mails so that they get opened, read, and acted upon requires a formula.

➤ **Start with a compelling subject line.** Ask a question, state a possible result, offer a valuable gift, or tell why you're writing. If there is an impending deadline, feature that in the subject line. And if you've properly captured your customer's name along with his e-mail address, you can speak to him by name in the subject line, too. Here are some subject lines I've used successfully:

> Gary, I'd Like to Interview You on Thursday . . .
>
> Until July 23rd: I Have a F*R*E*E set of Audio CD's for You! Just 3 Weeks Left.
>
> Hundreds of Speakers Will Be Joining Me. Will You?

➤ **Add a friendly salutation.** Use the recipient's first name, if you have it.† Otherwise, use a general form of address such as "Dear Busy Executive" or "Dear Mother of the Bride."

➤ **Create excitement in the lead paragraph.** Grab the reader's attention and give her a reason to keep reading. Perhaps you hint that you have a special offer just for her. Maybe you're offering a free giveaway, a special discount, or advance notice of a sale for e-mail customers only.

➤ **Describe the top three to five benefits.** Choose the most persuasive aspects of your product, service, offer, or free giveaway (if this is a two-step campaign).

➤ **Provide supporting information.** Testimonials, case studies, success stories, price comparisons, and other such details help to overcome any objections the reader may have before responding.

---

* To read more about writing direct-response copy, see Chapter 3, "Writing Ads That Make the Phone Ring."

† E-mailing through your shopping cart or e-mail broadcast service will enable you to personalize your e-mails.

➤ **Keep it short and compelling.** Include only the most compelling details in your e-mail. If your offer requires a lengthier discussion of why readers should respond, point people to your Web site for your long-form sales letter.

➤ **Break up the copy with bullets.** Lots of dense copy looks daunting and time-consuming to readers, so I always break up the copy by putting the benefits or case studies in bullet form.

➤ **Mention the offer.** If you don't have a Web site, write your offers directly in the e-mail using clear, simple language. You might choose seasonal offers, such as "Bring in your winter coat for dry cleaning before September 30 and we'll take $5 off." Or use the e-mail to bring in customers when it's slow—for example, "Enjoy a f.r.ee appetizer on us when you buy two dinners any Monday, Tuesday, or Wednesday evening." Be sure to put a time limit on the offer or require customers to bring in the e-mail as proof that they received the offer.

➤ **Tell the reader how to respond.** Always tell the customer exactly what to do, whether it's "Visit our Web site to learn more" or "Call us before noon on Thursday, March 8, to claim your f^ree gift."

➤ **Feature the link to your Web site.** If you want your customers to go to your Web site to read the complete sales letter, to download a coupon, or to take some other action, be sure to feature your Web site link prominently *at least twice*—somewhere in the second half of the e-mail, then again just before your signature.

➤ **Make it personal.** Today, too many e-mails end up sounding terse and unfriendly. "Who writes this stuff?" I often wonder. To combat this effect, inject some of your own personality into the e-mail. Remember, you're sending a message to people with whom you already have a business relationship. Make it friendly.

Comply with Spam Laws When E-mailing

Since January 2004, the U.S. government has regulated the transmittal of unsolicited e-mail, otherwise known as spam. One way to stay in compliance with these regulations is to first educate yourself on the CAN-SPAM Act,* but additionally, you should e-mail only to those people with whom you have a legitimate business relationship or who have requested to receive information from you (by opting into your free report or e-zine, for example).

The CAN-SPAM law

➤ **Bans false or misleading header information.** Your e-mail's "From," "To," and routing information—including the originating domain name and e-mail address—must be accurate and must identify the person who initiated the e-mail.

➤ **Prohibits deceptive subject lines.** The subject line cannot mislead the recipient about the contents or subject matter of the message.

➤ **Requires that your e-mail give recipients a method of opting out.** You must provide a return e-mail address or another Internet-based response mechanism that allows a recipient to unsubscribe from future e-mail messages sent to that e-mail address—and you must honor those requests.

➤ **Requires that commercial e-mail be identified as an advertisement and include the sender's valid physical postal address.**

Spam filters are software programs that shield consumers from receiving unsolicited messages. To ensure that your message has the best chance of bypassing these filters and being delivered, I recommend that you first check its content through one of the many spam checkers available online, such as www.lyris.com. They will compare your e-mail to known spam trigger phrases and give you a complete report on what needs to be changed. Many e-mail marketers insert special characters into words like *mo^ney, F.R.EE* and *in`come* to throw off spam filters.

---

* You'll find more information about CAN-SPAM at www.ftc.gov/bcp/conline/pubs/buspubs/canspam.htm.

Conduct a 28-Day Product Launch Campaign

Just two years ago, the Internet was instantly abuzz after a solo entrepreneur ran a sophisticated product launch campaign and sold over $1,000,000 worth of product in a single day. Soon, similar stories began making the rounds. And today, such results are *commonplace* among Internet marketers who have quietly incorporated these simple but superlucrative product launches into their marketing calendar.

Internet marketing strategist and behind-the-scenes advisor Jeff Walker was the first to perfect the *Product Launch Formula*—and today, more and more Web site owners and solo entrepreneurs are using his system to generate tremendous excitement and staggering revenue around a new product release or an existing product's rerelease.

All kinds of products and services are being sold this way, by the way—from e-books and coaching programs to memberships and consulting.

By Now You Should Have Done the Preparatory Work

While a four-week product launch is simple to execute, it does require some preparation—and some fairly dedicated focus time during the 28 days when you are executing the campaign. In other words, the product orders don't just appear in your Web site's shopping cart.

You have to drive them there.

To begin with, you should have followed the recommendations throughout this chapter and already have these promotional tools up and running:

➤ **A Web site designed to sell your product.** Simple Web sites created using direct-response copy are best.* Don't worry that you can't create elaborate graphics or flash animation. They are not required. In fact, these elements actually tend to detract from the sales process.

For the purposes of your product launch campaign, you'll first put

---

* See Chapter 3, "Writing Ads That Make the Phone Ring," for details on how to write compelling direct-response sales letters.

up a sales page that talks about the product to come but doesn't contain links that allow visitors to click and purchase yet. That fully operational "buy today" page will be added on Launch Day.

➤ **A shopping cart at your Web site to capture orders instantly.** A shopping cart allows visitors to your Web site to click on a link embedded in your sales letter and buy your product on a secure page that captures their credit card information and contact information. Excellent shopping carts (including the one used by countless Internet businesses) can be found at the Instant Income Resources Page (www.instantincome. com/resources.html).

➤ **A loyal subscriber list that you communicate with regularly.** The best 28-day product launches begin with a substantial and highly loyal list of e-zine subscribers, free report recipients, and other consumers who were driven to your site by your own efforts or by someone else who endorsed you. Once they opt in (register), keep the relationship going with a free mini-course delivered via autoresponder or other regular communication until you're ready to begin your product launch sequence.

➤ **An affiliate program that recruits Internet partners.** When you launch an affiliate program and give affiliates the tools they need to promote your e-zine, free report, or other list-building giveaway, your list will grow exponentially. Plus, these affiliates can become participating endorsers in your eventual product launch campaign.

➤ **A blog where your list can post responses to your e-mails.** In just a moment, you'll learn how to e-mail to your list and elicit responses that will help you not only develop your product but also develop the sales campaign as well. Asking your subscribers to post their responses at your blog brings a sense of excitement, community, and credibility to the campaign by showing the enthusiastic responses of other intelligent individuals who are also interested in you and your product.

Social Proof Helps Boost Excitement and Credibility

Populating your Web site, blog, and e-mail communications with customers' comments, video testimonials, questions, and input tells visitors to your site that other intelligent people are interested in your product, too. That's what Jeff Walker calls "social proof."

Removing from your Web page the 100 units of a bonus that were available on Launch Day but that have now been snapped up by 100 previous buyers is additional social proof that will convince visitors to act before other bonuses disappear, In fact, it's this social proof aspect of a campaign that is often the most compelling to prospective customers.

It Doesn't Require a Lot of Money

Notice that up to this point, you've spent very little money—if you've spent any money at all. Adding an extra page on your Web site costs nothing. Signing up for a shopping cart (if you don't have one already) costs about $79 per month. And sending out e-mails to your list through your shopping cart's list management function is free.

Yet despite your modest effort and negligible outlay, you stand to make *tens of thousands of dollars per hour* depending on your product, your price, your list, and your offer.

The Sequence Is Key

Not surprisingly, there is a specific sequence of steps to follow in executing a successful product launch campaign:

1. Ask the People on Your List about Their Biggest Problem

If you've been communicating with your subscribers all along—giving them valuable information and benefits for free—you can now send an e-mail 28 days prior to your intended launch date and ask your list to report back on the biggest problem they're experiencing.

For example, if you run a gardening site that gives away a free short course on growing vegetables, ask those on your list what their biggest challenge is in the area of vegetable gardening. Is it gophers, rabbits, blight, soil problems, insects, or something else?

Whatever it is, you want to hear about their biggest headaches, problems, and complaints. Why? Because good marketers know that consumers respond more readily and remain loyal longer if you take away their pain rather than simply make them feel good.

Take careful note of the responses you receive, as this feedback will literally help you write the promotional copy for the product you're about to launch.

2. Report on the Problems You Hear About

Keep the communication going by sending additional e-mails at four- to five-day intervals reporting on the feedback you've received. Eventually, one of these e-mails must casually introduce the fact that you are developing a product to address the needs you've been hearing about. In this e-mail, ask subscribers to help you develop the best possible product by hitting the reply button and telling you what should be in the product to best meet their needs.

Of course, your product may be 90 percent completed already, but be sure to leave room for adding components that will address the needs expressed by your list. Then, *tell your list* in the next few e-mails that you are adding specific components that will benefit them directly. You'll find that consumers respond better when they believe they've had a direct hand in the development of a product that fits their needs.

3. On Day 14 of the Countdown, Send the "Mission Critical" E-mail

While your list probably has an inkling that something is coming, this e-mail is the one that formally announces the product, gives its name, states what it will do, and—most importantly—sets the date of the launch. It also asks for any last-minute "mission critical" components that your subscribers believe must be included in the product when it is launched.

Rest assured that all this back-and-forth communication has not gone to waste. In fact, what you have done up to this point has laid the groundwork for a spectacularly successful Launch Day. You've started to build anticipation. You've let your list know that the product will be very focused on them. You've built reciprocity or a sense of payback among your subscribers.

4. E-mail Back or Post to Your Blog the Most Exciting Responses

Building excitement, enthusiasm, and anticipation is key. For the next 10 days of the countdown, you'll be sending e-mails every two or three days that report on the most exciting comments you've received—all the while sending readers to your blog, inviting them to teleseminars, answering their major objections, telling the continuing story, building tension, and creating the anticipation of a major event—your product's Launch Day.

5. Four Days ahead of Launch, Begin E-mailing Every Day

By the time the people on your list have followed your product launch campaign for 24 days, not only will they be primed to buy, but they'll be anxiously awaiting the launch date. In the four days remaining, send an e-mail every day that talks about how Launch Day will play out. Tell them the exact hour you'll put up the product announcement page and make the shopping cart operational. Talk about the bonuses you'll be offering (see the next section). Direct them to your blog to read messages from all the other people who are planning to buy . . . and so on.

6. On Launch Day, E-mail Instructions on How to Order

By the time Launch Day arrives, your subscribers should be anxiously awaiting your product's availability and be eager to buy as soon as your sales page is added to your Web site. If you've done your job, they'll literally flood your shopping cart with orders. Excitement will be high. The phone is likely to ring off the hook. Later in the day, send an e-mail that keeps the excitement going by reporting on some technical glitch or on the chaos that's taken over your office because of the overwhelming response. Be truthful, enthusiastic—and human.

Offer Bonuses That Expire within Hours

To heighten the response rate and get people to order immediately, plan a series of valuable bonuses that are withdrawn as the day progresses. You can even add a counter to your Web page that counts down a limited quantity of an extremely valuable bonus that you've set aside for the first 50 or 100 people who respond. If you want your list to buy within the first eight hours, offer a bonus that you pull from the Web page exactly eight hours later. Show integrity by offering, then pulling, bonuses—as you promised in your advance e-mails that you would.

Relaunch an Existing Product the Same Way

Even if you don't have a new product on the horizon, you can relaunch an existing one by simply polling the people on your list about their needs, then adding components that address those needs.

Follow the product launch sequence given here exactly as you would for a new product.

A Better Relationship with Your List

According to Jeff Walker, every entrepreneur who has used the Product Launch Formula* has reported a better relationship with his list than he had before. These entrepreneurs have customers and subscribers who are now more willing to buy—and who get more excited about responding to future offers.

Furthermore, these Internet entrepreneurs know that, in addition to the money they make from these campaigns, they derive even more important benefits. They gain momentum in their business—and the knowledge and confidence to replicate this strategy again and again, anytime, for any product.

That knowledge is priceless.

---

* You can read more about Jeff Walker's system at the Instant Income Resources Page (www.instantincome.com/resources.html).

CHAPTER 7

Finding Instant Income in Overlooked Assets

IN ADDITION TO THE traditional assets you may have in your business—machinery, furniture, your accounts receivable—you also have dozens of "hidden" assets that you've probably never thought about exploiting before. These are assets like your own business knowledge, the expertise of your employees, the downtime in your service department, your obsolete products, even your shipping cartons.

All of these things are *valuable assets* that can be easily turned into immediate cash. This chapter will help you identify them and prepare your company to profit from them.

Identifying Overlooked Assets

Finding the more unusual assets in your business will be much easier if you approach this treasure hunt like a marketer or a salesperson instead of like an accountant. Because, ultimately, you'll be looking for assets *that others will be happy to pay cash for.*

The first step is not to ask yourself what you have that's valuable, but to ask yourself, "What do other business owners need? What are they looking for?" While there is an infinite list of possible answers to this question, think through what other businesses in your industry or town would pay for:

➤ **Access to your customers?** If so, then your overlooked assets suddenly include advertising space in your shipping cartons, bag stuffers in your shopping bags, envelope stuffers in your invoices, hangtags or hang bags on your merchandise, free giveaways at your store, renting or joint-venturing your mailing list, the option to conduct evening workshops in your store, and so on.

➤ **Cheap sale goods or bargain services?** If so, then add to your list of overlooked assets your obsolete inventory, downtime in your manufacturing facility (when you can produce cheaper versions using leftover materials), bulk orders you would like to place but need someone else to help you meet the minimum order, and downtime in your various departments that lets you "hire out" your employees to provide services to other businesses or their customers.

➤ **Industry knowledge, training, or business contacts?** If so, then your own expertise (and that of your employees) can be sold via advisory services, consulting, coaching calls, teleseminars, workshops, a list of your suppliers, training programs for start-ups, and other such methods.

Do you see how thinking through what other business owners need will help you determine what valuable assets you have? Other businesses may also need

➤ Low-cost advertising options

➤ Something that they can't buy or produce themselves

➤ Additional products and services that they can sell to their customers

➤ Help with negotiating their deals

➤ Help in finding the right personnel

➤ Part-time labor on an occasional basis

➤ Proven advertisements that they can run in their local paper

➤ Sales scripts that work

➤ Internet knowledge

➤ Part-time use of someone else's shipping facility, kitchens, manufacturing plant, spare office or conference room, frequent flyer miles, and so on.

Of course, those are the types of things that *other business owners* need. But what do *consumers* want that you can find among your overlooked assets? They want

➤ **Someone else to manage things for them.** Can you assign service personnel to manage home projects for consumers in the morning or on weekdays when business is slow? Can you add a bridal registry or gift registry to your business? Can you access your supplier list to see if other businesses could provide other types of services that you don't provide? Can you turn an empty corner of your facility into a total makeover center that you rent to an outside company to use on weekends organizing people's finances, wardrobes, personal appearance, or career?

➤ **A better lifestyle for less money.** Can you discount your inventory overstocks, discount your services during slow times, or discount customers' annual subscriptions if they pay in full?

➤ **More free time, family time, and fun time.** Can you turn a portion of your facility into a classroom and sell unique leisure programs? Can you assign some of your employees to provide services for family groups? Can you take your current product line and package it with other components or services to produce hobby kits?

➤ **A fulfilling career.** Do some of your customers wish they could do what you do? If so, you can package your own expertise and help these customers start their own business using your business model.

Turning Your Overlooked Assets into Instant Income

Like selling any other product or service, turning your overlooked assets into cash requires packaging these assets in a way that makes them appealing and valuable to the consumer or to another business owner.

Remember that ideas don't sell very well. Saying, "We have this asset available" is never as compelling as detailing the benefits, giving examples of how the asset might be used, telling the story of why you're offering it, and other such actions.

➤ **Approach the ideal buyer.** Remember the first rule of good marketing? *Sell the right item to the right buyer.* Well, selling overlooked assets is no different. Once you have identified your list of overlooked assets, make a chart with a space next to each asset so that you can jot down who might pay money for that asset. For every asset you have, there is someone who desperately needs that asset *now*. Find that buyer and your job of creating Instant Income from overlooked assets will be a lot easier.

➤ **Package the asset for maximum revenue.** Show how valuable the asset will be to another business owner or consumer by treating it like any other product or service and writing about the benefits of buying it. Give it a name, develop a brochure for it (if necessary), develop a sales script for it, and so on.

➤ **Make specific offers.** Determine a price for your overlooked-asset package, then promote that package—and nothing else—in whatever marketing device you use. Offer it on a limited-time basis or a limited-availability basis. Or use one of the other proven offer types: discounted price, free bonus, "don't let competitors respond first," or free consultation.*

➤ **Offer it to your existing customers first.** Whether you sell to businesses or to consumers, people appreciate advance notice of unique sales or opportunities. In fact, you may sell out your overlooked asset just by alerting your current customers that it's available.

➤ **Use the Instant Income strategies to alert other likely buyers.** Before you invest too heavily in expensive marketing campaigns to the outside market, prove to yourself that the asset is salable by using some of the lower-cost Instant Income strategies to tell business owners and consumers that your overlooked asset is for sale:

Press releases	Internet affiliates
Teleseminars	Nontraditional salespeople
Viral reports	Outbound telemarketing
E-mails	Referrals from customers
Upselling	Endorsed offers by joint-venture partners
Online articles	Placing literature in targeted locations
Workshops	

---

* You can read more about how to communicate different types of offers in Sales Strategy 3, "Make Specific Product and Service Offers."

Liquidate Inventory Overstocks

We treat our obsolete inventory as a significant profit center for our business. By developing an entire liquidation strategy for older goods and obsolete designs, we instantly generate hundreds of thousands of dollars in additional revenue and recruit new accounts for our other products.

JEFF AUBERY
Owner of Golf Sales West,
Oxnard, CA

If you have slow-moving or obsolete inventory that's costing you money to finance and warehouse, you can generate Instant Income—and save money in the long run—by offering it to distributors and customers at a special liquidation price.

Jeff Aubery, a longtime client and one of the largest golf bag manufacturers in the country, not only liquidates existing inventory but actually *manufactures* additional units of older, "obsolete" designs specifically to sell at closeout prices. If a golf bag design is at the end of its two-year life cycle, he'll lower the price and manufacture an additional 5,000 to 10,000 of these obsolete bags—making tens of thousands of dollars extra, even when selling them at the lower profit margin. He not only treats his closeouts as a significant profit center in his business but also views them as an opportunity to create more sales to key accounts, as perfect starter products for smaller accounts, and as the best leverage of previously popular designs that are still serviceable but that are simply at the end of their one- to two-year popularity.

Manufactured closeouts, by the way, are only part of Jeff's total liquidation strategy. Another aspect is what Jeff calls "level pricing." He'll set one low wholesale price—say $49—on four or five different golf bags that previously sold for prices from $49 to $79—as long as retailers agree to sell them at the high retail price that Jeff dictates. Not only does Jeff liquidate his distressed goods this way, but he proves to retailers that his bags will sell at a high retail price—which, in turn, allows him to achieve many new customers for next season.

Finding Buyers for Obsolete Product

While ultimately there will be countless outlets for your obsolete product and overstocks, three of the most logical—and most immediate—potential buyers are your own customers, your competitors, and unrelated businesses whose customers would be perfect prospects for you.

➤ **Customers**. If you sell direct to consumers or end users and you can identify those people who have already purchased this product in the past, you can then use any of the compelling offers in the next section to sell your overstocked item to your remaining customers. Of course, if your customers are resellers, distributors, or other businesses that routinely buy for you, every one of them is a prime prospect for buying your closeouts.

➤ **Competitors**. Often your competitors will need certain kinds of products that they simply don't want to stock or manufacture themselves. If you have overstocks that fit their parameters, and that are also free of logos, labels, and other identifying information (including owner's manuals), you can often negotiate to sell your competitor the entire inventory at one time. Perhaps your competitor's company needs inventory to offer as a "special buy." Maybe it's looking for inexpensive merchandise to give away as a bonus with purchase. Or perhaps it simply needs a less expensive, value-priced item that will help it recruit new accounts. Whatever the motivation, a call to your competitor is worth your time—particularly if you can suggest possible sales offers or uses for your inventory.

➤ **Unrelated businesses**—In Chapter 2, "Getting Other People to Help Bring In the Cash," I recommended unrelated businesses as potential joint-venture partners, especially when their customers have the right *psychographic profile* to buy your product or service. Selling inventory overstocks to unrelated companies is no different.

Offers That Work for Selling Obsolete Product

Whether you decide to sell your inventory to your own customers or you liquidate it to someone else to sell to theirs, you'll need to keep in mind that certain kinds of offers work best for overstocks.

In general, buyers expect obsolete inventory and overstocks to be sold at a price that's well below full retail. But here's a technique for getting a reasonable price per unit, whether you're selling your overstock to consumers or to other companies: *charge an unusual price*. A price of $41.83, for instance, would actually be perceived as more of a bargain than $40.00 or even $39.99—because $41.83 looks like you took a pencil, did the math, and calculated the rock-bottom price that you need to get for each unit of the inventory. It may even look like you're selling it for hard cost only (making no profit whatsoever), even though your profit may be considerable.

➤ **"Reason Why"** sales. When you explain why the inventory has become obsolete or tell people why you're experiencing an overstock on this item, not only will you have a much more believable rationale for dropping the price but your customers will be more likely to buy in droves. Be truthful, even humorous, in describing your plight as the reason for why you must move the inventory immediately at a much-reduced price.

➤ **Bonuses**. An ideal use of obsolete (but still usable) inventory is to create a special offer that includes the item as a bonus with purchase. If the item sold well in the past, earned industry awards, or otherwise had a great run, talk about that track record in your sales copy, along with the item's benefits. Don't mention that the inventory is obsolete or languishing in your warehouse as the rationale for using it as a bonus. Instead, enthusiastically explain the tremendous value you're offering by combining the item with whatever else you are selling.

➤ **Twofers**. To clear out a substantial amount of inventory, why not make a two-for-one offer to those customers or accounts that have regularly bought this item in the past? In fact, you can create a special offer just for them—then tell them that it's exclusively for them in your letter, postcard, or e-mail. They'll appreciate you thinking of them first and may respond so enthusiastically that they become the only customer group you need to promote to.

➤ **Upsells**. If your obsolete or overstocked item is a natural add-on to current inventory that you sell, create a special offer, then train your sales staff or store clerks to upsell that item aggressively.*

➤ **Samples**. If you're a manufacturer and you have qualified prospects who need to see samples of your work, consider sending the obsolete item if it represents you well. Similarly, if you assemble literature packages containing small sample items, utilize the overstocks. Be sure that

* See Customer Strategy 2, "Upsell Customers at the Point of Purchase," for details.

any prospects to whom you send the package are truly qualified to make an immediate purchase upon receiving it.

➤ **Spiff* programs**—If you sell to retailers, resellers, VARs, or other dealers and distributors, you can develop a *spiff program* that pays your accounts an extra incentive or a portion of the inventory's wholesale price when they aggressively sell your inventory instead of other products that they might promote that week. Don't think of a spiff as cutting into your profit margin but rather as a way to recoup something from your deteriorating inventory.

You can also develop spiff programs for your own sales and order-desk personnel, offering an incentive that is perceived as having a high value—such as travel, gifts, and other items—but actually costs you very little. You'd be surprised how many employees respond to noncash compensation if it's appealing enough.

Provide Marketing, Sales, and Point-of-Purchase Materials

If you plan to sell any obsolete inventory or overstocks to outside companies, it's in your best interest to help with the marketing—even if you're considering selling the merchandise to a competitor. You'll probably sell the inventory for a higher price, or sell the inventory in its entirety rather than selling small quantities, if you can provide sales copy for the product, old promotional campaigns that worked, and other marketing ideas to help move the inventory.

At the very least, you should readily provide technical specifications, product usage information, and other key data that anyone would need in order to sell the merchandise effectively.

When you do the thinking for your buyer, you'll move the inventory that much faster.

---

* A dictionary of slang from the year 1859 defined a *spiff* as the "percentage allowed by drapers (cloth or dry goods merchants) to their young men when they effect sale of old fashioned or undesirable stock." Occasionally, the manufacturer rather than the employer pays this bonus directly to the salesperson.

Sell Excess Service Capacity

For past consulting clients who have completed their contracts with me, I offer a $750-per-month service where they can get one half-hour telephone consultation with me each month any time I have a cancellation. It's been a great way to monetize my excess consulting capacity and still profit from inevitable scheduling changes.

RICHARD SCHEFREN
StrategicProfits.com

Many small businesses—especially food establishments, personal service providers, and retailers—seem to have a slow day of the week or a slow evening. Many service companies have a difficult time booking house calls on weekday mornings and during the entire months of August and December.

If you experience "slow times" or have excess service capacity, you're perfectly positioned to turn these unique circumstances into Instant Income opportunities.

Motivate Your Customers to Buy from You When Times Are Slow

If your customers must be at home in order for you to make a house call and provide your service, why not offer a reduced rate to those who are willing to book their appointments early on weekdays? If you generally would not be booking appointments in the morning, but you *would* be paying your service staff to sit around waiting for the phone to ring, you can at least recover the cost of paying your staff for those times.

Discounting your excess service capacity or tempting customers with an additional bonus is also a great way to reactivate past customers who haven't done business with you in a long time. Telephone these customers and offer to clean an extra room free or detail a second car at half price or upgrade their cabinet and drawer pulls when they book repairs, cleanings, and installations during these slow times.

Make sure that the customer knows *why* you are offering this special deal and that when your schedule is fully booked, the special offer will expire.

Charge More for "Prime Time" Service

Depending on how well you market these slow times, you can actually *raise* your rates for "prime time," when your service people would be fully booked anyway, then keep rates at normal levels if the customer allows you to choose when your service people will arrive. Sometimes, it's as simple as asking customers whether they have flexible schedules (as many seniors and stay-at-home parents do) and can choose another time.

Unique Ways to Sell Excess Service Capacity

With a little creativity, you can turn downtime at your restaurant, day spa, hair salon, or other service business into an Instant Income opportunity.

For example, if you own a restaurant, you can generate business on slow nights by offering specially priced menus, live entertainment, or other incentives on those evenings. If that doesn't increase regular foot traffic, go back to your customer database and invite your best customers using two-for-one specials, entrée-plus-free-dessert, and so on. When things are slow, they'll enjoy excellent service, and you'll enjoy repeat patronage.

Alternatively, your restaurant could offer lower prices for large parties, meeting groups, and catering services. Start cooking classes. Offer wine tastings. Or, like one restaurant I know of, turn your dining room over to a local doctor or other professional who holds introductory luncheons or dinners for potential plastic surgery patients, high-net-worth investors, and other such groups. This is a great way for the practitioner to present his work in a leisurely setting, plus you make money by charging the doctor or advisor a per-plate amount for food, beverage, and service.

Other Ways to Use Excess Capacity

➤ If you have available floor space in your retail or industrial location, consider renting it out to another business or sole proprietor. A health-food store could rent space to a nutritionist, who in turn uses the foot traffic to give away a free analysis and consultation—selling the health-food store's products as part of her patient regimens.

➤ Consider opening a new business within your extra floor space. I know of one health club that turned over a portion of its square footage to a teen center for the summer. And many health clubs have offices for chiropractors, massage therapists, personal trainers, and other independent professionals on-site.

➤ The operations department of a medium-sized business could develop techniques for finishing its work quickly, then "rent out" the staff to other company departments that are behind.

➤ If you run a cleaning service for homeowners, why not develop a side business providing the same services to offices, job sites, filming locations, hazardous material spills, and other unique situations during downtime? The more you specialize, the more you can charge.

OVERLOOKED STRATEGY 3

Offer Credit Accounts a Short-Pay Option

I continually use the short-pay strategy to enlighten my customers regarding the creative use of credit. Offering the occasional short-pay option to select accounts makes the most of a company's sales potential, develops more loyal customers, minimizes bad debt and generates the most nimble cash flow possible.

CARL KENNEDY
Director, Home & Professional Products,
JL Audio

If your product or service has enough profit margin built into its price and you have customers who typically buy on credit, you can generate quick cash by offering your credit customers the option of paying less than the full balance due as a one-time incentive to pay off their outstanding balance immediately.

In the lending industry, these discounts are called *short payoffs* or *short pays*.

Similarly, if you offer any product or service on payments, you can start earning Instant Income—and locking in sales—by offering a full-pay option whenever you make a sale.

Approaching Customers with a Short-Pay Offer

While you would never want to reduce a customer's credit balance on a regular basis, you can offer a short-pay option to specific customers or specific categories of customers who purchased under certain circumstances. For example, if you have 100 customers who purchased a $2,000 item and still owe more than $1,000, you can offer them a 25 percent discount if they pay off the full balance due within 14 days.

Similarly, if you sell a product or service on a 12-month payment plan, you can contact customers during their fourth or fifth month to offer them a discount of 15 to 20 percent if they will make all their remaining payments by a certain date.

To make the most of this strategy, send letters or make phone calls to credit accounts with the "good news" that you are offering them a one-time discount if they will pay their full balance due within two weeks. If you've contacted them by phone, begin a consultative sales process by asking if that would be an offer that appeals to them. You can then ascertain if they are able to pay—and when they can send a check.

Of course, trying to get full payment after the fact is never as good as getting the money up front.

Always Offer a Full-Pay Option in the Future

While it continually surprises me, many customers will pay in full if that option is offered to them—especially if that option comes with some incentive for choosing to pay in full. Some people just like to pay cash for purchases and not have to worry about keeping track of monthly payments. Many people know that they have the cash now but aren't certain that they will in the future. Still others will pay in full if there is a bonus for doing so.

Whatever you sell, you should always reward these folks—and create more cash for yourself—by offering a full-pay option whenever you sell products and services that you would otherwise finance. What kinds of incentives can you use to encourage customers to pay in full?

- ➤ Bonus items that can be used with the original product or service that they purchased

- ➤ Discounts on future purchases

- ➤ Preferential treatment, such as access to special services, advance sales days, or other benefits

- ➤ A free service, delivered when your service people are sitting idle and not delivering services to full-paying customers

OVERLOOKED STRATEGY 4

Turn Your Top Employees into Expensive Experts

We combined our marketing expertise in the health and wellness field with additional industry research to publish the Ohio Health & Wellness Research Report. *We now sell that report—detailing the buying habits of consumers pursuing healthy and sustainable lifestyles—for $6,500 to businesses that want to market to this lucrative, untapped market. Most report buyers instantly become new clients.*

COLETTE CHANDLER
President, The Marketing Insider Inc.

Expert employees are the most valuable overlooked asset of any small business. They not only have unique expertise but are highly marketable, too. They've lived through your corporate history, learned new ways of doing things, and developed systems that work. Perhaps you've even invested in their education or turned over large areas of responsibility to them.

With very little effort, you can package their expertise in dozens of different ways, then sell it, trade it, rent it, loan it, or use it as a bonus to create Instant Income.

Employee Knowledge That Can Be Turned into Cash

Your employees know things. They know people, processes, procedures, and other particulars that could help grow a business, improve an individual system, or simply bring in more money.

That knowledge is worth cash—lots of it.

In fact, certain kinds of knowledge—especially knowledge that's needed by your customers and peers—can be turned into consulting revenue, project management revenue, more lucrative service contracts, and so on.

The most commonly marketed types of employee knowledge include the following.

Implementation and Installation Services

Without a doubt, the number one problem that most customers have is implementing, installing, using, or integrating the products, services, or advice you sell them. If you're a consultant, for example, your client companies are looking for a result, not just information and advice. If you have employees who are experienced at implementing the strategies you recommend and you aren't currently selling implementation services, start selling them immediately, even if it means sending your staff to the client's location for a period of time.

Most advertising agencies, public relations firms, and marketing firms, for example, have an entire team of employees who implement promotional campaigns using outside services. And here's a bonus: these agencies typically mark up the cost of the outside service by at least 15 percent as their fee for implementing the campaign.

You could learn a lesson here. If your clients are asking for help in executing the creative ideas or advice you give them, you could easily make one of your staff members an account manager to handle the implementation of the plan by outside parties.

Similarly, if you sell small electronics, equipment, parts, or machinery, for example, but you don't yet offer the services of someone to install these items, find one of your employees who can install them. Or negotiate a joint venture with an outside installer that you can refer business to for a percentage of the installation revenue.

Superior Technical Knowledge and Problem Solving

Companies both large and small are securing large contracts and creating additional revenues by bundling in the expertise of their top technical and scientific employees. *Fast Company* magazine recently reported on a sales strategy at IBM where nearly 3,000 researchers, including 2,000 Ph.D.s and 6 Nobel laureates, are paired with sales and marketing people in IBM's consulting services division to offer something that the competition doesn't: focused problem solving and access to future technology before the competition hears about it.*

Sales Strategies and Dialogues

Sales training is one of the most frequently purchased types of training in America. Every sales organization wants to increase its close rate and boost

---

* You can read more about this latest trend in the *Fast Company* article, "Brains for Sale," www.fastcompany.com/magazine/78/brains.html.

its average amount per sale. If your employees have this knowledge (and you can hone it into scripts, prospecting techniques, and closing techniques), you could "hire out" your staff to companies outside your geographic market area.

Artistic Expertise and Training

I once worked with a client in the faux finishing (elegant paint finishes) industry who started a school, a seminar business, and a national industry conference "selling" his employees' expertise and his own unique finishing techniques to other artists who wanted to upgrade their skills and build a more lucrative business.

New Business Development

Do your employees know how to find new business opportunities, negotiate deals, and otherwise create more money? If so, you can easily sell this type of expertise to novice entrepreneurs or start-ups by packaging new business development training into a coaching program, consulting contract, or call-in advisory service.

Sourcing

If your employees are masters at finding raw materials, locating unique services, securing international manufacturing, or uncovering other resources, you're sitting on a gold mine of expertise with a potential side business in referrals, where you get paid a percentage of all the business you direct to those resources. One of the more interesting businesses I've ever encountered was a man who sent a weekly fax offering closeouts from major manufacturers—including entire fleets of cars, container loads of soft goods, and other such items. Today, a business like that could easily be conducted via e-mail, with a Web site that described each lot of equipment and noted the price.

Industry Research and Market Intelligence

Perhaps your employees have researched a new market for your product or sifted through dozens of consumer groups to gain market intelligence that led you to substantially expand your business. If so, that research and knowledge is potentially worth hundreds of thousands of dollars in side revenue for you from other noncompetitive companies that can use it to build their business, too.

Don't Write It Off by Saying "Everybody Knows That"

What you may consider "everyday information" includes valuable business secrets, proprietary formulas, and hard-to-find expertise that can be turned into expensive knowledge products such as "how-to" courses, seminars, recorded products, and other such offerings.

If you think that what you know is not worth paying for, or that your industry doesn't have room for this type of thing, rest assured that it wouldn't be the first time I had heard that.*

In fact, high-priced, well-packaged knowledge products, training, and seminars are a typical "next step" for businesses that are already leaders in their niche but are also beginning to "max out" with the work they do, the services they provide, or the products they sell every day. It's also a logical next step for any business that can assemble a group of employees who—even though they're not household names—are marketable as experts because they have biographies and personal track records that lend credibility.

How to Package Employee Knowledge

In Part Three, "Going into Business with the Boss," I'll discuss in detail how employees can become "internal entrepreneurs" or *intrapreneurs*, not only benefiting personally from developing new side businesses *for you* but growing serious cash flow for you at the same time.

But before I discuss that lucrative business model, take a look at the most lucrative ways to package and sell your employees' knowledge or expertise:

➤ **Multimedia programs.** With digital camcorders available for under $500, you or a local video crew can inexpensively produce 30-minute "how-to" DVDs showing your employee teaching a specific process or procedure to other business owners or consumers. Combine these DVDs with a manual, a workbook, audio CDs, and other information that can be priced at $195 or more per kit.

➤ **Coaching, mentoring, and apprenticeship programs.** Some of the most lucrative knowledge products ever, these programs include regu-

---

* As the product developer and marketer behind many celebrity authors over the years, I've compiled all *my* knowledge into a course called How Experts Build Empires. You can read more about it at www.howexpertsbuildempires.com/empireplan.html.

lar phone calls, group teleseminars, resource materials, and more—priced at thousands of dollars per person. See the next strategy, "Sell Apprenticeships That Teach Your Business Model," for details.

➤ **Keynote speaking and breakout sessions.** Employees with specific knowledge and a flair for speaking can represent your company at industry conferences and other public forums, garnering new client prospects as a result, or even selling knowledge products at the back of the seminar room.

➤ **Prospecting seminars.** Turn your top salespeople into prospecting machines by sponsoring evening workshops open to the public. See Prospecting Strategy 1, "Conduct Preview Workshops and Start Speaking," for details.

➤ **Corporate training and train-the-trainer programs.** If your consulting firm specializes in labor relations, quality control, efficiency, or other subjects that benefit entire divisions of a client's business, you should immediately add on-site training to your consulting contracts. Your employees can even conduct a train-the-trainer program to teach your clients' human resources or technical personnel to lead this training in your absence. The long-term benefit of train-the-trainer programs is that, even though you are not on-site any longer, your client companies must continue purchasing your workbook, DVDs, and other materials for any new employees they train.

➤ **Subscription consulting.** Priced at $500 to $2,000 *per month* per person, subscription consulting programs turn your employees into a unique team of hired guns who provide monthly teleclasses, resource packages, industry updates, marketing and sales advice, and other such information on an ongoing basis.

➤ **Licensing.** If your employees have developed processes, product designs, artwork, or other types of intellectual property, check with your attorney to see if you can license these ideas, designs, and images to manufacturers, marketers, and other business owners for various uses.

Sell Apprenticeships That Teach Your Business Model

Janet Switzer was the ace up my sleeve when I realized I wanted to create a high-priced apprentice program. With her help and unique insights, I went on to rake in $173,000 in less than two weeks and oversell my program. Not bad for one idea.

YANIK SILVER
Creator of www.InstantSalesLetters.com

If you have broad working knowledge of your specific industry and can help novices learn the ropes while saving them time and money in starting or building their own business, you can earn hundreds of thousands of dollars by launching an apprenticeship program that is structured to bring about a specific result over a fixed period of time.

The apprenticeship concept is based on historical tradition. Two hundred years ago, a family would pay to "apprentice" a young son to the local blacksmith, carpenter, or other tradesman, who would teach the young boy everything he needed to know about that trade. It was not schoolroom-based; it was totally hands-on. The boy worked in the smithy or carpenter's shop, doing small tasks for the tradesman. Then slowly, over time, the boy would begin to do some of the actual work, and finally, he would be able to produce the end product for a customer.

Today, apprenticeship programs provide hands-on training for anyone who wants to immerse herself in a business, learn it, and move on to create that same kind of business for herself in a geographic market that is not competitive with yours.

Luckily, with modern technology, your apprentices don't even have to live in your own hometown.

Internet marketing expert Yanik Silver offered a $14,500 apprenticeship program in which apprentices chose one of Yanik's many ideas for businesses that he knew would succeed on the Internet but he didn't have time to launch himself. Over a year's time, Yanik worked directly with each apprentice to build an e-commerce business—from launching the Web site to securing the affiliate relationships to acquiring the products and making a profit.

At the end of the program, the apprentices took ownership of the businesses they had built with Yanik—and along the way they learned every detail of launching and operating a thriving Internet business. The program was so unique that it literally oversold by 68 percent in the first two weeks Yanik offered it, even though it was one of the most expensive programs in the Internet field.*

What You'll Deliver to Your Apprentices

Apprenticeship programs are priced in the thousands of dollars per person and are typically sold to novice business owners or individuals who want to receive an income from a certain business activity. As the "mentor," you'll want to deliver quality reference materials, one-on-one time with you over the phone, e-mail correspondence privileges, possibly live workshops, and usually group training forums that deliver general knowledge that everyone in the apprenticeship program needs to know.

Developing These Materials Quickly

Think through what you would need to do or have in order to build your business if it you had to start it all over again from scratch. Would you need front office forms, advertising campaigns, employee training systems, information on how to provide services, your vendor list, and other knowledge? Compile that knowledge into a manual, guide, recorded audio CD, or some other easy-to-access format that can help a novice replicate your proven systems.

Provide this information through a fixed curriculum as the program progresses—deliver an initial package, then periodic audio CDs, videos, printed manuals, monthly teleconference calls, sample advertising packages, strategy packages, access to your network of experts, and other bells and whistles. This way, you can produce the materials as you go along.

Marketing Your Program

There are several ways to market apprenticeship programs, all of which can be easily planned with a little brainstorming.

---

* Yanik Silver now sells a home-study version of his program. For details, visit the Instant Income Resources Page at www.instantincome.com/resources.html.

E-zine and E-mail Advertising

Seek out list owners or e-zines whose subscribers would be perfect prospects to purchase your apprenticeship program. Six months in advance of the start date, give the list owners and e-zine publishers prewritten articles and e-mails to send.* Direct those who respond to these e-mails to your Web site for more information, and be sure to put together a shopping cart page so that people can register online.

Direct Mail

Direct mail is still the most effective tool for marketing high-priced apprenticeship programs. And whether you use direct mail to generate leads to whom you later send an elaborate package, or whether you use the direct-mail piece itself to close the sale, you can put lots more information about your program's content and benefit in a written direct-mail letter than you can in an e-mail or even on a Web page.

Display Advertisements in Magazines

Running ads in magazines is an ideal lead-generating strategy because just one registration will often more than cover the cost of the ad. However, be aware that most magazines also reach thousands of people who will never be good prospects for you. It's best to run only in magazines that you're certain are read by qualified prospects. Trade magazines are ideal for this. General consumer publications are not.

Preview Teleseminars

Teleseminars are a favored strategy simply because they are so effective. Today, teleseminars are used to sell all kinds of programs, but they are especially effective in selling business how-to and apprenticeship programs because they can be targeted to prospects in specific industries.†

To get people on the call, use an e-mail or a postcard with enticing copy about what they can expect to learn from you. But make the teleseminar a real

---

* See Chapter 3, "Writing Ads That Make the Phone Ring," for details on how to craft e-mails that compel readers to register for your program.

† See Joint-Venture Strategy 4, "Conduct a Teleseminar with Your Joint-Venture Partner," for details on how to execute this strategy successfully.

learning experience, not just a big infomercial for your program. Additionally, be sure to record the call so that you can post it on your Web site. You can also create an audio CD of the call to send to people who did not "attend" the call itself.

Commissioned Salespeople and Outbound Telemarketing

If you've used the strategies just discussed to generate leads for your program, don't stop there. Close these prospects into your program using telemarketing follow-up by commissioned sales reps. Look around your sphere of influence. You can often find people who would make ideal salespeople—and who would work on commission only. Maybe they are stay-at-home parents, people in transition, retirees looking for something to do, or other types of people who would enjoy convincing others to join your program. Pay these reps commissions of 10 to 25 percent. The higher your program price, the lower the percentage.

Free Special Reports and Other Info Sales Devices

Once you've written your Web site copy or printed your brochure, be sure to turn the copy into a special report, white paper, or similar info sales device that has higher perceived value than a simple brochure. You can distribute these special reports in person, at trade shows, through the mail, or as a "bonus" included with another party's newsletter or other periodical.

Press Relations

If you're operating an apprenticeship program in a specific industry, you can often get written up in the "What's New" section of your industry's magazine or newsletter. Craft a well-written press release, mail it to the editor, then follow up by phone to provide any additional information the editor needs prior to publication. You may even land a feature article, particularly if you are offering a type of training that no one else is offering.

PART TWO

Instant Income
Overnight Audit

CHAPTER 8

Identifying the Hidden Income Opportunities in Your Small Business

NOW THAT YOU'VE LEARNED the seven major areas where Instant Income can be found in a small business, and also the strategies that can help turn these sources into cash, it's time to uncover the hidden income opportunities that are sitting in *your own business* right now. It's time to find the customers who will spend more money with you, the sales leads that need to be converted, the newspaper ad that could be repurposed, and the inventory overstocks that are ready to be liquidated.

But it's also time for you to create a plan for bringing the resulting income into your bank account. The *Instant Income Overnight Audit* is designed to do just that.

Page by page, it actually constructs a precise road map of the specific profit centers you'll concentrate on and the specific strategies you'll be implementing. By the time you've completed the Audit, you'll have a definitive list—in priority order—of the Instant Income activities you should be pursuing in your business.

You'll know which strategies to execute first, and you'll know which will be the most profitable for you.

The Audit is that effective.

And if you're currently employed by someone else? Then the next few hours will be the best investment you'll ever make in your own future. Because, once you determine these hidden income opportunities in your employer's business, you can easily present your written findings and negotiate an arrangement to be paid extra for working to bring in this newfound cash flow for the business—an opportunity that we'll talk more about in Part Three.

For now, start completing the Audit by simply answering the questions it asks. Quality thinking time is required; assign yourself some quiet space to do this.

If you prefer to type your answers and then have our online audit tool calculate your potential revenue and prioritize the list of profit centers for you, log on to our secure Web site at www.InstantIncome.com/audit.html. Use the passcode "iibookbuyer." No one but you and the Instant Income team will ever see your results (and only then when you specifically choose to do so).*

Completing the Audit Questions

Since we know from experience that the greatest amount of Instant Income can be made from existing customers, the Audit starts with this group. In fact, the first question asks you how you'll upsell existing customers at their time of purchase so that they buy a larger amount.

Let's take a look:

UPSELL OFFERS AT THE TIME OF PURCHASE: What else can you sell a customer or client at the point of sale? What would that be worth in Instant Income?

If a Customer Is about to Purchase This . . .	You Could Sell Also Them This . . .	If Just 20% Purchased the Additional Item, How Much Money Would That Bring You?
Digital Camera	memory card	$ 25,276
Digital Camera	leather camera case	$ 3,528
Digital Camera	aluminum tripod	$ 8,103
	Total Instant Income from Upselling	$ 36,907

If you know from experience that, when customers visit your camera store to buy a digital camera, they often add an expensive memory card to

---

* The Instant Income formula doesn't end with this book. In fact, trained business coaches are ready to work with you and your company as you implement the Instant Income strategies. Visit www. instantincome.com/coaching.html for details.

their purchase, why not create a special script for your checkout employees to help them "pitch" every single customer on the benefits and value of the added memory card?

Let's say that 890 customers visit your camera store every month. If just 20 percent of them—178 people—purchased the memory card at a retail price of $142, jot down $25,276 as the amount of income you would instantly add to your monthly revenue by executing this strategy.

Of course, the Audit will also reveal to you the business strategies that you can't afford *not* to execute. In other words, if *not* upselling memory cards is losing you $25,276 every month, wouldn't you make sure that your sales clerks pitch the card to every customer possible?

Similarly, if you offer a service and—with the right words—can get just 20 percent of your customers to agree to a higher-priced package of services, how much would it be worth to you to instantly begin offering the upgraded package to every customer who contacts you?

You can even use each Audit question to develop different scenarios—say, offering a $16 leather camera case versus offering a $35 photo gift card—to help you calculate which upsell offer would earn you the most money. In this way, the Audit can actually help you determine the exact techniques you'll be implementing—including which products, services, add-ons, and bundles you'll offer.

Let's look at another example.

CREATE ENDORSED OFFERS: Who do you know who has customers and/or prospects that would be perfect prospects for buying your product or service? How much newfound money could you create by negotiating these joint ventures?

Who Has Customers/Prospects That Need to Receive a Compelling Offer about Your Product or Service?	How Many Names Do They Have?	What Offer Would You Make to Those Names?	If Just 10% Purchased, How Much New Money Would That Bring You?
Sally's Boutique	200	wardrobe rework	$ 7,000
			$
			$
			$
			$
		Total Instant Income from Endorsed Offers	$ 7,000

If you know of an upscale dress shop that occasionally refers customers to you for alterations, you might determine that a joint-venture promotion is appropriate. Well, what if the shop sent a warm, caring personal letter to all its customers, recommending a complete wardrobe retailoring for any customers who had recently lost weight or been ill?

If just 20 of the shop's 200 customers called you for tailoring services within days of receiving the letter, what would that mean to your bank account?

Of course, those are just two examples from the dozens of questions, strategies, and profit centers that you'll find in the Audit.

Don't worry if you don't have all the necessary information to complete the questions in the Audit. You can always estimate for now, then go back later and put in real numbers. You're also not required to complete every question. If you don't have any sales leads yet or never experience slow times in your service business, for example, leave that question blank.

Prioritizing Your Strategies

Once you've completed all the questions that apply to your business or employer, it's time to rank your results in order—starting with the most lucrative strategies first.

Let's say that you know of a joint-venture partner who would start selling your product or service tomorrow as a necessary add-on. If—according to your calculations—that activity would net your company more income than any other strategy in the Audit, rank that strategy as number one—the first strategy you'll execute on your way to making Instant Income.

If holding a special sale and liquidating several thousand widgets from your warehouse would produce the second biggest chunk of cash, rank that strategy as your number two priority.

And if you determined that 364 of your one-time customers would—with the right sales script or phone call—convert into ongoing monthly customers, earning you the third largest amount of Instant Income, list that strategy as number three on your list.

Do you see how the Audit results easily produce a complete ranked checklist of priorities to focus on?

Of course, some strategies will clearly take more effort than others. In other words, some income isn't as "instant" as it might be with another business activity that can be executed more quickly. In that case, the easier of the two strategies should rank higher on your list.

➤ Chapter 1: Your Existing Customers

1. TRACK CUSTOMER PURCHASES AND CALL TO TAKE REORDERS. If you have customers who purchase on a regular basis but who haven't called you in some time, how much income could you make by calling them and taking their reorder?

Number of Customers Who Buy Regularly	What Item or Service Do They Purchase?	Amount They Typically Spend When They Order	Average Reorder Amount Expected	If Just 20% of Them Reordered, How Much Money Would That Bring You?
_____	|_____	$_____	$_____	$_____
_____	|_____	$_____	$_____	$_____
_____	|_____	$_____	$_____	$_____
_____	|_____	$_____	$_____	$_____
		Total Instant Income from Taking Reorders		$_____

2. MAKE UPSELL OFFERS AT THE TIME OF PURCHASE. What else can you sell a customer at the point of sale? What would that be worth in Instant Income?

If a Customer Is About to Purchase This . . .	You Could Sell Also Them This . . .	If Just 20% Purchased the Additional Item, How Much Money Would That Bring You?
_____	|_____	$_____
_____	|_____	$_____
_____	|_____	$_____
_____	|_____	$_____
_____	|_____	$_____
	Total Instant Income from Upselling	$_____

3. SELL PRODUCTS AND SERVICES ON CONTINUITY. What products and services could you deliver on a continual basis? What would you charge for them every month? How many one-time buyers would purchase on continuity instead?

Products or Services You Could Sell on Continuity . . .	Amount You Would Charge Every Month for Product/Service	Number of Customers Who Would Purchase Continuity Program	Amount of Monthly Revenue Your Continuity Program Would Bring You
_____	$_____	_____	$_____
_____	$_____	_____	$_____
_____	$_____	_____	$_____
_____	$_____	_____	$_____
_____	$_____	_____	$_____
	Total Instant Income from Continuity Programs		$_____

4. RESELL CUSTOMERS PRIOR TO THEIR CONTRACT RENEWAL DATE. If you have customers who have long-term contracts with you for services or other deliveries, how much income could you make by proactively selling them on a renewal?

Number of Customers Who Have Contracts with You	What Item or Service Did They Purchase?	Average Renewal Amount Expected	If 80% of Them Renewed, How Much Money Would That Bring You?
_____	|_____	$_____	$_____
_____	|_____	$_____	$_____
_____	|_____	$_____	$_____
_____	|_____	$_____	$_____
		Total Instant Income from Contract Renewals	$_____

5. REACTIVATE PAST CUSTOMERS AND PATIENTS. How much money could you create by turning past customers and patients into buyers again? What kind of specific offer would you make to entice them into doing business with you again? If just 20 percent of them purchased, what would that mean in windfall cash flow for you?

If a Customer Has Purchased This Item in the Past . . .	How Many of Them Would Purchase Again?	What Item or Service Would You Offer in Order to Reactivate Them?	If Just 20% Purchased That Item or Service, How Much Money Would That Bring You?
_____	|_____	|_____	$_____
_____	|_____	|_____	$_____
_____	|_____	|_____	$_____
		Total Instant Income from Reactivating Customers	$_____

➤ Chapter 2: Your Joint-Venture Opportunities

1. CREATE ENDORSED OFFERS. Who do you know who has customers and/or prospects that would be perfect prospects for buying your product or service? What offers would you make? How much newfound money could you create by negotiating these joint ventures?

Who Has Customers/Prospects That Need to Receive a Compelling Offer about Your Product or Service?	How Many Names Do They Have?	What Offer Would You Make to Those Names?	If Just 10% Purchased, How Much New Money Would That Bring You?
_____	|_____	|_____	$_____
_____	|_____	|_____	$_____
_____	|_____	|_____	$_____
_____	|_____	|_____	$_____
		Total Instant Income from Endorsed Offers	$_____

2. CREATE A REFERRAL CIRCLE OR PROFESSIONAL CONSORTIUM. Who else is selling complementary professional services to clients, companies, and consumers who might be perfect clients for you? If they referred business to you or included you in their contracts, how much money per client would you earn? How much net profit would be left over after paying a referral fee?

Who Is Selling a Product or Service to Your Ideal Customer or Client and Could Refer Business to You?	What Could You Sell to These Clients?	How Much Would You Earn for Each Contract?	How Much Would Your Net Profit Be after Paying Any Referral Fee?*	How Many New Clients Would You Get?	Multiply Your Net Profits by the Number of New Clients You Expect. How Much Money Will You Earn?
_____	_____	$_____	$_____	_____	$_____
_____	_____	$_____	$_____	_____	$_____
_____	_____	$_____	$_____	_____	$_____
_____	_____	$_____	$_____	_____	$_____
_____	_____	$_____	$_____	_____	$_____

* If required. Total Instant Income from Creating a Referral Circle or Professional Consortium $_____

3. SELL OTHER PEOPLE'S PRODUCTS TO YOUR CUSTOMERS. What else do your customers need or what else would they buy that you do not offer now? Who *does* offer that item or service? How many customers would purchase the new item if you offered it? How much Instant Income would you create for your business if you joint-ventured with that other business owner and sold the outside item to your customers?

Who Is Selling a Product or Service That Your Customers Need or Want?	What Is the Product or Service?	How Much Money Would You Make on Each Sale?	How Many of Your Customers Would Purchase the Outside Item or Service?	If Just 10% of Your Customers Buy, How Much Money Would That Bring You?
_____	_____	$_____	_____	$_____
_____	_____	$_____	_____	$_____
_____	_____	$_____	_____	$_____
_____	_____	$_____	_____	$_____
_____	_____	$_____	_____	$_____

Total Instant Income from Selling Someone Else's Product or Service to Your Customers $_____

4. CONDUCT TELESEMINARS WITH YOUR JOINT-VENTURE PARTNER. If your joint-venture partners got hundreds of potential customers on the phone to listen to your expertise and advice, how would you make money from that effort? What would you talk about? What would you sell? How would you determine which customers to invite?

If just 20 percent of them purchased what you offer, what would that bring you in Instant Income?

Name of Joint-Venture Partner . . .	Which List Segment Would You Invite?	What Could You Sell Them While You Are on the Phone with Them?	If Just 20% of Listeners Purchased, How Much Money Would That Generate?	What Would Your Income Be After Splitting with Your Joint-Venture Partner?
_____	L_____	L_____	$_____	$_____
_____	L_____	L_____	$_____	$_____
_____	L_____	L_____	$_____	$_____
			Total Instant Income from Teleseminars	$_____

5. BECOME AN ADD-ON TO SOMEONE ELSE'S PRODUCT. Complete the following chart to determine who might sell your product or service as a logical add-on to what they are selling customers. What would you offer? How many of the other company's customers might purchase your add-on? If just 50 percent purchased it, how much money would you make?

Who Is Selling a Product or Service That Needs Your Add-On?	Which Add-On Will You Pitch to This Potential Joint-Venture Partner?	How Much Money Will You Make on Each Sale?	How Many of Your Joint-Venture Partner's Customers Might Purchase the Add-On?	If Just 50% Purchased the Add-On, How Much Money Would That Bring You?
_____	L_____	$_____	L_____	$_____
_____	L_____	$_____	L_____	$_____
_____	L_____	$_____	L_____	$_____
	Total Instant Income from Becoming an Add-On to Someone Else's Product or Service			$_____

➤ Chapter 3: Advertising Activities

1. ASK CUSTOMERS TO TELL THEIR STORY. Do you have customers you could interview and then write a compelling testimonial-style advertisement about? What product or service would the ad sell? How much would you make from each new customer the ad produces? Can you estimate how many new customers would result from running the ad?

These Customers Have a Compelling Story or Result to Write About . . .	The Advertisement Would Offer This Product or Service . . .	How Much Money Would You Earn on Each Sale?	How Many People Might Respond to the Testimonial Advertisement?	If You Closed 30% of Respondents into Buying Your Product, How Much Would That Bring You?
_____	L_____	$_____	L_____	$_____
_____	L_____	$_____	L_____	$_____
_____	L_____	$_____	L_____	$_____
	Total Instant Income from Running Testimonial Style Advertising			$_____

2. BROADCAST A COMPELLING PRESS RELEASE. What would each press release teach the reader? What product or service would you mention in the press release? If just 10 people who read your press release eventually purchased from you, what would that be worth in Instant Income?

What Would You Talk about in Each Press Release?	Which Product or Service Would You Mention?	How Much Money Would You Make on Each Sale of That Item?	If 10 People Bought as a Result of Seeing the Release, How Much Instant Income Would That Bring You?
_____	_____	$ _____	$ _____
_____	_____	$ _____	$ _____
_____	_____	$ _____	$ _____
_____	_____	$ _____	$ _____
_____	_____	$ _____	$ _____
_____	_____	$ _____	$ _____
_____	_____	$ _____	$ _____
		Total Instant Income from Broadcasting a Press Release	$ _____

3. BECOME AN INDUSTRY EXPERT AND GET ON THE RADIO. What topics would you discuss on the radio? What special entry-level offer would you feature at your Web site for listeners to purchase? If just 10 people who heard you on the radio eventually purchased your highest-priced product from you, what would that be worth in Instant Income?

What Topics Would You Talk about on the Radio?	Which Product or Service Would You Mention?	How Much Money Would You Make on Each Sale of That Item?	If 10 People Bought Your Highest-Priced Item, How Much Instant Income Would That Bring You?
_____	_____	$ _____	$ _____
_____	_____	$ _____	$ _____
_____	_____	$ _____	$ _____
_____	_____	$ _____	$ _____
_____	_____	$ _____	$ _____
_____	_____	$ _____	$ _____
_____	_____	$ _____	$ _____
		Total Instant Income from Doing Radio Guest Appearances	$ _____

4. BUY ADVERTISING SPACE ON REMNANT. If you negotiated even a 20 percent discount off the ad rates you are paying now by purchasing remnant space, how much money would that save you? If you negotiated a 50 percent discount by buying on remnant, how much would *that* save you?

Name of Publication, Ad Topic, and Typical Size Display Ad You Regularly Buy	What Is the Cost of That Ad Space?	If You Negotiated a 20% Discount, How Much Money Would You Save on the Ad?	If You Negotiated a 50% Discount, How Much Money Would You Save on the Ad?
_____	$_____	$_____	$_____
_____	$_____	$_____	$_____
_____	$_____	$_____	$_____
_____	$_____	$_____	$_____
_____	$_____	$_____	$_____
Total Instant Savings from Buying Ad Space on Remnant	$_____		$_____

5. HOLD A SPECIAL SALE USING THE "REASON WHY." What rationale can you use to advertise a special sale? What would you sell? How many customers do you estimate would buy the special offer? How much would that be worth?

What Rationale Can You Use to Hold a Special Sale?	What Item Would You Sell?	How Many Customers Would Buy That Item?	How Much New Money Would That Bring You?
_____	_____	_____	$_____
_____	_____	_____	$_____
_____	_____	_____	$_____
_____	_____	_____	$_____
_____	_____	_____	$_____
_____	_____	_____	$_____
	Total Instant Income from Special Sales Using the "Reason Why"		$_____

➤ Chapter 4: Generating Prospects

1. CONDUCT PREVIEW WORKSHOPS AND START SPEAKING. When can you schedule an evening workshop, class, or lecture about your product or service? When is the next industry conference you might speak at? What package of goods and services will you offer at these events? How many prospects might attend? If just 10 percent of them bought the featured item, how much money would that bring you?

What Would You Speak About at an Evening Workshop or Conference?	Which Product or Service Would You Offer?	How Much Money Would You Make on Each Sale of the Item Offered?	If 10% of Attendees Bought as a Result of Hearing You, How Much Instant Income Would That Bring You?
_____	_____	$_____	$_____
_____	_____	$_____	$_____

_____	|_____	$_____	$_____
_____	|_____	$_____	$_____
	Total Instant Income from Preview Workshops or Speaking Engagements		$_____

2. RUN A TWO-STEP CAMPAIGN. What free giveaway item, informational report, or qualification process can you offer or advertise that would cause prospects to contact you for further details or to qualify? What product or service would that giveaway item ultimately sell? What would you make on each sale of that item when a prospect converts to a buyer? If just 20 percent of prospects buy, how much income will that bring you?

What Free Giveaway or Qualification Can You Offer?	Will You Distribute the Offer via Ads? How?	How Many People Do You Estimate Will Respond to the Two-Step Campaign?	How Much Would You Earn from the Sale of Each Item Advertised?	If Just 20% of Respondents Buy After Contacting You, How Much Money Would That Bring You?
_____	|_____	|_____	$_____	$_____
_____	|_____	|_____	$_____	$_____
_____	|_____	|_____	$_____	$_____
_____	|_____	|_____	$_____	$_____
		Total Instant Income from Two-Step Campaigns		$_____

3. PLACE YOUR LITERATURE IN TARGETED LOCATIONS. Where can you place literature that offers a specific product or service package? How much foot traffic do they get there? How many prospects might call you? What would you make on each sale of the package offered? If just 20 percent of the resulting prospects purchased, how much money would that bring you?

Possible Locations for Placing Literature . . .	What Product or Service Bundle Would You Offer?	What Would You Earn from Each Sale of That Item?	How Many Prospects Might Result from Placing Your Literature in Key Locations?	If Just 20% of Prospects Purchased, How Much Money Would That Generate?
_____	|_____	$_____	|_____	$_____
_____	|_____	$_____	|_____	$_____
_____	|_____	$_____	|_____	$_____
_____	|_____	$_____	|_____	$_____
		Total Instant Income from Placing Literature in Targeted Locations		$_____

4. ASK CUSTOMERS AND VENDORS FOR REFERRALS. What specific product or service package can you ask your customers to recommend to their friends and family? What product or service can your vendors recommend to their contacts? How many prospects might result from such a referral effort? How much money would you make if just a small percentage of these prospects purchased from you?

What Product or Service Would You Ask Your Customers and Vendors to Tell Their Friends and Contacts About?	What Would You Earn from Each Sale of That Item?	How Many Referrals Might Result from This Referral Effort?	If Just 20% of Referred Prospects Purchased, How Much Money Would That Generate?
_____	$_____	⌊_____	$_____
_____	$_____	⌊_____	$_____
_____	$_____	⌊_____	$_____
_____	$_____	⌊_____	$_____
Total Instant Income from Asking Customers and Vendors to Refer			$_____

5 MAXIMIZE YOUR TIME AT TRADE SHOWS. Of the trade shows you might attend, how many buyers who might be ideally qualified to purchase from you does the show management estimate will attend this year? If just 2 percent responded to your preshow marketing campaign, how many prospects would stop by your booth? If just 5 percent of those prospects purchased, how much income would that bring you?

What Trade Shows Could You Attend This Year?	How Many Attendees *Qualified to Purchase from You* Do Show Organizers Estimate Will Attend?	If 2% of Those Qualified Attendees Visit Your Booth, How Many New Prospects Would That Bring You?	How Much Would You Earn from the Sale of Each Special Show Package?	If Just 5% of New Prospects Purchase After Visiting the Booth, How Much Money Would That Bring You?
_____	⌊_____	⌊_____	$_____	$_____
_____	⌊_____	⌊_____	$_____	$_____
		Total Instant Income from Trade Shows	$_____	

➤ Chapter 5: Improving Sales Activity

1. CONDUCT FOLLOW-UP TELEMARKETING. What products and services have prospects inquired about but not yet purchased? How many people have inquired about each product? What would you earn on the sale of each item if these people *did* purchase? How much money would you make if your sales team followed up by telephone and closed just 20 percent of those prospects?

What Product or Service Have Prospects Inquired About but Not Yet Purchased?	How Many Prospects Have Inquired About This Product/Service?	What Would You Earn from Each Sale of This Item?	If Your Salespeople Sold Just 20% of Prospects, How Much Money Would That Generate?
_____	⌊_____	$_____	$_____
_____	⌊_____	$_____	$_____

		$_____	$_____
_____	|_____	$_____	$_____
_____	|_____	$_____	$_____
_____	|_____	$_____	$_____
	Total Instant Income from Conducting Follow-Up Telemarketing		$_____

2. START BUNDLING PRODUCT AND SERVICES. Which products or services would you bundle together into a higher-priced package? How many customers who are purchasing now would buy the package instead? What would you charge for that bundle? If you multiply the number of anticipated sales by the price you plan to charge, you can calculate how much money you'll make from each bundled item.

What Products or Services Would You Bundle Together into a Package?	How Many Customers Would Purchase the Package Offer Instead?	What Would You Earn from the Sale of Each Package?	Multiply the Number of Estimated Sales by the Price per Package to See How Much You'll Earn
_____	|_____	$_____	$_____
_____	|_____	$_____	$_____
_____	|_____	$_____	$_____
_____	|_____	$_____	$_____
_____	|_____	$_____	$_____
	Total Instant Income from Bundling Products and Services		$_____

3. MAKE SPECIFIC PRODUCT AND SERVICE OFFERS. Rather than talking about "quality, service, and value" in your sales pitches, why not make specific product offers at a specific price—with bonuses and other add-ons included? Determine which products you'll feature and what the price will be. If just 10 percent of prospects purchase the specific offer, how much will you make?

What Specific Product or Service Offer Would You Make, and What Would You Include in the Package?	What Price Would You Put on the Offer?	How Many Prospects Might Buy the Specific Package/Price Offered?	If Just 10% of Prospects Purchased the Special Offer, How Much Money Would That Generate?
_____	$_____	|_____	$_____
_____	$_____	|_____	$_____
_____	$_____	|_____	$_____
_____	$_____	|_____	$_____
_____	$_____	|_____	$_____
_____	$_____	|_____	$_____
_____	$_____	|_____	$_____
_____	$_____	|_____	$_____
	Total Instant Income from Making Specific Product and Service Offers		$_____

4. CREATE A DOWNSELL POSITION. If your salespeople are having a difficult time closing prospects into buyers, you should develop a downsell position that offers the prospect a less expensive item or a payment plan in order to save the sale. What can you offer? How many prospects will buy? What will that be worth to you?

When Prospects Balk At Purchasing This . . .	Your Salespeople Could Offer This . . .	What Price Would You Charge for the Downsell Item?	If Just 10% of Prospects Buy the Downsell Item, How Much Money Would That Generate?
_____	|_____	$_____	$_____
_____	|_____	$_____	$_____
_____	|_____	$_____	$_____
_____	|_____	$_____	$_____
_____	|_____	$_____	$_____
		Total Instant Income from Downselling	$_____

5. CONTRACT WITH NONTRADITIONAL SALESPEOPLE. Who is already interacting in a sales capacity with people who would be perfect prospects for you? How would you compensate these salespeople for bringing in new customers? How many new sales might you capture if you recruited these salespeople to help you sell?

Who Is Already Interacting with Your Ideal Customer in a Sales Capacity?	How Many Sales Might You Capture from Their Effort?	How Much Would You Earn from Each Sale?	How Much Would Your Net Profit Be After Paying Their Commission?	Multiply Your Net Profits by the Number of New Clients You Expect. How Much Money Will You Earn?
_____	|_____	$_____	$_____	$_____
_____	|_____	$_____	$_____	$_____
_____	|_____	$_____	$_____	$_____
_____	|_____	$_____	$_____	$_____
_____	|_____	$_____	$_____	$_____
_____	|_____	$_____	$_____	$_____
_____	|_____	$_____	$_____	$_____
	Total Instant Income from Contracting with Nontraditional Salespeople			$_____

➤ Chapter 6: Making Instant Income on the Internet

1. LAUNCH A VIRAL REPORT AND SQUEEZE PAGE. What kind of special report can you produce to entice others to "pass it along"? What product or service would the report discuss? If 10,000 visitors clicked through to your Web site as a result, what would you try to sell them? If 3 percent of them* bought, what would that be worth to you?

* 3% of 10,000 visitors is 300 buyers.

What Topic Would You Talk About in a Special Report That Would Remain Timely and Newsworthy?	Which Product or Service Would Your Free Report Attempt to Promote or Sell?	How Much Money Would You Make on Each Sale of That Promoted Item?	If 300 People Bought as a Result of Seeing Your Report, How Much Instant Income Would That Bring You?
_____	|_____	$_____	$_____
_____	|_____	$_____	$_____
		Total Instant Income from Sending a Viral Report	$_____

2. RECRUIT AFFILIATES FOR A 24-HOUR CAMPAIGN. If you knew that dozens of Internet affiliates would be e-mailing their lists on your behalf during a single 24-hour period that is sure to drive massive online sales, what would you offer for sale? What would the price be? If one-half percent (0.5%) of e-mail addresses buy, how many sales would result? What would that be worth to you in Instant Income?

What Product Would You Offer during the 24-Hour Campaign?	What Price per Unit Would You Charge?	How Many E-mails Would You and Your Affiliates Send on That Day?	If 0.5% of E-mail Addresses Buy Your Offer to Get the Bonuses, How Much Income Would That Bring You?
_____	$_____	|_____	$_____
_____	$_____	|_____	$_____
		Total Instant Income from 24-Hour Campaigns	$_____

3. DRIVE BUYERS TO YOUR WEB SITE WITH ONLINE ARTICLES. What types of articles can you write that make a case for your product or service in a newsworthy way? What product or service would you mention in the press release? What free downloadable giveaway item can you feature in the resource box? If just 10 people who read your article eventually purchased from you, what would that be worth?

What Topic Would You Talk About in Each Article That Would Always Remain Timely and Newsworthy?	Which Product or Service Would Your Free Giveaway Attempt to Promote or Sell?	How Much Money Would You Make on Each Sale of That Promoted Item?	If 10 People Bought as a Result of Seeing Your Article, How Much Instant Income Would That Bring You?
_____	|_____	$_____	$_____
_____	|_____	$_____	$_____
_____	|_____	$_____	$_____
_____	|_____	$_____	$_____
		Total Instant Income from Writing Online Articles	$_____

4. BROADCAST INTERNET-ONLY OFFERS VIA E-MAIL. Whether you own a retail store, a consulting business, a service location, or some other type of business, what introductory offers can you make via e-mail in order to prompt customers to give you their e-mail address? What offers can you send later? Which customer segments would you send them to? If just 10 percent of customers purchased the offer, what would that be worth?

What Introductory Offer Would You Make in Order to Capture E-mail Addresses?	What Price per Unit Would You Charge?	How Many New Customers Do You Get per Month?	If 10% of New Customers Buy the Introductory Offer, How Much Instant Income Would That Bring You?
_____	$_____	|_____	$_____

Which Later Offers Would You Make to These E-mail Addresses?	What Price per Unit Would You Charge?	How Many Customers Are in Each List Segment You Intend to E-mail?	If 10% of Customers Buy the E-mailed Offer, How Much Instant Income Would That Bring You?
_____	$_____	|_____	$_____
_____	$_____	|_____	$_____
_____	$_____	|_____	$_____
		Total Instant Income from Broadcasting Offers Via Email	$_____

5. CONDUCT A 28-DAY PRODUCT LAUNCH. What product or service could you create excitement for during the 28 days leading up to its launch or rerelease? If just 1 percent of your customers* purchased it, what would that mean in Instant Income?

Product or Service Package You Would Launch or Rerelease . . .	Offers, Bonuses, and Take-Aways You Would Incorporate into the Launch . . .	Amount You Might Earn from Each Package Sold	If Just 1% of Customers Purchased the Package, How Much Money Would That Generate?
_____	|_____	$_____	$_____
_____	|_____	$_____	$_____
* Or your Internet affiliates' customers.	Total Instant Income from Conducting a 28-Day Product Launch		$_____

➤ Chapter 7: Sell Your Overlooked Assets

1. LIQUIDATE INVENTORY OVERSTOCKS. If you have obsolete inventory or slow-moving inventory, how much cash might you generate if you used the Instant Income strategies to create a special sale, bundled package, or other offer?

Obsolete or Slow-Selling Inventory Items Still in the Warehouse . . .	How Many Units of Each Item Are Available for Immediate Sale?	Amount You Might Earn from the Sale of Each Unit	Multiply the Number of Units of Inventory Left by the Dollar Amount per Unit You'll Charge
_____	|_____	$_____	$_____
_____	|_____	$_____	$_____

		$	$
_____	|_____	$_____	$_____
_____	|_____	$_____	$_____
_____	|_____	$_____	$_____
_____	|_____	$_____	$_____
_____	|_____	$_____	$_____
_____	|_____	$_____	$_____
_____	|_____	$_____	$_____
_____	|_____	$_____	$_____
_____	|_____	$_____	$_____
_____	|_____	$_____	$_____

Total Instant Income from Liquidating Inventory Overstocks $_____

2. SELL EXCESS SERVICE CAPACITY. Are your service personnel sitting idle during certain times rather than performing on-site service calls or delivering services at your facility? Could you create a special offer to prompt customers to book appointments for those times? Is there another way to monetize your service downtime?

Service Downtime Typically Occurs on These Days or during These Hours or during These Months . . .	What Special Offer Could You Make in Order to Book These Times?	Amount You Might Earn from Each Special Offer Sold	Multiply the Number of Bookings You Expect by the Amount You'll Charge per Booking
_____	|_____	$_____	$_____
_____	|_____	$_____	$_____
_____	|_____	$_____	$_____
_____	|_____	$_____	$_____
_____	|_____	$_____	$_____
_____	|_____	$_____	$_____
_____	|_____	$_____	$_____
_____	|_____	$_____	$_____
_____	|_____	$_____	$_____
_____	|_____	$_____	$_____
_____	|_____	$_____	$_____
_____	|_____	$_____	$_____
_____	|_____	$_____	$_____

Total Instant Income from Selling Excess Service Capacity $_____

3. OFFER CREDIT ACCOUNTS A SHORT-PAY OPTION. If you have customers who purchased on a payment plan, how much of a discount or "short pay" would you be willing to offer if they paid their balance due in 10 to 14 days? If just 30 percent of credit accounts acted on the offer, how much cash would flow into your bank account?

How Many Credit Accounts Do You Have (by Category) with Balances Due?	What Is the Average Balance Due on These Accounts?	Would You Accept as Payment on These Accounts 80% of the Balance Due? 70%? 60%?	What Would the Average Balance Be on These Accounts after the Discount?	Multiply the Number of Accounts Outstanding by the Average Balance Due after Discount
_____	$_____	|_____	$_____	$_____
_____	$_____	|_____	$_____	$_____
_____	$_____	|_____	$_____	$_____
_____	$_____	|_____	$_____	$_____

Total Instant Income from Offering Credit Accounts a Short-Pay Option $_____

4. TURN YOUR TOP EMPLOYEES INTO EXPENSIVE EXPERTS. Do your employees have expertise that you can sell or otherwise monetize? If so, jot down the type of expertise, how you would package it, what you might charge for it in the marketplace, and how many customers you believe would purchase that expertise.

Type of Expertise Your Employees Possess That Could Be Marketed or Monetized . . .	How Would You Package the Expertise? What Offers Would You Make?	Amount You Might Earn from Each Package Sold	Multiply the Number of Sales Expected by the Amount per Package to See What You'll Earn
_____	|_____	$_____	$_____
_____	|_____	$_____	$_____
_____	|_____	$_____	$_____
_____	|_____	$_____	$_____
_____	|_____	$_____	$_____
_____	|_____	$_____	$_____
_____	|_____	$_____	$_____

Total Instant Income from Selling Employee Expertise $_____

5. SELL APPRENTICESHIPS THAT TEACH YOUR BUSINESS MODEL. If you could package your business model for start-ups or others in your industry who lack the specialized training you have, what could you charge for that package? $5,000? Even $15,000? How many of these apprenticeships might you sell in your market?

Basic or Advanced Functions of Your Business That Could Be Marketed or Monetized . . .	How Would You Package the Apprenticeship? What Offers Would You Make?	Price You'll Charge for Each Apprenticeship Sold	Multiply the Number of Sales Expected by the Price per Apprenticeship to See What You'll Earn
_____	|_____	$_____	$_____
_____	|_____	$_____	$_____

Total Instant Income From Selling Apprenticeships $_____

PART THREE

Going into Business with the Boss

CHAPTER 9

Embracing Intrapreneurship

FOURTEEN YEARS AGO, I was a hard-working employee. Like 112 million other employees of small businesses in America, I collected a paycheck, got two weeks' vacation every year, and worked diligently to do a good job for my employer. I enjoyed the work I did every day. I felt that I was making a contribution to the company.

At the time, I never dreamed that I'd be an entrepreneur, doing what I'm doing today. I had been an employee all my life. But a year-long stint as an *intrapreneur* gave me the confidence, knowledge, and discipline I needed to eventually go out on my own.

In the midst of a major restructuring at the company where I worked, I was offered the "job" of a lifetime—an opportunity to market full-time the published works I had helped develop over the previous three years. I jumped at the chance to maximize what I saw as my employer's finest and most valuable asset—its intellectual properties. Having helped to develop these books, tapes, home-study courses, and training modules, I knew exactly what I could do with them, where I could sell them, whom I could joint-venture with, and how to enroll others in the process of expanding that area of the business.

I immediately saw the vision of what the publishing division could be like. And, of course, I had been trained over three busy years to execute some very powerful marketing and sales campaigns.

I quickly made a deal with my employer to work on commission, making a percentage of the revenue I brought in. I wrote a 28-page catalog, worked with our outside fulfillment and customer service center, recruited a national sales force of inbound telemarketers, and reorganized the existing publications and courses into 327 different product offerings.

Within just a few months, I had nearly doubled my previous salary. Plus, I had the independence—and the independent decision-making authority—to work on something I took pride in.

While I had never been an entrepreneur, I had become an *internal entrepreneur.*

I took a hidden opportunity in my employer's business and made extra money exploiting it. But more than that, I took on a challenging new role, learned skills that I never would have gained otherwise, and became a more confident, more marketable professional as a result. That's what the experience did for me.

And it's what *intrapreneurship* can do for you.

What Intrapreneurship Is—and Isn't

In my experience, most small business owners are thrilled when an employee approaches them and says, "I know how we can make more money around here. I'm willing to do the work. I want to help contribute to your bottom line." This enthusiasm is not surprising when you consider that your employer's responsibilities are great, and cash flow is a constant worry.

So when you offer to alleviate this worry—and generate additional cash for the business—not only will your proposal be met with appreciation but your employer will be much more open to rewarding you with extra pay for the expanded role you're offering to take on.

I like to think of intrapreneurship as "going into business with the boss." In truth, it's a joint venture where *you* create revenues in dozens of ways that your employer hasn't identified yet, then *your employer* shares the additional revenues you've created outside of your regular job duties. Additionally,

- ➤ You still keep your regular job (or get promoted into a better one).

- ➤ You utilize your employer's existing resources, product lines, customer list, industry contacts, inventory, and market posture.

- ➤ You have reasonable autonomy to execute the strategies you choose.

- ➤ You become a valued revenue producer rather than a tolerated revenue consumer.

Of course, the idea of intrapreneurship is not new. In fact, many large corporations pay their employees for ideas. But most small businesses have never heard of it. This is surprising when you consider that most small businesses are actually better able to initiate, manage, and benefit from these employer-employee relationships.

In case you're wondering, intrapreneurship is *not*

➤ **More work for the same pay.** "Thanks for the idea, Jim. Let me add that to your current job description."

➤ **The duties you were hired to perform in the first place.** "You're supposed to be doing that now, Miss Smith. It's good to see you'll finally be doing your job."

➤ **Part ownership in the company, unless that is the deal you negotiate.** "You mean you want equity in the business!?"

To prevent these reactions, take a look at the presentation strategies I give you in Chapter 11, "Planning Your Meeting with the Boss." If you are properly prepared, you should encounter little, if any, of this type of negative reaction to your proposal.

Finding Hidden Opportunity in Your Employer's Business

To begin your adventure as an internal entrepreneur, start looking for ways to instantly improve the revenues at your employer's business. While many employees recoil at the idea of working harder to make the boss more money, intrapreneurs welcome this opportunity, because they know that they'll get a bigger paycheck right along with the owner.

To find the extra money hiding in your workplace, read through the strategies in the first seven chapters of this book. Determine which ones your employer is failing to execute. Then complete the Instant Income Overnight Audit to identify those strategies that will generate the greatest revenue (and the most extra income for you). Those strategies should be pursued first.

In the seven major areas where Instant Income can be made in a small business, you'll be looking specifically for

➤ **Customers** who have purchased something once and now need to be sold more goods and services. Logical upsells that your salespeople aren't currently pitching. Repeat customers who could be offered a continuity program or monthly delivery. Customers whose contract is about to expire, and who could be sold a new one. Past customers or clients who could be reactivated.

➤ **Joint-venture opportunities** with others in your industry who could send you new customers immediately. Other professionals or referral sources that you can align with. Other products and services that you could offer to current customers or outside products for which yours could become an add-on.

➤ **Advertising** outlets that would be perfect for direct-response or testimonial-style advertising. Company activity that could be written about in a compelling press release. Advertising budgets that could be cut by negotiating remnant pricing.

➤ **Prospects** sitting in your database or unique groups within your industry who are not currently being targeted but who could be pursued and then converted into buyers via evening workshops, teleseminars, trade shows, two-step campaigns, and other such techniques.

➤ **Sales enhancement opportunities** that are not currently being used, such as bundling, downselling, and follow-up telemarketing. Nontraditional salespeople who could help generate Instant Income. Specific product offers that could improve sales.

➤ **Internet activity,** Web site programming, e-mail offers, and other Internet campaigns that are not currently being conducted but that could mean tens or hundreds of thousands in new monthly revenue streams for your employer.

➤ **Overlooked assets** that are sitting around waiting to be exploited, marketed, packaged, sold, or traded.

Ultimately, your goal is to (1) find strategies you can implement as an intrapreneur, then (2) present those strategies in a written plan to your employer via a closed-door meeting, (3) negotiate an arrangement to earn extra pay for implementing those strategies, and (4) take charge of executing your very first campaign to bring in the money.

Once you've identified the hidden income opportunities in your employer's business, it's time to move to the next chapter and create your written plan using the Instant Income Overnight Audit.

CHAPTER 10

Gathering Information for the Overnight Audit

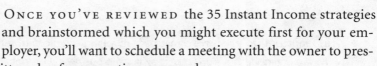

ONCE YOU'VE REVIEWED the 35 Instant Income strategies and brainstormed which you might execute first for your employer, you'll want to schedule a meeting with the owner to present your written plan for generating more cash.

The Instant Income Overnight Audit is the tool you'll use to produce that written plan.

You'll find the Overnight Audit in Chapter 8, "Identifying the Hidden Income Opportunities in Your Small Business," or you can use the online version to quickly prioritize which strategies you should execute first to produce maximum income. The online version even delivers your plan in a professional-looking format for you and your employer to review.*

To gather the information required to complete the Audit, you'll need to access specific information within your employer's business. Here's how to begin.

Start with Your Own Department. Whether you're in sales, accounting, customer service, or the warehouse, you should look around your own department and determine which of the Instant Income strategies could be used to create cash immediately.

---

* Visit www.instantincome.com/audit.html for the online version of the Instant Income Overnight Audit.

Use the information you gather about inventory overstocks, sales scripts, advertising campaigns, Internet activity, and other aspects of the business to complete the related questions in the Audit.

If you don't have access to certain types of other information because of your current position with the company or the department you work in, here are some alternative ways to gather the information or estimates you'll need for the Audit.

Interview the Staff in Other Departments. Your fellow employees should be open to your making informal inquiries about their department. While they may not give you exact numbers, response rates, and other confidential information, they'll probably at least give you an overview of what they do, how they contribute to cash flow, and, specifically, whether they already execute the income-generation strategies described in this book. (This will help you avoid suggesting an intrapreneurship deal involving something your company is already doing.)

Try using the following script when asking for information from other departments:

> "Hi, Jonathan. Do you have a minute? I'm taking an informal survey on ways we can generate extra cash flow for the business. I've looked at my own department, but I was wondering if I could ask you a couple of questions that would help me educate myself about _____ (sales, our Web site, the warehouse, our advertising campaigns, how we prospect for new customers)."

Ask Customers about Their Preferences. If you work at any job where you come into contact with customers, ask them about their needs, problems they're not able solve, what kinds of other products they might be able to use, why they don't buy from the company on a regular basis, how you might improve their buying experience with your company, and so on.

Start Researching the Industry for Possible Joint Ventures. One of the best intrapreneurship deals is to initiate and manage joint ventures with outside parties. Joint ventures—and the revenues they produce—are almost like miniature, self-contained profit centers that have identifiable sales, separate reporting, and unique activity that can be easily differentiated from your employer's normal business.

By researching possible joint-venture partners, you can at least complete the joint-venture section of the Overnight Audit.

Investigate Media and Message-Delivery Options. If you educate yourself about dozens of low-cost ways to broadcast a press release, get featured in an e-zine, do voice-mail broadcasts, or execute any of the other Instant Income strategies, you could easily use this information to rank which strategies would be the most profitable—and the lowest risk—for your employer.

CHAPTER 11

Planning Your Meeting with the Boss

MEETING WITH THE BOSS OR OWNER of the company needn't be daunting. In fact, with a little advance planning and some written notes, the overwhelmingly positive outcome may surprise you.

To make the most of the intrapreneurship deal you'll be suggesting, take steps before the meeting to prepare yourself, your pitch, and your deal points.

Step 1: Complete the Overnight Audit

When you have completed the Overnight Audit, you'll have in your hands a road map of strategies ranked in the order in which they should be executed. (If you complete the Audit online, our system will rank them for you.)

To prepare written notes for your meeting, simply print out those strategies that will earn the greatest—and quickest—amount of income for your employer. Then, add to that printout a brief description of how you'll execute each strategy. Review the individual strategy sections in Part One for details on executing each strategy successfully.

Step 2: Write Down Your Deal Points

Have you thought about what you want in exchange for executing the Instant Income strategies and bringing in new revenue for the company? While it may be easy to say "more money," the reality is that there are many other deal points to consider besides just more pay.

In the next chapter, I'll give you a step-by-step lesson in how to negotiate the deal. But suffice it to say that you *could* be paid in any number of ways, including a percentage of the revenue you bring in, a flat fee per project, a percentage of the money you save your employer, a fee paid by your joint-venture partners, a finder's fee, an Internet affiliate commission, and many more.

Other deal points to plan for include when you'll be paid, who will own the ads you write or the sales strategies you develop, who will manage the project, who will pay the expenses of executing your strategies, how reporting will be done, and other such issues.

Step 3: Approach the Actual Decision Maker

Who will you be ultimately making your intrapreneurship deal with? Be aware that it may not be your immediate supervisor. In fact, if you approach your immediate supervisor, there may be a risk that your supervisor will ignore your ideas at the moment, then later present your plan to management as his own.

What can you do to prevent this outcome?

If your company is small enough that you're in daily communication with the owner, speak privately with her to schedule a meeting. Plan to have her set aside at least 45 minutes to discuss your plan in detail.

If your company is large, consider approaching the owner's personal assistant about a "personal matter" you would like to speak to the owner about confidentially.

Step 4: Write Your Agenda for the Meeting

Meeting with the boss can be intimidating. So do yourself a favor by writing a short agenda to help you stay on track with your discussion points. I don't recommend that you give this agenda to your employer—just study it ahead of time, then keep it with you for reference during the meeting. A good sample agenda might read like this:

Tell Mr. Jones Why I Asked for This Meeting

- I've always been interested in ways to help the business do better, but I didn't have the confidence to speak up about it until now.

- Then just last week, I discovered a series of small business strategies that fit perfectly with all the things I've been wanting to suggest to you. These strategies can be implemented very quickly, and they tend to bring in cash flow very quickly, too.

- I did an intensive survey of many of the activities of the business, and I found 16 different areas where I believe I could apply these strategies and—by myself—bring in more cash for you.

- I'd like to present these ideas to you, then talk about how I can fill a new and unique role here at the business, being paid to create cash for you in areas that are outside of my regular job.

Present the Overnight Audit to Mr. Jones

- I conducted an informal audit of a few of the different departments, and I have a written document that shows where the most money can be made first.

- If you look on Page 1 of the audit, you'll see the 16 areas where money is waiting to be brought in:

  - We have 627 units of Product XYZ in the warehouse that I would like to liquidate for cash via a unique promotion to our customers that tells the story of why we're reducing the price this one time only.

  - I discovered that about 35 percent of all customers in our retail store end up buying the special of the day when it is offered to them. I'd like to develop a script for our order desk to use to upsell telephone customers in the same way, since they are not using an upsell script at the order desk now.

- I found 47 possible joint-venture partners whose customers would be perfect buyers for our Model 4500 Widget. We don't do any joint ventures like this now, but I estimate that working with even five of these outside parties could bring in about $82,000 extra each month.

- There are 622 Web sites that publish newsletters about camping and outdoor living. I'd like to start an article campaign on the Internet to sell our Model 6255 Home and Recreation Unit to individual consumers. Since we currently truck everything to wholesalers, I've identified three call centers and fulfillment houses that would ship individual orders.

- And so on.

Tell Mr. Jones I'm the Best Person to Bring in the Money

- I have an entire strategic plan that I'm finalizing that will allow us to begin bringing in this cash.

- While I know we have marketing people and salespeople here at the company, I believe I'm the best person to bring in this money because, based on my informal audit, I'm the only employee who has identified these profit centers and has had the initiative to research ways to turn them into cash.

- I'm motivated enough to do my regular job *plus* oversee the new revenue streams I've just discussed with you.

Tell Mr. Jones I Want to Make a Deal

- Mr. Jones, the reason I wanted to meet with you privately is that I'd like to discuss an unusual arrangement. I'd like to become an internal entrepreneur within your company. I'd like to do my regular job *plus* be allowed to execute these strategies in other areas.

- Like other entrepreneurs, I'd like to share in the profits when I bring in this cash.

Tell Mr. Jones What My Deal Points Are

- I ask to be paid only *after* the money comes in. I'm that confident that these strategies will be successful.

- I'd like to be given the autonomy to initiate these arrangements and manage these revenue streams—always seeking your approval before sending a promotion, spending money for marketing, or speaking with our most important customers.

- As part of the process, I'd like to get ongoing advice from the company that first gave me these Instant Income strategies.*

- I'd like to initiate third-party reporting where necessary to assure both of us that these strategies are the true source of the revenues.

When you plan ahead and practice your talking points, you'll be more confident during your meeting and better able to represent yourself as a competent intrapreneur. In addition, some of the best advice I can give you is to simply believe in yourself. You can do this.

---

* The Instant Income Business Enhancement System helps you develop substantial additional expertise (see the ads at the end of the book). Trained business coaches are also available to work with you personally as you implement the strategies in your employer's business. For details, visit www.instantincome.com/coaching.html.

CHAPTER 12

Negotiating a Deal That Brings You More Pay

MOST EMPLOYERS I'VE MET are exceptionally fair people. They like paying good employees good money, and, in truth, they probably wish they had more money to lavish on their best and brightest.

They're also entrepreneurs at heart. They got where they are today by being creative, flexible, and open to pursuing unusual opportunities.

Your intrapreneurship deal is one of those opportunities.

In fact, when faced with an employee who is as motivated as you are—one who not only has done the advance research, but also plans to work even harder to benefit the company—most employers will work just as hard to craft a compensation arrangement that is fair and sensible.

Employees Rarely Get Paid for Ideas

One of the reasons I encourage you to attend the meeting with a fully developed plan in writing is that employees of small businesses rarely get paid *extra* for ideas. They get paid by the hour, they get paid for their work product, and they get paid for results.

But they rarely get paid for an idea.

That's why you *must* go to the meeting with a definitive plan for *what you will do* to make the company more money. When you present an entire program, complete with estimates and even sample promotional pieces, it will be virtually impossible for your employer to dismiss you by saying, "Thanks for the idea."

Go prepared with your research, two copies of the Overnight Audit, a list of the tasks you'll do, any suppliers you've found, any pricing notes you've taken, any revenue estimates you've projected, the date by which you expect to be able to launch, how your project might benefit or affect other departments, and other such information. These are the kinds of details that high-level managers and executives discuss. You should plan to do the same.

But more importantly, the more your "fingerprints" are all over these profit centers, the more justified you will be in asking to be paid extra for creating them.

"This Is Way Better than a Business Plan"

You should also go to the meeting armed with a package of sample ads, telemarketing scripts, spreadsheets, supplier brochures, and anything else you can use to make your case.

One client I consulted with quietly recruited the chief financial officer as a mentor, a champion, and a sounding board before going to the president of the organization. Because my client hadn't fully developed his idea yet, the CFO said simply, "Show me a business plan." While this dismissal could have been the death knell for my client's intrapreneurship idea, I quickly helped him put together a presentation that was much more exciting than just numbers and paragraphs.

You see, the trouble with business plans is that they're boring.

What's worse, *they don't describe exactly what will be done to bring in the revenue.* Compare that to a proposal you might assemble with sample ads, new sales scripts, exact offers designed for specific customer segments, new product bundles at better margins, and so on. A proposal like this will make the entire project so much more real and exciting to your employer that it's likely that he won't even ask you for a business plan.

Talk about the Revenue Before You Talk about the Revenue Sharing

In negotiating any deal, I don't like the other party to think about the "what ifs" too much. I'd much rather give him *actual* plans to dwell on.

I now extend the same advice to you.

If you can get your boss excited about the marketing and cash-flow outcomes, about the new energy in the sales department, about the empty shelves in the warehouse, and about the Web site that's now promoting the company to eager buyers—trust me, the deal points between you two will almost become secondary to your discussion.

And that's exactly where you want them to be.

Your discussion in this meeting should take a two-pronged approach: (1) extra revenue that could be generated from existing customers, and (2) additional customers that could be generated by your campaign.

Only after you've discussed these two points should you ask to share in the revenues you create—or begin discussing how you'll split the money.

Present Your Plan as Separate from Your Regular Job

Of course, central to your discussion should be your pronouncement that you have identified brand-new revenue streams for your employer that are outside of your regular employment—and, indeed, outside what others at the company already do. (Be sure to review any employment agreement you've signed.)

"This is something I'm very passionate about," you can say. "It's an area that I've been researching on my own."

Not only do you think it will serve existing customers better, but you think it will drive new customers to the company.

"I also believe I can create a phenomenal revenue stream from it," you should say, "but I have to be honest. You hired me to do the job I do now. This is way outside that job, so I'd like to talk about an intrapreneurship deal where—in addition to my regular job and my regular pay—I'd be compensated extra for doing this work and creating this additional revenue stream."

Don't Leave It to Your Employer to Suggest the Form of Compensation

Since it's likely that your employer has yet to encounter an intrapreneurial offer from an employee, it's probably safe to say that she also has no idea how to compensate you for your efforts. That's why you should always have in mind *before the meeting* how you would like to be paid and how much you would like to earn when you create new revenue streams for the company.

Different Ways to Get Paid

In your negotiations, it's always a good idea to strike a balance between what it's worth to your employer to have you bring in this revenue and how much effort, focus, and resources will be required from your employer and your coworkers.

One way to start the compensation discussion is to say, "Actually, I *have* thought about the amount of extra money this campaign will produce, and I'm convinced that there will be enough margin for us to split the proceeds 50/50." Another way to approach the discussion is to say, "I'm willing to be paid solely out of the proceeds I bring in. But I *do* want to be treated like any other joint-venture partner by sharing in the results 50/50."

If a 50/50 split isn't acceptable to your employer, ask what percentage he feels *would* be fair. Then go from there.

To help you think through the possible compensation deals, I've listed the more common ones here. But be aware that your—and your employer's— imagination is the only limiting factor. Anything goes if it's acceptable to both of you.

Percentage of Gross Revenues

I've listed this compensation method first because it's truly the best way to get paid. Not only is it easy to calculate but it's also easy on the accounting department because it fits into that department's software as a simple sales commission. Depending on the percentage you negotiate, you can even increase the price of a product or service to cover your percentage—then use your good marketing techniques to convince customers to pay the higher price.

I've been paid between 15 and 50 percent of the gross revenues on projects I've been involved with. And while much depends on the amount of profit connected with a particular product or service that you might promote, you should be aware that any percentage within that range will be very fair.

Percentage of Net Revenues

I never recommend accepting compensation on a "percentage of net" basis— mainly because the net profits are always changing (even on the same product), and this figure is simply too time-consuming to calculate. In order to calculate the true net profits, you would have to wait for invoices, shipping documents, potential refunds, calculation of overhead attributable to the project, and on and on. Instead of focusing on your work, you'll be haranguing the accounting department.

That said, I've mentioned it second on the list because it's very popular with employers and joint-venture partners. It's how they think. It's how they're accustomed to looking at reports. They want to be sure that all their costs are covered—and then some—before they split the proceeds.

One way to keep your employer happy is to agree to a percentage-of-net arrangement *but calculate that percentage just once at the beginning of the project.* You can then *convert that net figure into a percentage of gross profits* and include that fixed percentage in your written agreement. For example, if you'll be selling an item for $300 and the net profits are $200, on which you make 40 percent, multiply 40 percent by $200, then represent your $80 commission as 26.7 percent of the gross retail price when it comes time to write your agreement. I'll talk about written agreements at the end of this chapter.

Fixed Commission for Each Unit Sold

Just as in the previous example, you can elect to be paid a fixed amount per item sold. This is an easy deal for employers to make because they readily understand sales commissions and are accustomed to signing commission checks for their salespeople.

Of course, if you're developing an Internet affiliate program for your employer, one way to calculate and keep track of your commissions is to simply sign up as an affiliate yourself, or sign up as the party responsible for signing up other affiliates. Check your shopping cart software to be sure this function is included.

Fixed Monthly Retainer Based upon Additional Duties

If your employer balks at giving you a percentage of revenues or a commission because she doesn't want to open her accounting books to you, you can suggest that she just pay you a monthly retainer based upon the extra work you'll be doing. Estimate the number of extra hours you'll spend each month, then don't agree to accept less than your current hourly wage for those estimated additional hours.

Job Promotion with Commensurate Salary Increase

For many employees, a big promotion with a substantial raise is an almost un-attainable goal. But by the time you get done executing your very first cam-paign, you'll realize how deserving you truly are of a bigger job with the higher pay that goes along with it.

If this compensation method is acceptable to you, make the most of it by investing that extra income in your financial future rather than by expanding your lifestyle and consuming it.

Flat Fee for Executing Specific Strategies or Completing One-Time Projects

Marketing firms, business consultants, Internet affiliate managers, advertis-ing agencies, and public relations firms all get paid thousands of dollars a month *minimum* by the typical small business client. You should accept *no less* than $50 per hour—depending on your expertise—for executing specific strategies or completing one-time projects. And upwards of $100 per hour is not uncommon.

Getting Paid by a Joint-Venture Partner

Managing joint ventures—particularly if your employer does not seek out and conduct joint ventures now—is one of the easiest intrapreneurship deals to do. And it's by far one of the easiest ways to get paid because you can simply agree to be paid by the other party out of the proceeds of the joint venture.

Of course, this works only if your joint venture is set up with the other party collecting the customer's money. But if you choose a joint-venture part-ner to whom your employer can completely outsource a new service or prod-uct delivery function, not only is the sales reporting easy but often the joint-venture partner will pay you a finder's fee or other revenue split with a simple letter of instruction from your employer.

Additional Nonmonetary Benefits Based upon Results

I'm not a legal advisor or an accounting professional, but I can tell you that making more money is sometimes secondary to other benefits that you might earn. If this is your situation, talk to your employer about nonmonetary forms of compensation that work better for you.

Perhaps more than money you need flextime, telecommuting privileges, extra vacation days, a company car, or other benefits. Be sure to check with your accounting professional to ensure that you are properly reporting these benefits on your tax return.

Similarly, can you execute the Instant Income strategies and earn income while you are on maternity leave, family care leave, or sabbatical?

Part Ownership in the Company

This is the brass ring of intrapreneurship deals, but it's not impossible to negotiate. If you bring a substantial new revenue stream to the company, with the result that its flagging profits are transformed or its owner finally gets to pursue semiretirement, you deserve to "run things" along with your employer—and benefit from the change in finances.

The percentage of ownership that you negotiate is up to you, but a good way to get started is to gradually buy a percentage of the company over time as you bring in new revenues.

Part Ownership in a Spin-Off Company

If you have a brand new product, service, or market in mind for your intrapreneurship project, a spin-off (or separate company) is an ideal way to maximize your contribution.

You'll need to agree on who will put up the resources required to start the new company, but suffice it to say that many of the Instant Income strategies are ideal for start-ups and spin-offs because they tend to create cash quickly with very little cash outlay. If you choose a product or service that can be created as you make sales—that is, that doesn't need to be manufactured or purchased in quantity in advance—both you and your employer could launch a very profitable spin-off within weeks of your initial meeting.

Your Compensation Should Be Ongoing

The last thing you want to do is work yourself out of a job. I've seen people get fired, get a better job, or otherwise be forced to leave their current employment for personal reasons. If you have set up healthy revenue streams (particularly those that require no oversight by your employer, such as viral

Internet campaigns), you should ideally be paid for those revenues even after you leave your company's employ.

This happens only in a perfect world—unless, of course, your employer agrees *in writing* to continue these payments even after your employment ends. An even better safeguard than an agreement is to set up these revenue streams using a third-party billing service, which splits the money and cuts separate checks for both you and your employer based on written instructions signed by both parties during the set-up phase.

Be Sure to Get Everything in Writing

It almost goes without saying that you should put every deal point in writing. It's not that your employer will be deliberately dishonest (most aren't). It's just that people often forget what was discussed days ago—let alone months ago.

To get you started in documenting your deal, you can review a sample deal-point memo at the Instant Income Resources Page.* While the memo is not guaranteed to be specific to your situation or circumstances, you'll find sample language, sample compensation ideas, and other content that will provide discussion points for your ultimate deal.

Visit www.InstantIncome.com/resources.html to download the sample deal-point memo and other important information.

Additional deal points that you'll want to consider in finalizing your agreement with the boss are

- ➤ How often you'll get paid

- ➤ Whether a refund reserve will be established for refunds and how often that reserve will be "swept" and distributed to you

- ➤ Who owns the marketing pieces, ads, and sales scripts you'll write

- ➤ What remedies you'll have if your employer doesn't pay you

- ➤ Whether others will participate in the revenue splits—such as salespeople or customer service personnel

---

* You should always get professional legal counsel whenever you are putting an agreement in writing. The deal points you'll find online *must* be altered for your specific circumstances and to comply with the laws of your state. Do not use the sample deal-point memo as written. It is for educational purposes only.

- How reporting will be done

- Who will pay the expenses of the project

One Final Word: Don't Quit Your Day Job

Despite your best efforts, your employer simply may not be open to growing the company in the way you suggest. Some business owners believe that growth leads to more work or more hassle. This is not true in most cases, but sometimes you just can't get around another person's belief system.

If your employer says no to your intrapreneuring proposal, don't be discouraged. You are a talented and highly motivated individual who can easily pursue alternative methods of getting ahead.

Don't quit your job. Instead, read through Part Four of *Instant Income*, "Becoming an Occasional Entrepreneur," for advice on directing your energy toward creating additional streams of income outside your regular employment. With what you've accomplished to get this far, you're now entrepreneurial material. Don't let a negative response from one person stop you from earning Instant Income.

Creating Your Task List and Taking Charge of Your Very First Campaign

BY THIS POINT, you've successfully negotiated your deal with the boss. And now it's time to create the list of task items you'll perform as you execute your very first strategy. Rest assured that the most difficult work—Going into Business with the Boss—is already behind you.

Now it's time to relax and plan your first project.

To simplify your planning, you should know that the process of executing any Instant Income strategy can always be reduced to four basic action areas:

➤ Getting your message and your product ready

➤ Order taking, upselling, and customer service on Launch Day

➤ After-launch fulfillment and reassurance

➤ Future reselling and cross-selling

To keep track of individual tasks within these four action areas, you'll need to create one large master list of to-do items *in the order in which they need to be accomplished*—with columns off to the side for due dates, the party responsible, contact information, costs, and other notes.

I always use the spreadsheet program Microsoft Excel because it's simple to use, it lets me create lots of columns, and I can highlight certain tasks in color for easy reference. You can use any system you choose (even keeping all your notes in a spiral binder if you want), just as long as everything is written down. I've provided a sample spreadsheet from one of my actual campaigns—a new product launch at a trade show—later in this chapter.

Of course, this task-by-task implementation plan is also a good blueprint if you're executing any sort of strategy for yourself. In other words, you don't have to be an employee to use this planning format.

Get Your Message and Your Product Ready

Critical to your first successful campaign will be the e-mail copy, upselling script, online article, trade show promotion, or other message that you'll be using. Spend time getting these messages right. Review Chapter 3, "Writing Ads That Make the Phone Ring," for a lengthy tutorial on writing direct-response ads—the best chance you'll have for success with your campaign.

In addition, you'll need to prepare your product or service bundle and your sales and ordering mechanisms. While your prelaunch to-do list may look significantly different, here is a list of possible task items to help you get you started:

➤ Decide whom you'll market to.

➤ Decide how you'll deliver the message to those people.

➤ Check on space and materials deadlines for magazines and newspapers if you'll be placing display advertisements.

➤ Book advertising space (at remnant rates, if possible).

➤ Decide what the product or service bundle offered will be.

➤ Decide what the upsell product or service offered will be.

➤ Recruit affiliates or joint-venture partners.

➤ If you are offering a new product or service bundle, decide what the offer, pricing, packaging, delivery, and other product features will be. If you are offering an existing product or service bundle, compare the components against what you know the market wants, then make adjustments, if necessary.

➤ Write the marketing copy for the e-mail, direct-mail package, postcard, newspaper ad, or other advertisement.

➤ If Internet affiliates will be helping you promote your offering, create and deliver tools for them along with complete instructions for launching the promotion.

➤ Prepare order-taking mechanisms—Web site, telephones, call center, in-store retail clerks, and so on.

➤ Create the artwork for the advertisement (if display ads are being used). Create any two-step conversion package that is needed.

➤ Prepare any sales scripts, prepare upselling scripts, and train sales or retail staff on the product or service.

➤ Deliver artwork to the periodical, upload the Web pages, release the press release, or otherwise activate your promotion

Take Charge on Launch Day

If you've prepared adequately, the launch of your promotion should go smoothly. In fact, many strategists are so accustomed to preparing and activating campaigns that they're already working on the next one by the time Launch Day occurs. (This is particularly true if you've placed an advertisement in a trade magazine that had a 60-day advance deadline.)

On Launch Day, you'll want to personally take charge of the activity. And while that day can get very exciting, be aware that—depending on the type of strategy you used—responses from customers could come in slowly at first, rather than deluge your sales department, as with other types of strategies you might have used. Be assured that *any response should be welcomed and appreciated.* Just be sure to prepare your sales team and yourself—and your boss—for the right level of response, however small at first.

Of course, if you are using any type of outbound telemarketing strategy (such as Customer Strategy 1, "Keep Track of Customer Buying Patterns, Then Call to Take Reorders," or Sales Strategy 1, "Conducty Follow-up Telemarketing and Voice Broadcast Campaigns,"), you may want to make some of these calls yourself, just to get an idea of the feedback being received from customers. Feedback will help you make immediate adjustments in any sales script, upselling script, or bonus descriptions that you've written. I always work in conjunction with my salespeople on Launch Day to update their sales

Due Date	Resp Party	Task Item	Call to Activate OR Deliver to...	Done?
2 Dec.	Jim Client	Advise Victoria to book two rooms for staff members by Jan. 9	Victoria	✓
12 Dec.	Victoria	Ask Jim Client to approve staff list	Jim Client	✓
12 Dec.	Victoria	Check with Show Promoter to see if Jim's room has been booked	Kristin Promoter	✓
16 Dec.	Janet	Deliver draft of audio workbook guts to Jim Client	Jim Client	✓
16 Dec.	Janet	Deliver draft workbook cover artwork to Jim Client	Jim Client	✓
16 Dec.	Janet	Deliver draft audio entrapments artwork to Jim Client	Jim Client	✓
16 Dec.	Janet	Deliver draft CD face artwork to Jim Client	Jim Client	✓
16 Dec.	Jim Client	Return marked-up audio cover artwork to Janet Switzer	Janet Switzer	✓
16 Dec.	Jim Client	Return marked-up CD face artwork to Janet Switzer	Janet Switzer	✓
16 Dec.	Jim Client	Return marked-up audio entrapments artwork to Janet Switzer	Janet Switzer	✓
16 Dec.	Victoria	Acquire 3,000 carbon-imprintable credit card slips from bank	Jim's Merch. Acct. Bank	✓
16 Dec.	Victoria	Acquire four manual credit card imprinters with Jim's merch. acct. #	Jim's Merch. Acct. Bank	✓
20 Dec.	Jim Client	Return marked-up audio workbook to Janet Switzer	Janet Switzer	✓
20 Dec.	Victoria	Book airfare for staff going to event (Jim Client + five staff above)	Airlines	✓
22 Dec.	Janet	Get format requirements from media duplicator for audio masters	Media Duplicator/Lee	✓
28 Dec.	Victoria	Advise Show Promoter of names of staff members	Kristin Promoter	✓
31 Dec.	Jim/Janet	Record audio tracks for audio CDs (215 minutes + 7 minutes of segue)	John Doe Studio	✓
6 Jan.	Janet	Deliver final audio CD masters to media duplicator	Media Duplicator/Lee	✓
6 Jan.	Janet	Deliver final workbook text pages PDF file to printer	Web Press Printers	✓
6 Jan.	Victoria	Ship credit card slips and imprinters to hotel/get documents from Janet	Pauline	✓
9 Jan.	Janet	Order materials-handling services for day-direct shipment	Expo Handlers	✓
9 Jan.	Victoria	Book rooms for Jim Client and all staff members at hotel	Orlando Hotel Conf. Ctr.	✓
10 Jan.	Janet	Deliver final audio CD face artwork to media duplicator	Media Duplicator/Lee	✓
10 Jan.	Janet	Deliver final workbook cover artwork to printer	Web Press Printers	✓
10 Jan.	Janet	Deliver final entrapments artwork to media duplicator	Media Duplicator/Lee	✓
10 Jan.	Victoria	Fax in credit card authorization for materials handling	Expo Handlers	✓
10 Jan.	Victoria	Ship testimonial poster to hotel	Pauline	✓
13 Jan.	Janet	Do artwork for booth posters/mount onto foam core	Quick Printer	✓
13 Jan.	Janet	Produce Banner artwork for 10-foot banner	Jim Client to approve	✓
15 Jan.	Janet	Design product order form	Janet/Pauline	✓
17 Jan.	Janet	Last day to order materials handling—MUST ORDER ONLINE	Expo Handlers	✓
17 Jan.	Janet	Print product order form	Quick Printer	✓
17 Jan.	Janet	Ship product order form to hotel	Pauline	✓
20 Jan.	Victoria	Purchase product bags and ship to hotel	Pauline	✓
20 Jan.	Victoria	Do artwork for stand-up acrylic sign-holder; ship to hotel	Pauline/Quick Printer	✓
27 Jan.	Victoria	Get cash box together with $20's and $1's for booth ($1,000)	Jim's Bank	✓
28 Jan.	Janet	Pack easels, desk accessories, book-signing pens and ship to hotel	Pauline	✓
29 Jan.	Media Dup.	Deliver finished audio product cartons on skid packs to hotel	Media Duplicator/Lee	✓
29 Jan.	Team	Set up Jim Client's product booth and booksigning table	8:00am–6:00pm	✓
30 Jan.	Team	Work at Jim Client's booth	10:00am–7:00pm	✓
31 Jan.	Team	Work at Jim Client's booth	8:00am–6:00pm	✓
1 Feb.	Team	Work at Jim Client's booth	8:00am–12:00pm	✓
1 Feb.	Team	Dismantle booth and coordinate return shipping of materials	12:00pm–5:00pm	✓

scripts. As the calls come in, they will test different dialogues, and once we figure out what works, we don't change it again for that product or service.

After the Launch, Fulfill Orders and Reassure the Customer

Most new marketers don't realize that a certain amount of postpurchase regret occurs sometime after a customer buys something. Some customers may immediately feel guilty about spending so much money. Others may experience embarrassment later that day when they need to justify the purchase to their spouse or family. Still others may call you for a refund weeks afterward when they get their credit card statement and decide that they are over their limit again. Whatever the reason, you need to be aware of this phenomenon and take steps to make sure that your product stays sold.

What can you do?

To cut down on returns or cancelled orders, *you must immediately communicate with customers* to reassure them that they have made a smart purchase. Remind them of the benefits they'll begin to enjoy once they have the product in their hands and are using it. Give them additional ways to use the product, or tell them what they can expect when they first open the box or first come in for an appointment. This tends to "future pace" customers, getting them to think about the future rather than dwelling on their current thoughts about their purchase. These messages are best (and most economically) sent via e-mail, but I've also received phone calls from companies I've purchased from.

Another way to cut down on returns is to bundle into your product offer some sort of service that can be delivered immediately. This service will cut down on returns, because customers will often assume that since they've already used a portion of what they bought, they cannot reverse the purchase.

Additionally, frequent future communication and bonding with the customer is important because—human nature being what it is—most people will not seek a refund from a friend or someone with whom they have a good business relationship. They're much more likely to seek a refund from a stranger, since they don't have to wrestle with their conscience.

Resell and Cross-Sell Customers in the Future

While the first three steps in any strategy launch may be logical to you, many of you will be surprised to hear that the marketing doesn't stop once you make the sale. You'll need to continue marketing after the sale in order to retain customers and sell them more things later. This is where a lot of even savvy marketers really leave a lot of money on the table.

It's not enough to make the first sale.

You have to keep your buyers engaged with your product, excited about their potential results, and engaged with your community of customers and—if appropriate—with you personally as their expert of choice.

To stay in communication effectively enough to resell additional products and cross-sell other products and services, you should also include in your product delivery cycle a point at which you'll start selling buyers your next product or service. Perhaps you include a flyer in the shipping carton, schedule them for a telemarketing follow-up call from your salespeople, invite them to a teleseminar, or send them a personal letter.

You can also put on your marketing schedule future dates when you'll offer these customers early-bird specials, advance notice of special sales, last-minute deals, overstock discounts, and other offers.

PART FOUR

Becoming an Occasional Entrepreneur

CHAPTER 14

Finding Opportunity Everywhere

I AM CONSTANTLY AMAZED and humbled by the unique and unusual ways in which people make money. And while lots of business owners have mastered the art of developing interesting profit centers for their business, some of the most exciting revenue streams that I see today are developed by *employees of these small businesses* who are making money outside their "regular" job.

While these workers love the security, variety, and steady paycheck of their 8-to-5 career, they also enjoy making tens of thousands of dollars extra for themselves by executing short-term, minimum-commitment strategies several times a year.

I call these folks *Occasional Entrepreneurs.*

And if making money on the side interests you, but you don't want the commitment of running a part-time business all year round, then using the Instant Income strategies to make extra cash at night, on weekends, and during holidays is for you.

What Do You Love to Do?

I also believe that you have inside of you some one thing that you are truly passionate about—something that, regardless of what you do for a living now, you would pursue as your lifetime's work *if only you could earn enough money doing it.*

Like the college professor who writes articles for hire, the aerospace manager who sells Native American crafts at weekend powwows, or the stay-at-home mom who runs a podcasting Web site for other stay-at-home moms, being an Occasional Entrepreneur lets you pursue your passion. It lets you make money in ways that work for your lifestyle, your family commitments, and your schedule.

Freedom to Find Opportunity Everywhere

Of course, being an Occasional Entrepreneur gives you freedom—in deciding on the kinds of projects you take on, in choosing whom you want to work with, and, ultimately, in making independent decisions about your finances.

In the following chapters, I not only detail the exact steps required to become an Occasional Entrepreneur, and make money outside of your regular job, but also introduce you to the types of "businesses" that can generate cash quickly using the Instant Income strategies. Many of these occasional projects require only your own expertise; there are no cash outlays for staff, inventory, special equipment, or ongoing expenses. Instead of burdening yourself with these expensive annoyances, I show you how to minimize the *hassle factor* so that you can focus on actually executing the short-term, minimum-commitment strategies I've detailed in this book.

For instance, instead of starting a brick-and-mortar business that requires up-front cash, ongoing rent, personal guarantees, and regular business hours, I want you to be free to concentrate on finding the best moneymaking projects for your expertise and skill set, rather than tying yourself to a product or service long-term because you have "invested" in the business.

Instead of spending your time running the business, I want you to automate the most time-consuming work using inexpensive services and software that are available to everyone. Instead of being tied to a side business that takes up every weekend, I want you to work nights, weekends, and holidays during a two- or three-week period, then take the next three or four months off while still enjoying the income you created. Instead of working at a second job, I want you to evolve to creating a second income stream.

Do you see the difference in mindset—and the difference in approach—that being an Occasional Entrepreneur offers you?

Pay Off Your Debt and Start Building Lifetime Wealth

Of course, earning extra money on the side benefits you in many *other* ways, too.

For instance, imagine how your lifestyle would change if you made just an extra $1,000 a month. Suddenly, you could begin to pay off your debts, invest more money for retirement, send your children to private school, move to a better neighborhood, hire a housekeeper and gardener, spend $12,000 a year on luxury vacations, increase your charitable donations, help your elderly parents with in-home care, and start spending more on your own health and well-being. You would probably feel less stressed about your finances, you would actually use your vacation time from work, and you would probably find ways to work smarter at your regular job so that overtime and weekends at the office became a thing of the past.

Then, once you started paying down your debt and living better, you could start building a financial future by investing just half of that $1,000 each month. For instance, it might surprise you to know that investing just $500 a month at 10 percent interest would generate $1,094,385 over 30 years. Investing the full $1,000 would generate over a million dollars in just 22.5 years.

And if your Occasional Entrepreneurship projects generated $3,000 to $7,000 each? You could invest $5,000 a month and retire in style with a $100,000 annual income after just 15.4 years.*

That's when the prospect of becoming an Occasional Entrepreneur gets really exciting.

---

* Visit www.monkeychimp.com to determine your own future investment values using its compound interest calculator. A $100,000 per year retirement income requires $2.2 million invested at 10 percent interest.

CHAPTER 15

Occasional Income Sources That Bring in the Cash

IN THE WORLD OF BUSINESS TODAY, there are probably a million ways to make a million dollars. And when it comes to making something a lot easier (like $100,000), the list of possible opportunities increases exponentially.

So which of these opportunities are right for you? More importantly, which opportunities work best with the Instant Income strategies?

What Makes an Income Opportunity an Instant Income Opportunity?

This section discusses 13 criteria that I look for in any business opportunity—whether it be full-time, part-time, or occasional. While these criteria are important enough when you're producing any business income, they become even more important when you're seeking to create quick cash. The more of these criteria that are met by your chosen opportunity, the easier it will be to use the Instant Income strategies to generate revenue quickly.

Let's take a look.

Potential Buyers Can Be Identified and Located

Many potential businesses have prospective customers who are *everywhere* and *nowhere* at the same time. They're everywhere, but you can't identify who they are, what niche markets they're associated with, which joint-venture partners they might already be customers of, and so on. This makes your advertising and marketing job much more difficult. But think how much easier your promotional efforts would be if you could clearly identify *exactly* where to find these prospects—on the Internet, in your local geographic market, within specific industries, and as past buyers of other companies.

Start-Up Costs Are Low

I'm not a big fan of spending money to launch a business, particularly an occasional one. Instead of budgeting tens or hundreds of thousands of dollars, think about funding your start-up costs out of sales by spending just $200 to run a press release, $50 to conduct an introductory teleseminar, or nothing at all to make a deal with your very first joint-venture partner.

There Is the Potential for a High Price, a Sizable Margin, or Volume Sales

Some industries have products and services that can be sold for very high prices, have profit margins over 75 percent, or offer the promise of selling consistently large quantities. Knowledge products fit this description, as do many professional services.

It Matches Your Skills, Passion, Personality, and Expertise

Much of what I teach in *Instant Income* helps position you as not only the ideal provider of your product or service but also a major authority on the subject. If you're not comfortable in this role, either reconsider whether you want to pursue this opportunity or decide whether you could instead take on a "reporter" role—being a messenger for industry information, rather than a leading expert.

Competitors and Potential Joint-Venture Partners Abound

I never worry too much about competition. To me, competition is simply an indicator that there's a viable market for the product or service that you're selling. Besides, there are a number of ways to differentiate yourself in the marketplace. Not only that, but the existence of numerous competitors and others operating in an industry simply means more potential joint-venture partners for your occasional pursuits.

Advertising Opportunities Are Inexpensive and Accessible

Nothing is worse than an industry in which the only way to reach potential buyers is a $30,000 ad in a single trade publication. When deciding if an opportunity is for you, be sure to research all possible advertising outlets available for reaching your niche market.

Monthly Maintenance Costs Are Low

Ongoing monthly costs such as rent, leases, Yellow Pages advertising, and other recurring costs can be devastating for occasional businesses. If you decide to incur an ongoing charge, be sure that the cost goes directly to create revenue, such as a call center or shopping cart service, or that the cost is negligible, such as Web hosting.

It Creates an Impressive Result That Can Be Advertised

I discussed in Chapter 3, "Writing Ads That Make the Phone Ring," how testimonials and case studies from happy clients and customers should be an important and compelling part of any advertising campaign. If the occasional opportunity that you are contemplating delivers results that can be talked about in your advertising campaigns, so much the better.

Expenses Can Be Paid as You Make Sales

I dislike up-front costs of any kind. In my experience, many of the things that are paid for in advance are never actually used because of delays, finding a better solution, and simple changes of plan. Luckily, many types of occasional business projects allow you to pay for the cost of goods, cost of service delivery, sales commissions, and other costs of running the business *after* you receive the revenue from any sales that are made.

The Product Can Be Downloaded or Is Otherwise Easy to Deliver

One of the reasons I like selling knowledge products is that they are easy to deliver, particularly as e-books over the Internet. Countless thousands of Occasional Entrepreneurs have written an e-book around their area of expertise, launched a one-page Web site designed to sell the e-book, then recruited hundreds of affiliates to promote the e-book for them. Their shopping cart software automatically delivers the e-book to the buyer as a downloadable file.

Other products and services are also easy to deliver if you can drop-ship the product from the manufacturer directly to your customers, warehouse the product with a fulfillment center that will ship upon receiving an e-mail from you, or contract with a joint-venture partner to deliver a service while you concentrate on marketing the service on an occasional basis.

Deadlines and Other Market Forces Cause People to Buy Now

In the advertising world, shortages and deadlines are wonderful things. By appealing to that natural human emotion *fear of loss,* deadlines force buyers to make a decision and to take action before a certain date. In fact, deadlines are so powerful that, even if none exist in your contemplated opportunity, you can often create them through well-written advertising copy. Of course, a genuine deadline is an even bigger benefit.

What kinds of deadlines can you build a business around? Government filing deadlines; back-to-school deadlines; business-reporting deadlines; fixed-date events, such as weddings and product releases; the date after which an investment will no longer be possible; and seasonal deadlines such as Mother's Day, graduation, and even flea season for pets.

Other market forces can be just as effective as a deadline in driving sales. These include genuinely limited supplies of rare items, the limited time available for some expert to consult privately, and other such limitations. Examine your intended occasional opportunity to see if it has some "deadline" aspect to it or if you can create scarcity in your advertising using other market forces.

You'll Be Selling a Consumable Product or Recurring Service

The best occasional business opportunities let you sell a customer once, then collect money from that customer for a very long time. In fact, given a choice, most marketers would prefer to sell subscriptions, memberships, and other continuity programs. It's how you leverage your limited time as an Occasional Entrepreneur.

If you have an idea for an occasional business, think through what you might be able to offer on an ongoing basis. Since you may not want to be tied to the business year-round, also think through how you might fulfill these ongoing orders or deliveries throughout the year. Can you contract with an outside firm to do it? Can you produce all the items over just two or three months, then take the rest of the year off while a college student that you hire ships them out?

Or can you simply become a representative, reseller, or affiliate for other people's continuity programs? Occasional opportunities that fit this qualification include network marketing companies, Internet membership sites, and becoming an outside sales rep for another company. You can even meet once a month with potential customers and clients, booking all your sales over a single weekend, then outsource the fulfillment to the company you're representing. You could very effectively become a manufacturing consultant, a nutritionist, or some other type of expert who meets with clients, sells them on a program, then turns over the order to a manufacturing company, vitamin company, or other provider that is in the business of providing customer service and fulfillment on an ongoing basis.

There Are Logical Upsells and Downsells

Even better than selling one product or service is selling a bundle of products and services through good upselling techniques. If the occasional opportunity you're contemplating allows you to sell additional items or services, so much the better.

Alternatively, you should always look within any opportunity for a downselling position, such as a lower-priced option, a payment plan, or an entry-level item or service.

Business Categories That Are Favorable for Making Instant Income

Of course, some businesses just don't work for Occasional Entrepreneurs. For obvious reasons, retail and manufacturing aren't conducive to making Instant Income on an occasional basis, except on a very small scale. The cost to purchase inventory to stock a retail store, the cost to tool up your manufacturing facility, and other burdensome start-up costs and ongoing management requirements make retailing and manufacturing inadvisable for Occasional Entrepreneurs.

That having been said, it *is* possible to run a retail or manufacturing operation part-time if it involves highly specialized one-of-a-kind items that you enjoy making and that you can sell at a very high price—unique jewelry, intricate model ships, hand-tied fishing flies, couture clothing, and other limited-manufacture items. Alternatively, you could start a Web site to sell *the parts needed to make these items* to other hobbyists. Or consider approaching a large retail chain's clothing or accessory buyer to sell a large quantity of your unique item in a single order that you fulfill over 30 to 60 days.

Still, for most Occasional Entrepreneurs, retailing and manufacturing take too much time and effort. There are much easier ways to make Instant Income on an occasional basis. For instance, there are more than half a dozen major categories of small business *besides* retailing and manufacturing, most of which are much more conducive to creating cash quickly:

➤ Consulting   ➤ Services

➤ Professional practice   ➤ Network marketing and direct sales

➤ Wholesaling/distribution ➤ Knowledge products/publishing

➤ Investments/holdings

Notice that in this list, I did not mention e-commerce as a category. That's because the Internet is not a business. It's a marketing and advertising delivery tool that helps you automate and sell more of the product or service you're already selling.

That said, however, take a look at the list again. There *are* categories that are naturally favorable for making Instant Income with very little effort and with even fewer start-up costs. These categories—consulting, services, network marketing, and knowledge products—also meet many of the ideal criteria for occasional opportunities that I mentioned at the beginning of this chapter.

Consulting on an Occasional Basis

If you have knowledge or expertise that others don't have, you can earn a superb income as an occasional consultant. In fact, thanks to the Internet, there are numerous Web sites that will connect you with companies that are looking for start-up advice, product development assistance, labor relations guidance, and countless other help. (See the next chapter, "Minimizing the Hassle Factor," for details on these online consulting forums.)

To best market yourself, first determine who needs what you know and which niche markets these buyers belong to. Then target your online marketing and your direct-mail letters to reach these buyers. Online articles, free reports, free assessment tools, and other helpful documents are good ways to familiarize potential clients with your specific expertise.

Providing Services on an Occasional Basis

Many thousands of people offer services on an occasional basis—whether it's professional organizing, tax preparation, party planning, interior decorating, weed clearing, grant writing, holiday gift buying for corporations, magic acts, or one of the hundreds of other types of services that consumers and businesses will pay for.

Almost anything you love to do that is also physically impossible, bothersome or time-consuming to others can be turned into an occasional service earning Instant Income. The key to marketing yourself as a service provider on an occasional basis is to approach *other* providers from whom these consumers and businesses are already buying.

Network Marketing and Direct Sales on an Occasional Basis

While most network marketing companies would like you to pursue their opportunity on a full-time basis, the truth is that they are equally welcoming to—and ideally structured for—Occasional Entrepreneurs. With products, services, sales tools, and fulfillment policies that favor Occasional Entrepreneurs, it's no wonder that the network marketing industry has grown from humble beginnings to an $82 billion industry worldwide.

In addition, if you have any international aspirations for your business, many of the more established parent companies have branched out into Europe, Asia, South America, republics of the former Soviet Union, and even Africa.

Having worked with a number of successful parent companies, direct sellers, and network marketing leaders, my experience is that reaching the most prospects possible with product information and the benefits of the business opportunity is key.

Of course, Instant Income can be made—and is made—by many thousands of participants, even though 85 percent of the participants spend fewer than 30 hours a week on their business.* Network marketing is an ideal occasional business.

Selling Knowledge Products on an Occasional Basis

There's a host of reasons why I've enjoyed working with authors and experts over the years—in addition to all the other businesses I've advised. Publishing is exciting, the margins are superb, there's little or no competition within the different categories of subject matter, and the methods used to market published works and other knowledge products are easy to execute and manage.†

In addition, with the advent of the Internet, almost anyone can easily and inexpensively promote himself as an expert and sell knowledge products and services.

How is Instant Income made on an occasional basis in the knowledge products industry?

➤ Set up a Web site selling an e-book, online course, or newsletter.

➤ Offer coaching over the phone on specific days of the month or week.

➤ Accept paid speaking engagements on an occasional basis—or speak for free, but sell consulting services, a coaching program, or products at the back of the room.

➤ Write a nonfiction book and sell it for an advance on royalties to a publishing company, which will distribute the book through normal bookstore and trade channels.

➤ Begin consulting and training for corporations that need your expertise.

➤ Become an info-marketing consultant who locks up the rights, then leverages the knowledge assets of other companies.

---

* Source: DSA's *2002 National Salesforce Survey*.

† As the expert behind many top celebrity authors, I've compiled my entire system for generating income through selling knowledge products. To learn more, visit www.howexpertsbuildempires.com/mavericks.html.

CHAPTER 16

Minimizing the Hassle Factor

EVERY WELL-MANAGED BUSINESS has systems in place that enable the company to run smoothly without the owner or senior management overseeing each individual transaction or process. Your occasional business can—and should—operate the same way.

When you automate your sales function, your customer service, your billing activity, your telephone system, your prospecting for new customers, and other functions, you reduce the day-to-day annoyances of running a business so that you can focus on the most important aspects: advertising and marketing. You also give yourself the freedom to step away from the business for a period of time. Occasional Entrepreneurship can work only if you have effective systems in place.

Technology Makes It Possible

Luckily, today we live in an age in which the technology to help you run your occasional enterprise is cheap, available, and—most importantly—understandable by the average nontechnical person. Not only that, but these systems have the added benefit of making you and your "company" look bigger, more professional, and more established than you truly are.

Solo entrepreneurs have known about these systems for years. Now it's time for Occasional Entrepreneurs to follow suit.

In her exceptional book *The Accidental Millionaire,* my good friend Stephanie Frank details many powerful strategies for organizing small enterprises, including one that has literally transformed my business. Instead of constantly reinventing individual processes or re-explaining established systems to new vendors or virtual help that I might bring on, Stephanie urged me to write down how each transaction is performed, then keep a notebook of these individual explanations that can be photocopied or e-mailed any time I launch a new project.

This way, everyone knows which technologies we use, how they're set up, and how they can be monitored and updated when necessary. This allows me to delegate 100 percent of certain functions to other people, so that I can focus on what I do best.*

What Hassles Do You Need to Minimize?

Over a decade ago, the term *virtual company* came into use to explain the idea of a company—or a solo entrepreneur—that brings together independent project managers, personal assistants, sales representatives, Web site developers, and other nonemployee contractors to work on various projects or particular aspects of the company. What developed eventually was, in my opinion, the least expensive and most effective way to run a small enterprise.

Now, a decade later, technology has replaced many of these contractors, making small businesses and occasional enterprises easy to set up and even easier to operate.

The following are the more common types of business functions that can now be performed inexpensively by technology and outside resources. But because the services available are constantly changing, with new ones becoming available nearly every day, *specific companies and technologies are recommended by name* only at the Instant Income Resources Page at www.instantincome.com/resources.html. You'll find my own personal recommendations there, including many of the vendors I currently use to run my own business—plus tips for using each service effectively.

> ➤ **Automated telephone systems and answering services.** Today, the technology exists for you to receive calls and automatically route them to your contractors, your sales representatives, or yourself, via landline

---

* You can get a free copy of Stephanie's system by visiting the Instant Income Resources Page at www.instantincome.com/resources.html.

or cell phone, wherever in the world you may be. These services will even announce your caller and allow you to choose whether to take the call or let it go to voice mail.

➤ **Live answering services.** Teams of trained professionals now exist the world over to answer your company's phone 24 hours a day, 7 days a week, in English and in numerous foreign languages. These services typically capture the caller's name, telephone number, e-mail address, and message, then e-mail you each message as it comes in. They can also input orders directly into your Web site, transfer calls to you or to other people, take workshop registrations, do basic inbound telesales, and more—all for a modest price.

➤ **Voice broadcasting.** For solo and occasional entrepreneurs who don't have dedicated salespeople, voice broadcasting lets you send a marketing message in your own words to your customers and prospects by recording a message, then uploading the phone numbers you want it sent to. You can choose whether to deliver the message only when a live person answers or solely when the call goes to voice mail.

➤ **Customer service and help desks.** Typically the most time-consuming part of an occasional enterprise, customer service can now be performed largely on the Internet. If you sell to thousands of customers, you can begin recording welcome messages, how-to messages, answers to frequently asked questions, and other such information, then posting them on your Web site. Numerous technologies exist to "learn" the most frequently presented problems and direct customers to the answers, which are continuously collected into a "smart" database over time. For high-paying clients, however, it pays to address these issues yourself, or at least hire a part-time virtual account manager who can learn your business and interface with clients.

➤ **Fulfillment centers.** Facilities exist that will receive your orders (even e-mailed from your Web site) and ship out your products for a small per-order fee. That means no shipping out of your garage and no hiring people to help you. In addition, these centers will warehouse your goods and even take care of reordering them from your suppliers when inventory runs low.

➤ **Project managers, Web site developers, writers, and other creative people.** Today, Web sites abound that will connect you with people who can write articles, design Web sites, develop newsletters, write proposals, and perform virtually every creative task in between. Most of these Web sites are free to you, the buyer. They charge the provider a fee to bid on your project instead.

➤ **Virtual assistants.** Many solo entrepreneurs I know have an assistant who answers their phone, sends out their letters, and coordinates their projects—yet they've never met that assistant in person. Virtual assistants are easy to find and hire, even if you need them for only a limited time. They typically work by the hour or on a monthly retainer based upon anticipated duties.

➤ **New business development for consultants.** Web sites are springing up every month to help connect consultants with clients who need their help and expertise. These sites typically list projects without contact information, then require you to pay a small fee to access individual project information and communicate directly with the company that is hiring.

➤ **Agents and publicists.** If you are a consultant who is quickly becoming an expert in your field, and you have aspirations of writing a book, licensing your work, getting on the six o'clock news, or becoming an on-air radio or television talent, you should be aware that there is an entire industry of licensing agents, literary agents, publicists, talent agents, and others who are ready to help when you and your product (or brand) are marketable.

➤ **Speakers' services and bureaus.** There is a handful of Web sites that will connect you with organizations that need speakers on different topics, either locally or across the country. You typically either pay a subscription fee to access new speaking opportunities as they are posted to the Web sites or pay to list yourself as a speaker who is available for certain topics. Speakers' *bureaus,* which are much more difficult to be accepted by, will represent you to their list of clients for highly paid keynote speeches and other presentations once you have a track record or national persona. Speakers' bureaus typically charge you 25 to 30 percent of the fees received from the client who hires you to speak.

➤ **Marketing, press relations, and advertising.** This category is full of Web sites and other services that will broadcast your press release, send out your autoresponder messages, announce your affiliate program, announce your workshop, and carry out other such operations. Whatever you want to do, the chances are good that the technology exists to automate it. And the good news is, many of these services are free.

➤ **Web site shopping cart and affiliate tracking system.** If you review Chapter 6, "Making Instant Income on the Internet," you'll soon discover that selling products and services on the Internet can be easily automated by subscribing to a full-featured shopping cart service. These services automate your Web site sales, product delivery, affiliate tracking, autoresponder follow-up, and other such functions. If you sell a digital product or e-book, some shopping cart services will even pay your affiliates for you out of the proceeds earned at your site each month.

➤ **Expert help and coaching as you implement.** While there are many business "advisors" out there whom you could hire to help you implement, regrettably few of them have extensive experience in guiding Occasional Entrepreneurs through the actual steps required to bring in the cash. The coaching professionals—who work with Instant Income customers—have the finest track record in the industry for helping Occasional Entrepreneurs and full-time small business owners to build their business. Each coach is also a successful entrepreneur and has broad experience in stepping small business owners, solo entrepreneurs, intrapreneurial employees, and Occasional Entrepreneurs through implementing the Instant Income strategies. You can find out more about them at www.instantincome. com/coaching.html.

CHAPTER 17

Earning Extra Income Whenever You Need It

As I noted at the beginning of this book, your business is a valuable asset. It gives you the ability to collect money for goods and services. It lets you create continual cash flow from loyal customers. It lets you conduct promotions, run advertisements, and broadcast e-mails that drive eager buyers to your door. And if your bank account is in trouble, it's also your single best opportunity for generating cash virtually overnight.

Not surprisingly, your *occasional business* is no different.

When you set up your occasional enterprise with the marketing systems, customer communication systems, and product delivery systems that I've talked about in this book, you have in place everything you need to create cash whenever you want it. Suddenly, being an Occasional Entrepreneur becomes not just random efforts at executing the Instant Income strategies but the deliberate exploitation of your own business whenever you need cash.

A Short Checklist of Systems You Must Have in Place

Instead of scrambling to establish these systems every time you want to execute one of the Instant Income strategies, why not make it easy on yourself and put these systems in place before you start? In order to maximize the Instant Income strategies, here is the short list of systems you'll want to have in place. And while it *is* possible to read about a strategy and execute it the very next day, dealing with the response might be overwhelming if you don't have these systems already in place.

➤ **Customers and prospects of your own in a database** (or someone else's customers that you access via a joint venture). The easiest way to generate Instant Income is by sending a special offer to your existing customers. Alternatively, you can negotiate with other business owners to send an offer to their customers. And if neither of you has records of who these customers are? An alternative is to make verbal offers to customers who call in or visit the store.

➤ **Order-taking functions.** Whether you employ a staff to book orders, hire a call center to do so, allow your joint-venture partner to collect the money, or use a shopping cart function at your Web site, you must have a way to take orders, assure customers that they have made the right decision, and process the payments.

➤ **A Web site that sells you and your product.** If you use any of the Instant Income strategies that are best executed by driving prospects to a Web site, you must have a Web site that includes at least a landing page that features your sales letter, a shopping cart to take orders, and a thank-you page to reassure customers and tell them how their product or service will be delivered. See Chapter 6, "Making Instant Income on the Internet," for more details.

➤ **A product or service delivery method.** Whether you deliver your product or service yourself or contract with an outside fulfillment center, joint-venture partner, or manufacturer to do so, you must have the delivery method established prior to executing any of the Instant Income strategies.

The Quickest Way to Instant Income

Of all the Instant Income strategies you might use, a few top my list of the quickest ways to make extra cash when you need it:

1. Upsell customers at the time of purchase.

2. Send a special offer to your customers.

3. Send endorsed offers to another company's customers.

4. Broadcast a press release.

5. Run a direct-response or testimonial-style advertisement.

6. Invite your customers (or someone else's) to a teleseminar.

Of course, not all of these strategies may be appropriate for you. For instance, if your niche market is very narrowly defined, then running a direct-response ad in the local newspaper won't work for you. Always use your best judgment before executing any of these strategies. And remember, this book describes 29 *other* ways to make Instant Income.

PART FIVE

Turning Instant Income into Lifetime Wealth

CHAPTER 18

Using the Instant Income Strategies to Build Lifetime Wealth

WHILE MOST OF THIS BOOK has focused on creating income in the short term, the truth is that mastering—and then *implementing*—the Instant Income strategies on a regular basis can also deliver lifelong benefits in the form of greater financial independence, earlier retirement, far less stress, and a superb quality of life.

Think about it.

If you approached your business as a true investment vehicle—one that not only serves its customer, but also *helps build lifetime wealth for you as its owner*—your everyday business priorities would shift immeasurably. Suddenly, you would set up systems that would keep the business running smoothly so that you could focus on implementation. You would concentrate more on proactively creating new profit centers that bring in the cash. You would aggressively seek out joint-venture partners, chart an annual marketing calendar, develop smart new strategic alliances, find new ways to leverage your Internet presence, and work with a business advisor to keep you on track.*

---

* Highly trained business coaches are ready to help you stay focused on creating cash. Visit www.instantincome.com/coaching.html.

And all of those daily small annoyances that go along with running a small business? They would instantly fall into proper perspective compared with generating cash flow for your ultimate benefit. After all, if you're not running the business for your own financial gain and professional satisfaction, why are you running it at all?

Entrepreneurship Equals Financial Freedom

Implementing the Instant Income strategies—as a business owner, an employee, or an Occasional Entrepreneur—also helps you maintain a much clearer focus on your desired financial goals. For one thing, relentlessly pursuing cash flow forces you to think about your finances in general, about your financial future, and about how much money will ultimately make you and your family happy.

Of course, I'm no investment guru. And I'm not about to tell you what to do with the money that these strategies produce.

But I am suggesting that if you developed a plan to invest some (or all) of what you earn with these cash-flow techniques, you would also be taking the first step toward financial freedom. When you have invested capital that generates enough monthly cash flow to support you and your lifestyle without your having to work even one day a year, that's financial freedom. Entrepreneurs who are financially independent work when they want to . . . *if they want to.*

Decide What "Wealth" Means to You

Of course, you *could* achieve financial freedom and then go on to attain any conceivable level of financial success you desire, depending on your level of expertise, your diligence, where your business is now, and your ability to put the Instant Income strategies to work.

But have you actually thought about what you want? Have you thought about what "wealth" means *to you?* Have you researched what it would cost to pay your bills, travel in style, send your children to the best schools, give back to your community, and fund other activities that are important to you? If you haven't already, take steps to do so now. Only when you know these costs can you truly begin to use the Instant Income strategies as tools for building lifetime wealth and independence.

In fact, for every new expense you would *like* to incur, there's an Instant Income strategy that can help you *first create the cash flow* that you'll need in order to pay for it. With this "earn-it-first" approach, you'll find your consumer habits suddenly becoming more thoughtful, your buying sprees less impulsive, your debt reduction more important, and your savings much more aggressive.

A perfect example of this is my own situation. When I first launched my Web site to help authors, speakers, and consultants become "infopreneurs," selling books, seminars, and other knowledge products,* I also decided that I wanted the revenues from the Web site to go toward fulfilling some of my own financial goals. When it became apparent that 20.8 percent of all visitors who opted into my free report series *also bought my $97 entry-level product,* it became equally apparent that I could reach my financial goals a *lot* faster if I simply focused on driving massive traffic to my free report series.

Do you see how the Instant Income strategies can help you fulfill *your* goals? Do you also see that implementing the Instant Income strategies on an ongoing basis can help you achieve a lifetime of wealth and freedom faster than you had previously thought possible?

To start planning how *you* will use the strategies to build wealth, let's take a look at the next chapter, "Integrating the Strategies into Your Day-to-Day Business."

---

* To see this campaign in action, visit www.howexpertsbuildempires.com.

CHAPTER 19

Integrating the Strategies into Your Day-to-Day Business

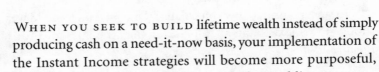

WHEN YOU SEEK TO BUILD lifetime wealth instead of simply producing cash on a need-it-now basis, your implementation of the Instant Income strategies will become more purposeful, more calculated—and a lot less exhausting. Instead of scrambling to put together promotions when you're in dire need of cash, you'll seek to integrate them into your day-to-day business as an important part of the systems I've talked about over the last few chapters.

You'll not only refine those systems by installing the Instant Income strategies but also think through how to set up your systems so that the Instant Income strategies are executed repeatedly as part of a predetermined plan.

A Strategy-by-Strategy Guide to Long-Term Integration

When approached from a wealth-building perspective, each Instant Income strategy fits into your business in a specific way. Take a look at each of the 35 Instant Income strategies to see how to integrate them into the day-to-day operation of your business:

Customer Strategy 1: Reorders. Add fields to your database that record "product purchased" and "date of most recent purchase." Then assign someone to print a list of customers who regularly purchase a consumable product, and make telephone calls to capture their reorders.

Customer Strategy 2: Upsell. Train your staff using upselling scripts that you write, then schedule 8 to 12 upselling offers per year, changing them seasonally or to coincide with specific offers that you're promoting. Add language to your Web site's shopping cart, thank-you page, or landing page that upsells buyers.

Customer Strategy 3: Continuity. If this is appropriate for your business, develop a recurring delivery, monthly subscription, or membership-type product or service, then begin promoting it—both as a new product or service and as an upselling offer that you make to customers who would otherwise purchase one time only.

Customer Strategy 4: Resell. To best integrate this strategy, add a field to your database that captures "contract expiration date," then print out two months in advance the names of any customers whose contracts expire in the next 60 days. Call these customers to renew their contract.

Customer Strategy 5: Reactivate. Using the "date of most recent purchase" field discussed earlier, print out a list of customers every 45 to 90 days, then assign an employee (or hire a part-time person) to telephone them or mail them an offer that entices them to begin doing business with you again.

Joint-Venture Strategy 1: Endorsements. To continually cultivate joint-venture partners who can send endorsed offers, you'll need to first develop an offer that works. Once you have results, assign an employee to research and call new joint-venture prospects. Set a goal of approaching a certain number of prospects each week.

Joint-Venture Strategy 2: Referral Circle. Don't let the members of your referral circle or professional consortium fail to promote you to their clients. Schedule monthly mailings—via e-mail or post office—then offer to do the mailings if your circle members will provide the names.

Joint-Venture Strategy 3: Outside Products. As part of your marketing calendar (see the next chapter), schedule a series of product mailings, some of which may offer other people's products and services on which you get paid a commission. Add links at your Web site for other products that you promote as a paid affiliate.

Joint-Venture Strategy 4: Teleseminars. Many businesses hold teleseminars monthly, each featuring a different guest selling a product. Research coaching programs and monthly teleseminar series that might feature you as a guest expert, then contact them. Follow up by sending your written teleseminar outline that sells your product.

Joint-Venture Strategy 5: Become an Add-On. Once you have established these relationships, regularly maintain literature at your joint-venture partners' place of business, schedule flyers to go into their shipping cartons, or offer to do regular mailings to their customers. Schedule these activities so that you don't forget them.

Advertising Strategy 1: Testimonial Ads. If you own a business or practice where customers wait in your lobby, keep clipboards handy so that customers can complete a survey while they're waiting. Add blank lines for comments about their experience. Structure questions so that you capture compelling stories, then contact customers to write ads about them.

Advertising Strategy 2: Press Release. Plan and schedule an entire year's worth of press releases (15 to 20) at one time, then hire a writer to write them for you all at once. Put all 15 to 20 release dates on your calendar to remind you to broadcast the press releases.

Advertising Strategy 3: Get on the Radio. Produce an electronic press kit and e-mail local stations monthly, citing a current news tie-in. Or consider buying time on a local station and hosting your own radio show if you believe you'll recruit new customers this way.

Advertising Strategy 4: Remnant Advertising. Start researching appropriate publications for your business, then contact the advertising representative to begin the remnant negotiations. Plan your advertising calendar a year in advance.

Advertising Strategy 5: "Reason Why" Sales. Plan in advance what you want to sell at a particular time of year, then, 60 to 90 days beforehand, seek out a rationale that you can add to the campaign. Schedule this so that you won't forget it.

Prospecting Strategy 1: Workshops. Produce an advertisement, letter, e-mail, or other device that compels prospects to register for your event. Schedule events regularly. To speak at industry events, produce a speaker's kit that you send 10 to 12 months in advance.

Prospecting Strategy 2: Two-Step Campaigns. Determine the advertising outlets that are available to you, then develop campaigns that fit those outlets. Produce your giveaway item, then structure the data capture mechanism. Finally, plan any follow-up contact that the resulting prospects will receive to convert them into buyers.

Prospecting Strategy 3: Place Literature. Keep a list of locations where you've placed your literature rack, then add to the list by recruiting new locations. Schedule regular replenishment of the racks or displays. Train your staff on any offers in the literature.

Prospecting Strategy 4: Ask for Referrals. Schedule regular mailings or e-mails to customers making a special offer and asking them to refer their friends and family. Produce literature or other samples that customers can pass on. Make a list of all vendors, then start calling to be referred to their customers.

Prospecting Strategy 5: Trade Shows. Determine your entire year's schedule of trade shows in advance, then plan the special offers and preshow promotions that you'll conduct. Program your lead follow-up system so that prospects from each show are converted to buyers.

Sales Strategy 1: Follow-up Telemarketing. Start by acquiring contact management software, then capture all data during an initial call from a prospect. Make it part of each salesperson's job to routinely schedule follow-up appointments. If you don't have your own sales force, budget for regular voice broadcasts.

Sales Strategy 2: Bundling. Revise your product and service offerings to sell bundled packages wherever possible. Redo existing advertising (or create new offers) to sell these bundles. Finally, recruit outside parties to deliver bundled components or bonuses, if necessary.

Sales Strategy 3: Specific Offers. Plan in advance what you want to sell at specific times throughout the year, then start writing those campaigns early. Segment your database so that specific customers or prospects can receive specific offers (if appropriate).

Sales Strategy 4: Downsell. Write a downselling script, then train your salespeople to determine when a downselling offer is appropriate. Hold at least biweekly training meetings with your sales staff to help them articulate the script properly.

Sales Strategy 5: Nontraditional Salespeople. Create a shortlist of 10 to 12 people whom you will contact about selling for you in addition to their other work. Develop the sales tools they'll need. Then plan regular training "calls" that you hold as a group, conduct individually, or record on tape or CD to update salespeople on current offers and proven sales techniques.

Internet Strategy 1: Viral Report. Set up your Web site's "name squeeze" page to capture a visitor's name, e-mail address, and zip code before allowing the visitor to download your free giveaway. Once visitors register, send them to a thank-you page that not only provides downloading instructions but also encourages them to click over to read your sales letter. Embed links to your shopping cart into your sales letter. Put links in your free viral report that drive readers to your sales page. Finally, allow affiliates to redistribute your report after registering at an affiliate sign-up page. Write an introductory e-mail that they can download and send to promote the free giveaway to their list.

Internet Strategy 2: 24-Hour Strategy. Schedule three or four of these campaigns during the year, then begin recruiting affiliates 90 to 120 days in advance. Recruit bonus providers. Set up your landing page and bonus download page. Program your customer follow-up autoresponders to deliver messages after customers buy.

Internet Strategy 3: Online Articles. Plan and write 20 articles of interest about your area of expertise (or hire someone to write them). Then schedule and budget for broadcasting them every 10 to 14 days.

Internet Strategy 4: E-mail Campaigns. Plan a year's worth of offers for individual products or services, including the special pricing, unique product bundle, time limit, and so on. Schedule these promotions to go to your e-mail list on specific dates. Alternatively, program these promotions into your autoresponder so that visitors and buyers receive prescheduled offers at specific intervals in the future.

Internet Strategy 5: 28-Day Launch. Schedule three or four of these campaigns over the year for specific product bundles, then begin writing the necessary e-mail communications in advance, leaving room for current information or feedback from your blog. Set up your blog page and landing page (sales letter). Program prewritten appeals into your autoresponder.

Overlooked Strategy 1: Liquidate Overstocks. Schedule inventory regularly in order to identify overstocks or obsolete products. Identify likely bulk buyers in advance or determine in advance any special offers that you can promote to your customer list.

Overlooked Strategy 2: Service Capacity. Determine those weeks or days during the year when you experience a drop in business, then either (1) save money by scaling back your staff during those times or (2) send special promotions three or four weeks ahead of those downtimes.

Overlooked Strategy 3: Short-Pay Offers. Offer full-pay pricing as a way to capture cash from members and subscribers up front. If some do elect the payment plan, determine when the most breakage occurs, then program your autoresponder or database to send short-pay offers 30 days ahead. Alternatively, write a series of short-pay offers to past-due accounts.

Overlooked Strategy 4: Employees. Produce a survey to determine what employees know that is marketable. Schedule specific days each month when employees can "consult" or provide other services. Promote the new service or develop a new profit center around the employees' expertise.

Overlooked Strategy 5: Apprenticeships. Systematize your own business, then carefully record the documents, systems, and strategies that you are using to successfully build your business. Keep them in a notebook or file cabinet. Structure your apprenticeship program, then begin promoting it in such a way that new apprentices can join any time.

CHAPTER 20

Developing Your One-Year Income-Generation Calendar

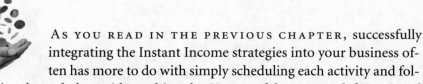

AS YOU READ IN THE PREVIOUS CHAPTER, successfully integrating the Instant Income strategies into your business often has more to do with simply scheduling each activity and following through than with anything else. Yet one of the greatest deficiencies of most small businesses is they do not establish any type of annual marketing calendar, nor do they follow one. Instead, they approach income generation haphazardly—or worse, they approach it only when they need money.

You have the ability to overcome this deficiency in your own business—*and even outmarket your competitors*—simply by developing a calendar that keeps you focused on creating cash and customers.

Start with the List of Strategies You Would Like to Pursue

To begin developing your annual calendar, make a list of all the strategies and activities you've read about in this book that you would like to pursue or that you know you should be pursuing. These may be *recurring activities* such as sending out press releases, or they may be *one-time efforts* such as a trade show or a holiday sale. Whatever is on your list, start penciling in the *fixed-date* campaigns first. This will allow you to focus on deadlines that are fixed by other people and therefore are out of your control. Later, you can pencil in those campaigns that you can choose to run at any time.

What are some fixed-date campaigns to schedule first?

➤ Trade shows

➤ Guest appearances on teleseminars

➤ Directory deadlines

➤ New product launches

➤ Customer reorders

➤ Customer contract renewals

➤ Service downtime and slow periods

➤ Government deadlines

➤ Speaking at industry conferences

➤ Yellow Pages ad deadlines

➤ Special advertising pull-outs

➤ Holiday sales/seasonal offers

➤ Limited-time offers/ products

➤ Inserts in third-party shipments

Of course, your list may contain other fixed-date deadlines that are particular to your industry. But whatever they are, pencil them into your calendar, then count backward the number of days or weeks you'll need in order to prepare and launch a successful campaign.

For example, since you learned in Prospecting Strategy 5, "Create Instant Income at Trade Shows," that at least six weeks are needed to plan an exhibit and conduct preshow marketing effectively, first schedule the show, then count back six weeks and set that day as the deadline by which you will have booked your exhibit space, rented your booth (if necessary), and developed your preshow marketing materials. Schedule execution of your preshow mailings, phone calls, e-mails, and other communications during the remaining six weeks before the show.

Similarly, if you know that a government deadline is fast approaching and you perform a service that helps consumers or business owners meet this deadline, count back the number of weeks you will need in order to perform the service adequately, and then count back 90 to 120 days prior to *that* in order to effectively prospect for new clients and close them into contracting for the service.

Of course, you could develop the systems you need quickly, then implement the Instant Income strategies for quick cash. But why stress yourself if it's unnecessary? If you have plenty of time to prepare, take advantage of it.

Schedule Recurring Promotions

Regular press releases, online articles, autoresponder e-mails, preview workshops, radio shows, display advertising, referral circle mailings—these are all examples of strategies that you will be executing on a repeat basis. Once you have the date-specific promotions listed on your calendar, begin to fill it in with repeat promotions. You might even set some rules for yourself, such as "all e-mails are sent on Tuesdays," "trade publication ads are due the twentieth of the preceding month," "customer renewal voice broadcasts are done the fifth of every month," and so on.

Give Prospects Time to Receive Your Promotions and Respond to Them

I recommend that you count backward far enough to schedule all the marketing activity that you know you'll want to do. Give yourself time to produce the materials required (the brochure, the e-mail series, the telemarketing scripts, and other documents), but also allow time for people to receive those materials and respond to them.

Different marketing vehicles have different response times. For example, e-mails create the quickest response—often within minutes of your sending them. Outbound telemarketing can be very fast at generating cash if your salespeople can reach prospects by telephone—and if you have a mechanism to handle return phone calls.

One of the slowest, but still effective, means for marketing high-priced products and services is direct mail. Be aware that over the last few years we've seen lag times as long as three weeks before the majority of the responses come in. People are busy. They often sort their mail over the trash can. However, if your mailing looks compelling and grabs their attention, they *will* set it aside to read later. For your most important deadline-driven promotions, do *not* send direct-mail packages within four weeks of any major event. Use outbound telemarketing instead.

Afterword

I'VE TAUGHT YOU A NUMBER of new skills through the pages of *Instant Income*, but you will achieve the biggest benefit only when you actually implement what you have learned. Using the Instant Income Overnight Audit, get started *now* on a plan to implement just one new strategy in your small business. If you're an employee, start researching *now* where hidden income opportunities are lying dormant in your employer's business. If you're an Occasional Entrepreneur, think through your next moneymaking project and determine which Instant Income strategies will help maximize the effect of your short-term effort.

Read and reread this book, marking it up with notes about how you'll use the strategies, what you'll say to your employer, which joint-venture partners you might approach, and so on. Often you'll have the biggest insight, idea, or revelation when you read *Instant Income* the second or third time. If you know you'll need to enroll others in the implementation process eventually, give them their own copy of *Instant Income* so that they, too, can mark it up, make notes, and learn.

And finally, don't end your education with these last few pages. Instead, visit the Instant Income Web site for additional training, resources, and information. You can find the following types of help by pointing your Web browser to

Instant Income Overnight Audit: www.instantincome.com/audit.html
Sample deal memo for your employer: www.instantincome.com/resources.html
Resources mentioned in *Instant Income*:   www.instantincome.com/resources.html

People who can help you as you implement:	www.instantincome.com/coaching.html
Free gifts to give to your customers:	www.instantincome.com/freeB-to-B.html
Instant Income e-training program:	www.instantincome.com
Instant Income guide for your industry:	www.instantincome.com/plans.html
Teach Instant Income to your reading group:	www.instantincome.com/turnaround.html
Report to Janet about your successes:	www.instantincome.com/stories.html

But before we end our time together and you rush to the Web site to get started on the Overnight Audit and claim your additional gifts, let me say that you have the power within you to change your business, the compensation arrangements of your employment, and, indeed, your own financial future simply by mastering the Instant Income strategies and implementing them in your life or workplace.

Not only will you grow as a person but you'll bring others along, too. Imagine if every small business started truly maximizing its daily activities and hidden assets. The economy as a whole would benefit, entrepreneurship would be much more exciting, and business owners and employees alike would raise the level of their work, their professional relationships, and their outcomes. It's a fact that the more you help others grow, the more they'll want to help you succeed. Folks just naturally support those who have supported them.

And finally, please let me know how you're benefiting from implementing the strategies in this book. My goal is to build a worldwide community of like-minded, forward-thinking, proactive, and super-savvy entrepreneurs who regularly use the Instant Income strategies in their business, side projects, or workplace. I look forward to hearing about your success.

Access These Powerful Online Tools *Free* When You Purchase the *Instant Income* Book!

Free Online Audit Gives You a Complete Written Plan for Executing the Strategies!

Let the online version of the Instant Income Overnight Audit help you plan, organize, and prioritize your Instant Income strategies. Log on now to www.instantincome.com/audit.html and use the passcode "iibookbuyer" to access this powerful planning tool. Then watch as our secure online engine steps you through completing all 35 of the Instant Income opportunities in your business or workplace. Simply key in your answers to the Overnight Audit questions and our system will calculate your expected income, compile your plans into a neatly organized written document, and even prioritize which strategies you should pursue first to make the most income quickly. Your data are always secure—only you and the Instant Income team will ever see them (and then only at your request).

Free Sample Deal-Point Memo* Gives You Deal Points for Going into Business with the Boss!

If you're employed by a small business and would like to get paid more to create cash using the Instant Income strategies, this sample deal-point memo will get you started. While the memo is not guaranteed to be specific to your situation or circumstances, you'll find sample language, sample compensation ideas, and other content that will provide discussion points for your ultimate deal. Log on to www.instantincome.com/resources.html to download the sample deal-point memo and other important information.

Free Instant Income E-training Program Helps You Implement Key Strategies!

When you visit www.instantincome.com, be sure to register for Janet Switzer's Instant Income E-training Program, designed to deliver ongoing strategies, implementation guidance, and other training information via e-mail.

---

* Please be advised that Janet Switzer is not a lawyer and that neither she nor her company, Success Resources International Inc., is dispensing legal advice. Professional legal counsel should always be sought whenever you are negotiating a deal or putting an agreement in writing. The document you'll find online *must* be altered for your specific circumstances and to comply with the laws of your state. Do *not* use the sample deal-point memo as written. It is for educational purposes only.

Index

About the Author

A 22-YEAR VETERAN of the marketing and advertising field, Janet Switzer is unique among experts as the woman who has developed and executed the day-to-day income-generation strategies of many of the world's top celebrity entrepreneurs: *Chicken Soup for the Soul* cofounder Jack Canfield, underground marketing guru Jay Abraham, celebrity speaker Les Brown, Internet income expert Yanik Silver, and master motivational speaker Mark Victor Hansen, among others.

Today, she's the *New York Times* and *USA Today* best-selling coauthor of *The Success Principles: How to Get from Where You Are to Where You Want to Be,* published in eight languages worldwide.

As well, she's the creator of the Instant Income series of small-business books, multimedia training courses, public seminars, coaching programs, and industry guides designed to help small businesses and at-home enterprises generate immediate cash flow and develop long-term revenue streams. Ms. Switzer is a powerful and dynamic keynote speaker who speaks to thousands of entrepreneurs, independent sales professionals, corporate employees, and industry association members around the world on the principles of success and income generation. Additionally, she works with corporations to support their dealers and distributors in selling more of the company's products and services through Instant Income training tools and customer outreach programs.

Janet Switzer is a featured expert in the motion-picture documentary, *U R Pre-Approved,* documenting the personal finance and debt crisis in America. She's a popular radio talk show guest and has been featured in the *Wall*

Street Journal, USA Today, the *New York Times, Time Magazine, US Weekly, Metropolitan Magazine, Costco Connection,* and countless other periodicals and newspapers worldwide. Additionally, as one of America's most respected authorities in the knowledge products industry, Ms. Switzer helps experts build publishing empires around their business strategies, training concepts, industry expertise and unique market posture. Her multimedia short course—*How Experts Build Empires: The Step-By-Step System for Turning Your Expertise into Super-Lucrative Profit Centers*—is the industry's definitive work on the subject of developing and marketing information products. (Visit www.howexpertsbuildempires.com.)

To find out more about Janet Switzer, *Instant Income* products, and Ms. Switzer's availability to speak for your next event, call (805) 499-9400 or visit her Web site at www.instantincome.com.

Permissions

I acknowledge the many individuals who granted me permission to reprint the cited material:

Brian Tracy. Author of *The Way to Wealth*. Reprinted by permission.

Mark Victor Hansen. Co-creator of the *Chicken Soup for the Soul*® series. Coauthor of *Cracking the Millionaire Code* and *The One Minute Millionaire*. Interviewed by author. Reprinted with permission.

Jack Canfield. Co-creator of the *Chicken Soup for the Soul* series. Interviewed by author. Reprinted with permission.

Jennifer Schwabauer. Interviewed by author. Reprinted with permission.

David Deutsch. Top direct-response copywriter, marketing consultant and author of *Think Inside the Box*. www.thinkinginside.com. Reprinted with permission.

Dr. Len Schwartz. Founder of Market Domination Specialists, LLC. (877) 204-2739. Reprinted with permission.

Garret Wood. Reprinted with permission.

Clate W. Mask. Reprinted with permission.

Carson Conant. Nightingale-Conant Corporation. Reprinted with permission.

Patrick Henry. The Fishing Coach. www.fishingcoach.net. Reprinted with permission.

David Vallieres. InfoProduct Lab LLC. Reprinted with permission.

Ken Keis, MBA. Reprinted with permission.

James E. Smith. Interviewed by author. Reprinted with permission.

Robert Hamm. Interviewed by author. Reprinted with permission.

Matt Bacak. #1 Bestselling author and mentor. Reprinted with permission.

Randall Blaum. President, Marketing Experts International. www.randallblaum.com. Reprinted with permission.

David Scotland. CEO, Marketing Experts International. Reprinted with permission.

Cheryl Scales. Entrepreneur and Innovator. Interviewed by author. Reprinted with permission.

Michelle Anton. Producer and author of *Weekend Entrepreneur*. Interviewed by author. Reprinted with permission.

Jeffrey Wycoff. Vice-President, Sirius Products Inc. Reprinted with permission.

Les Brown. President and CEO, Les Brown Enterprises. Interviewed by author. Reprinted with permission.

Kathryn Dunn. K. Dunn & Associates, a performance-based marketing firm. (800) 553-0135. Reprinted with permission.

Ernest L. Salazar II. Reprinted with permission.

Richard B. Schefren. Reprinted with permission.

Mitchell Carson. Interviewed by author. Reprinted with permission.

Gary Handwerker. CEO, Handwerker Consulting. Interviewed by author. Reprinted with permission.

Robert Handwerker. YellowPageAdvice.com. Interviewed by author. Reprinted with permission.

Mark Romero. Reprinted with permission.

Joel Block. Reprinted with permission.

Dan Mozersky. Reprinted with permission.

Stephanie Frank. Author of *The Accidental Millionaire* and founder, Stephanie Frank Worldwide. www.StephanieFrank.com. Interviewed by author. Reprinted with permission.

Peggy McColl. Reprinted with permission.

Krizia DeVerdier. Reprinted with permission.

Jason Potash. Interviewed by author. Reprinted with permission.

Joel Comm. Reprinted with permission.

Jeff Johnson. Receive free training from Jeff Johnson at www.SuperAffiliateCoachingClub.com. Interviewed by author. Reprinted with permission.

Jeff Walker. Creator and publisher of the *Product Launch Formula*. Interviewed by author. Reprinted with permission.

Jeff Aubery. Interviewed by author. Reprinted with permission.

Carl Kennedy. Reprinted with permission.

Collette Candler. President and Sr. Marketing/PR Consultant, The Marketing Insider Inc., and an expert on consumer health trends and behavior. Reprinted with permission.

Yanik Silver. Creator of www.InstantSalesLetters.com. Interviewed by author. Reprinted with permission.

NEED ONGOING ADVICE AS YOU IMPLEMENT THE INSTANT INCOME® STRATEGIES?

Running a business can be hard work. There are so many decisions to make. And cash-flow is always a priority. But what if you had a coach—a seasoned, experienced business professional—supporting you, month after month, as you implement the Instant Income strategies, put your systems in place and manage your new-found revenue streams?

You can get this support-when you join the...

INSTANT INCOME COACHING PROGRAM

Your coach will help you look at where you are now—then work with you to create a personalized plan for getting to where you want to be. Whether you're a business owner, an employee or just considering starting a business of your own, your coach can be there for you—advising you, providing accountability, working with your unique strengths and challenges, and moving you forward on your path.

Find out today how your Instant Income Coach can help you:

• **Build a personalized financial and business-building plan**

• **Determine which strategies to execute to improve cash-flow**

• **Discover what you'll need to achieve your business goals**

• **Reduce the headaches and challenges of running a small business**

• **Set your plan in motion—so that Instant Income is an automatic process**

Visit www.instantincomecoaching.com today for details!